"WHY DO I HAVE THE FEELING I'M ABOUT TO BE SEDUCED?"

Lucas's voice was low, his eyes gleaming like polished gems.

"Am I being that obvious?" Jennifer swallowed, surprised at the steadiness of her voice. In her mind, conflicting thoughts played a tug-of-war over the rights and wrongs of the course of action she was about to undertake. But with a few simple words and provocative moves she'd committed herself totally to this moment. There was no backing out now.

In a sudden panic she tried to interpret his expression, but all she saw was his desire and determination to finish what she'd begun. She shivered as though chilled, then felt his arms encircle her. Her pulse leapt wildly as she watched his lips slowly descend to hers. Then, closing her eyes, she gave herself up to the magic of his kiss.

ABOUT THE AUTHOR

Like her characters in *Moment of Madness,*
Evelyn A. Crowe makes her home in
Houston, Texas. Although she enjoys city life,
Evelyn likes nothing better than to slip away to the
country for a little fishing and dreaming, something
her characters also like to do. Readers who enjoyed
Evelyn's second book, *Charade,* will be glad to
know that its main characters appear in *Moment of
Madness.* Her next Superromance *Final Payment,* to
be published in the summer of 1986, concludes this
four-book series with a wonderful reunion scene.

Books by Evelyn A. Crowe

HARLEQUIN SUPERROMANCE

112—SUMMER BALLAD
160—CHARADE
186—MOMENT OF MADNESS

These books may be available at your local bookseller.

Don't miss any of our special offers. Write to us at the
following address for information on our newest releases.

Harlequin Reader Service
P.O. Box 52040, Phoenix, AZ 85072-2040
Canadian address: P.O. Box 2800, Postal Station A,
5170 Yonge St., Willowdale, Ont. M2N 6J3

Evelyn A. Crowe

MOMENT OF MADNESS

Harlequin Books

TORONTO • NEW YORK • LONDON
AMSTERDAM • PARIS • SYDNEY • HAMBURG
STOCKHOLM • ATHENS • TOKYO • MILAN

Published November 1985

First printing September 1985

ISBN 0-373-70186-1

For my editor, Margaret Learn,
who's always willing to listen,
and for Marianne J. Crowe, my mother.

PROLOGUE

THE SMALL, BLUE GRANITE DANCE FLOOR at Boccaccio's gleamed with minute diamond sparkles, defying the scuffing and scraping of shoes that persistently tried to grind away its brilliance. Shoulder to shoulder the after-work crowd swayed slowly, hypnotically, their eyes closed against the fatigue of a long day, waiting for the rapidly consumed alcohol to take effect and send them spiraling into a false sense of euphoria.

The long, brass-trimmed bar was lined three deep as customers jockeyed politely for their drinks. Bright smiles flashed; voices rose louder in a kind of desperation as men and women, Houston's single elite, vied for one another's attention. They were forlorn souls, looking for company to chase away their loneliness—all except for a couple tucked away in a shadowy corner. At first their presence brought envy and suspicion, but they were quickly forgotten in a frantic search for a night's companionship.

At a distance the tall, model-thin woman bespoke money and beauty. From her handmade Italian shoes to the classic lines of the Chanel suit and the unmistakable Valentino silk blouse, she reeked elegance. It wasn't until a closer glance that an observer realized that the subdued lighting blurred the harsh lines of her face, hiding the heavy makeup and the candlelight added a sparkle to the lifeless, overbleached hair.

In reality Susan McCord was as hard and cold as arctic ice. Her blue eyes glittered, and her glossy red lips thinned now in anger.

"Damn you to hell," she spit. "Just give me my twenty-five thousand dollars and stop trying to pick me for free information." She lifted her drink and took a hefty gulp as she watched the man across from her with narrowing eyes.

He grinned, shrugged and shook his head. The light caught the tiny circlet of gold in his left ear, making it flash almost in warning. "You're a greedy woman, Susan," he stated snidely in his Oxford English.

"No, just a good businesswoman." She held our her hand, wiggling her fingers impatiently until a thick brown envelope was slapped into her palm. "And you needn't be contemptuous of me, not after all you've done." One long, pointed nail neatly sliced open the envelope, and she ran a thumb over the crisp new thousand-dollar bills, mentally counting them. "I wonder what Lucas DeSalva would do to you if he knew you were stealing him blind of his precious electronic secrets?"

"Shut your mouth, you bloody bitch."

The low growl brought Susan's head up in fright. Never in all her dealings with this elegant stranger—for that's what he still was, despite their many meetings—had he ever once lost his cool British reserve when she'd deliberately needled him. She met the controlled fury in his eyes as his mouth curved into a tight-lipped smile.

"You're a fine one to talk about screwing your friends, when you've set up your own stepsister to take the rap if Lucas finds out. From what you've told me about Jennifer McCord, it would be like tethering a lamb before a hungry panther."

Her thinly plucked eyebrows rose arrogantly. "Scruples? Surely not." She picked up her drink, then quickly set it down when she felt the tremor in her hand. "We made a deal before we started on this course of action—no questions. My motives are simple—money. I've never asked yours and don't intend to. But I'll tell you this. When my stepsister fell ill and was going to be forced into dropping out of graduate school, I saw a way out and a chance to settle some old scores."

Susan reached across the table and covered his long-boned hand with her own. "Let's not fight." She dropped her voice to a suggestive purr, studying his face for any change in expression; when none came and he eased his hand from hers, she shrugged and leaned back. In all their meetings he'd never tried to seduce her and it rankled her that a man with his sex appeal and obvious appetite didn't use sex as a tool or lever. He was damn good-looking and lately she'd been wondering what he'd be like as a lover. She watched him now as he idly glanced at his watch and noticed for the first time that evening the white band of skin around his little finger, as if he'd worn a ring there for many years and had suddenly lost it or forgotten to wear it. She was about to ask, but he stopped her.

"I have an appointment in fifteen minutes, Susan. Is there anything else you have to tell me?"

"Oh, yes. But I need another drink, dear. And I don't give a damn if you're late for your other appointment. What I have to tell will be better than a few hours in some whore's bed and save you the cost of a night's fun."

"Love, you wound me. I've never had to pay for any of my pleasures." He smiled and raised his hand for the waiter's attention, holding up two fingers to signify the number of drinks he wanted. "One more quick drink, Susan. Then I go whether you've told me this breathtaking news of yours or not.''

"Tell me something. Is your date male or female?'' she prodded, looking pointedly at his earring.

"My darling girl, you and I are two of a kind. What's your preference these days?'' He watched with savage pleasure as the unbecoming red washed up her neck and cheeks.

"You really are a bastard. Thank heaven we won't be meeting like this much longer.''

"What the hell do you mean?'' He hunched forward. "If you're thinking of backing out now you—'' He broke off as the waiter brought their drinks.

"I'd say one more good piece of information ought to do it.'' Susan leaned forward, too, her face close to his. "The big one,'' she taunted. "The one you've been waiting for. The one that will make your dreams for destruction come true. Lucas called to double-check security, so you know what that means?''

"He's suspicious,'' he hissed, "and traced the leaks to your company?''

"Don't be stupid,'' she smiled. "Why would he check security if he wasn't about to give us a big translating job? Why?''

"Dammit, Susan!'' Her companion's anger blasted across the table, but his voice trembled with an undercurrent of excitement.

Susan wondered fleetingly if his renewed animation was due to the fear of being caught or the sadistic enjoyment he would eventually take in facing Lucas and explaining why he had double-crossed him. She propped her chin on her folded hands and smiled. "This time it's going to cost you three times what you've been paying.''

"Seventy-five thousand dollars! You're crazy, Susan.''

"No, just practical. Once the information is in your hands I'll never see you or your money again. It will be every man for himself then." She rotated the cold glass between her hands. "The way I've set it up, Lucas is going to suspect and accuse Jennifer. When and if she can convince him of her innocence, he'll realize I was the one and come after me. I plan to be gone by then—happily hidden away in Europe where no one can ever find me."

"You must really hate your stepsister," he mused out loud. "Do you have any idea what a man like Lucas is capable of doing to her?"

"What do I care what happens to the little bitch." She tried to calm the ripple of excitement that coursed through her veins. "It will be her problem, won't it?" Susan gulped down the rest of her drink, stuffed the money-filled envelope in her purse and reached for her briefcase. She moved to stand up, but strong fingers clamped around her arm and pulled her back into the chair with a jolt.

"You can throw Jennifer to the wolves if you want to, but let me remind you of what we agreed on at the beginning. If you're caught you don't implicate me, and I do the same." He applied more pressure to her arm till he had the satisfaction of seeing her flinch. "I meant what I said, Susan. If Lucas finds out about me through you before I'm ready—" he lowered his voice "—I'll kill you with my bare hands. Now what's this new development and when should I contact you next?"

"I don't know yet what it ties into, but it's big. Have I ever steered you wrong? Just give me a couple of months." She looked pointedly at his hand on her arm. "You're hurting me," she protested, but the fingers only tightened more, until she bit her lips to stifle a whimper.

"You'd better be right about this, Susan." He eased the pressure of his fingers but didn't let go. "Have you ever thought about what will happen if Lucas catches up with us?''

The question caught her off guard and a momentary flash of fear shone in her eyes. ''Jail, I guess.''

He threw back his head and laughed, but the sound held no humor. ''Oh, no love. That would be too easy, too quick. Lucas DeSalva will take care of us personally. His Spanish heritage would demand revenge. No, no. He'd never let the law become involved. And it wouldn't surprise me to see Jennifer McCord at his side if the day ever comes when we face each other.'' The man's mouth twisted malevolently. ''When Lucas gets through with her, she'll want the pleasure of taking care of you herself.'' He released her cold arm suddenly, as if he'd touched something dead.

Susan sucked in a shaky breath at his words and strove to retain her confident composure. She failed, but blustered on. ''First of all, Lucas will never find me in Europe and second...I couldn't care less what happens to Jennifer McCord. From now on she's on her own.''

Say I'm weary, say I'm sad,
Say that health and wealth have missed me,
Say I'm growing old, but add,
Jenny kissed me.

Rondeau 1838

CHAPTER ONE

SHE WAS BEING WATCHED!

All day long she had had a sense of foreboding—a persistent feeling she was being followed. No, not all day. Just since Susan had informed her she was to meet Lucas DeSalva to review the translations she'd completed. Of course she was crazy. Who would want to shadow her every move? She tried to pinpoint when the suspicion started and realized it must have begun when she left the office early to run some errands before her business appointment. At first she had shaken off the feeling as being fanciful, but she was too levelheaded to imagine such a thing. Now she wasn't so sure. Once again as she sat alone in the cocktail lounge of the Westin Oaks Hotel, waiting for her client, she had the same strange sensation that the watching eyes were close—too close.

Jennifer McCord picked up her glass and sipped nervously at the dry white wine. Her violet eyes deepened in thought. She hadn't wanted to be here and she definitely didn't want to meet Lucas DeSalva. Since she'd taken over the DeSalva account three months ago and caught her first glimpse of Lucas in the newspaper, she'd begun a daily search of the gossip and business columns for a word or picture of him. But her interest went beyond the business side of Lucas. She was far too attracted to the man himself, and the feelings made her uncomfortable. She thought cynically that only a gifted psychiatrist could explain her newfound obsession.

She took a quick sip of wine, set the glass down and let one finger absently circle the thin rim. A frown marred her smooth high forehead. Every time she saw his face she could feel a warmth wash over her and her hands would begin to tremble. Maybe she was losing her mind.

Hadn't she spent the better part of her adult years clawing her way to independence, haunted by nightmares and memories of the past? She'd promised herself long ago that it would be a cold day in hell before she became the fly in the trap she'd watched her mother become. Never would she be subjected to the abuse and cruelty her mother had tolerated. But, now, to realize she had a childish crush on a man she'd only seen in the newspapers was worse than humiliating—it was disgusting.

Her finger stopped caressing the glass and she brought the rim to her lips and finished off the remainder of lukewarm wine in an unladylike swallow. What an ironic joke life was playing on her. In ten minutes she was about to meet the specter of her dreams. No, she silently amended, her nightmares.

Jennifer shifted uncomfortably. She hated the position she'd been placed in. Her apprehension of sitting alone in a cocktail lounge, even one as elegant as this, grew with each passing minute. The lounge was situated just off the lobby of the hotel, and the murmur of happy voices proved too inviting to the weary shoppers and afterwork crowd from the connecting Galleria complex to pass up. She gazed at her wristwatch, counting each sweep of the second hand. How long, she wondered, was she going to have to wait?

Two drinks and twenty minutes later she began to feel the uneasiness of a woman stood up. Angrily she crossed her legs beside the small round table, quickly tugging her lilac silk skirt over he knees, diverting a few hungry stares to the slim calves and shapely ankles. Her anger rapidly changed to nervousness as she wondered if Lucas had been detained and wouldn't show up after all. But surely if that were the case he'd have the courtesy to let her know. Wouldn't he?

"Ms McCord."

Jennifer jumped at the intrusion, her head jerking up at the sound of the female voice. Not recognizing the woman, she scowled, then remembered her as the hostess who had seated her earlier, taking her name and that of her expected companion. At her expression of concern, Jennifer's wildly beating heart plummeted. Lucas wasn't coming and she'd have to walk out of the place *alone*.

"Ms McCord, Mr. DeSalva called and asked that you please forgive him—" *Here it comes,* Jennifer thought, bracing herself. "—for being late. He was unavoidably detained and will join you in about ten minutes. He also asked that I serve you another drink while you wait." She smiled, understanding Jennifer's uneasiness.

Jennifer returned the smile. "Thank you," she said in a strangled voice. How, she asked herself, could she look forward to meeting Lucas and also dread it? Was it possible to feel this wild heart-stopping excitement and at the same time a dark premonition of doom?

Ten minutes! Automatically she reached for her drink, then stopped. Instead she picked up the *Wall Street Journal* she'd brought along, smoothed its folded pages out and pulled the small candle lamp closer, pretending to read. As her gaze settled on the black print, her interest was renewed, even though she'd practically memorized the lengthy article.

There was something hypnotic about a man with so much control over the lives and destiny of other people. She tried to tell herself she was repelled by his power, but the aura of ruthlessness seemed to hold a gripping fascination for her. Lucas ruled DeSalvas with total dictatorship, a domain that consisted of an electronic company, oil wells, real estate, a bank or two in South Texas and a large family-owned ranch in the Texas Hill Country that raised celebrated cattle and quarter horses. DeSalvas empire encompassed the globe, and the reins were held exclusively by one man.

What further amazed Jennifer was the fact that Lucas had assumed responsibility for the huge conglomerate at the age of twenty-two, after his father's forced retirement following the tragic accident that killed his mother and young sister. Though Matthew DeSalva had fully recovered from his injuries, his grief had dimmed his interest in the business and he'd turned the empire over to a reluctant Lucas.

Jennifer took a sip of her wine, continuing to read. She smiled at the next bit of information. It appeared that DeSalvas business associates resented an inexperienced playboy taking control of the vast holdings. However, after eleven years they had come to respect his business acumen and judgment. It was rumored that Lucas ran his companies with an iron hand and an eagle eye and that very little, if anything, escaped his notice.

Jennifer often speculated about a company the size of DeSalvas using her stepsister's company. Admittedly Susan hired some of the best translators for McCord's Translation Services. Still, it puzzled her that an international company like DeSalvas didn't have its own linguistics department.

Suddenly, she froze. The tingling at her nape was now creeping slowly down her backbone. The sensation was so powerful that she jerked her head up and her gaze searched the packed room. This time, in desperation, she allowed herself to make direct eye contact with an interested stranger. But when she met only invitation and desire, her gaze hastily shifted, seeking the one pair of eyes that had been spying on her.

She was about to give up the hunt, when she found herself staring into a pair of silver eyes, narrowed in contemplation. These were the ones, the eyes that had followed her, prying. Relentlessly they scrutinized her, judging her reaction. She had no conception of the features framing the empty, soulless eyes as their glances remained locked. Her vision began to blur and she had a sudden wild thought that he would never release her. She battled to break the invisible hold he seemed to have on her, but the stranger was the first to break away. Jennifer pursued the path of his gaze as if his eyes were magnets compelling her to trail behind him.

Was her mind playing tricks? Or, as her eyes followed his, did the room darken slightly? Her heart pounded with expectancy as a cloak of intimacy wrapped around her in a warm embrace. The sounds of voices and the sharp tinkle of ice against glass faded to a low murmur. She knew instinctively where and to whom those silver eyes were leading her as surely as if he had whispered the name in her ear. It was then that she spotted the three new arrivals waiting to be seated.

Jennifer leaned back into the shadows. Her breath hung painfully suspended in her throat and her eyes widened with anticipation. Forgotten was the silver-eyed stranger as she recognized the profile of the tall man across the room. With him so close now, she was suddenly inexplicably hesitant to look at him just yet, so her eyes slid to his companions. Though she thoroughly inspected the other man and the diminutive woman beside him, she kept Lucas in her peripheral vision, not wanting to let go totally.

She closely observed the two towering men laughing with their small companion till they spotted the other man making his way toward them. A man, Jennifer noticed, with silver eyes that now blazed to life as he wrapped the tiny woman in a tight embrace. Finally she let her gaze shift to the man she'd secretly hated for having occupied her thoughts for so many months.

Now, she congratulated herself, she could be rid of this haunting attraction. For some unknown reason she'd become fascinated with a man she'd never met, only seen in photographs. She'd let her imagination run wild and had become caught up in her own fantasies. But this meeting was her chance to dispel her obsession once and for all. No flesh-and-blood man could be as desirable or as compelling as the image she'd conjured up in her mind.

Uninhibited, she let her eyes roam slowly, intimately over the lean body. Though he was dressed in what she was sure was the finest in tailoring, the three-piece suit hid nothing of the power of the man. His shoulders were broad, yet he had a sleek quality, a long leanness that could be deceptive. There was an essence of mystery in his proud stance, a natural arrogance in the tilt of his strong jaw.

The shock of reality shot through every nerve of Jennifer's body like a current of electricity. He was no longer a figment of her imagination but a flesh-and-blood man. She could almost feel the vitality, the earthy sensuality that emanated from him. The air seemed to leave her lungs as she struggled to regain her equilibrium. She wanted to cry out at the unfairness of it all. How could she rid herself of such a powerful attraction when she was almost reeling from his presence and he still hadn't even looked in her direction.

Lucas DeSalva, in person, reeked with sex appeal, and it didn't go unnoticed by others, either. She watched the hostess talking to Lucas as she led him in Jennifer's direction. He walked with the loose-limbed control of an animal confident of himself and any territory he chose to claim and Jennifer suddenly felt like a cornered fox.

She quickly shoved her hands beneath the tabletop and snatched the napkin from her lap, wiping her sweaty palms. Her lips seemed parched and her throat hurt from the knot of panic as she lifted her eyes to the approaching man. Swallowing hard, she tried valiantly to slow the heavy pounding of her heart.

Candlelight ricocheted off his black hair and illuminated the wide, intelligent forehead, marked by dark eyebrows above equally dark eyes. She knew every line in the rough-hewn face by heart and for the first time, her dreams fused with the living, breathing man. She shook her head in protest at the wild thoughts that ran rampant through her mind. It wasn't fair, she protested. She didn't want a man in her life—real or fantasy.

Lucas moved like some great marauder stalking an unknown prey, and having caught the scent, he stopped across the table from Jennifer and rested his beautiful, long-boned hands on the back of a chair. Their eyes locked and she felt herself tumble into the depths of dark green eyes. A deep forest green that reminded her of spreading oaks casting shade beneath a relentless sun—a haven to get lost in. She could feel the coolness now and smell the freshly cut grass of summer and newly tilled soil, fragrant and welcoming. She wondered why she would think of him as a man of the land, instead of the business executive he was.

She watched as the high autocratic nose flared slightly. His hard jaw clenched, and the square chin with its deep cleft seemed to jut out just a little farther than normal. But, then, as if something passed across his face and took away the latent anger, he smiled. Two long creases accented the sides of his firmly held lips, softening the stern face. With a quizzical look he asked, "You're Jennifer McCord? Susan's sister?"

His mellifluous voice rolled over her, soothing her ragged nerves, slowing the heavy thudding of her heart. She caught herself just in time to stop the soundless whistle from forming behind her lips. She had never expected him to have this effect on her. "Stepsister, Mr. DeSalva."

"Lucas, please." He pulled out the chair and sat down. "There's no need for formalities between us, is there?"

"N-no," she stuttered at the intimacy in his voice. There was an inexplicable, hard glitter in the green eyes, and Jennifer wondered what was wrong.

LUCAS ORDERED A ROUND OF DRINKS from the hovering hostess. With deliberate slowness he pulled a lighter and a pack of cigarettes from his inside coat pocket, shook one out, put it between his lips and flicked the lighter into a blue flame, all the while studying Jennifer beneath drooping lids. He let his eyes touch quickly on the braided and coiled honey-blond hair before his gaze traveled to tilted violet eyes and a wide sensuous mouth, then on to the determined, dimpled chin. She definitely was not what he'd expected as Susan's younger sister. Now, dammit, he'd have to change his whole strategy. Or would he?

He had come prepared to do anything to get the information he wanted. Somehow he couldn't see his plan working on this young woman. Damn that lying, thieving bitch to hell and back for sending this dewy-eyed... He was at a total loss for words to label her. Maybe this was what Susan had planned, though, to throw him off the scent. Now all he had to do was find out to what extent Jennifer was involved in her sister's thievery.

His lips curved in a wicked smile. He'd see how far Jennifer McCord was willing to go and how many lies she was prepared to tell. He braced his elbows on the table and leaned forward. "Well, Jenny, why has your sister been keeping you under lock and key?"

"Stepsister," she reminded him, and watched the chiseled lips smiling at her. But instead of the warm glow she'd first experienced, she now felt as if a Siberian wind had draped her in a frosty shroud. She fumbled for the briefcase in the chair next to hers. "I've brought the German and French translations you wanted to go over."

He waved away the folder she held out to him. "Not here, honey. Didn't your sister tell you those papers are highly confidential?"

"Stepsister, and yes, as a matter of fact I'm fully aware of their content and importance, Mr. DeSalva—"

"Lucas, please," he interrupted, his body motionless.

"You see, I did the translations. I thought you knew Susan turned your account over to me about three months ago."

"Did she now?" Three months! He felt ready to explode. Two months ago Kane and Shasta Stone, special people with special talents, had turned up the biggest leak ever from DeSalvas through the European computer industry. Actually, it wasn't until that very morning that an inside source let it slip that Jennifer was the only one working on the DeSalvas account, and Kane immediately set to work checking her movements. They had even switched the meeting place from DeSalvas' to the hotel across the street so Shasta, Kane and his own brother, Brandon, could get a good look at their prime suspect. Lucas's hands itched to reach across the small table and shake her by her slim shoulders till she confessed.

He inhaled deeply and shifted his gaze across the room, meeting three worried pairs of eyes. They knew the signs of his simmering temper and were silently warning him to play the game out—get as much information as possible. He shook his head slowly. Play it cool, he reminded himself sarcastically. This woman and her stepsister had only cost him more than a million dollars so far. "How long have you worked for your sister, Jenny? Or is it a partnership?"

"Stepsister," she said slowly striving to control her temper.

"Sorry."

He didn't sound sorry to her.

"I guess it's confusing with both last names being McCord, but I'm sure Susan referred to you as her sister?" He left the question hanging in midair.

Jennifer leaned back in her chair, trying to get away from the telling light and collect her thoughts. For some reason Lucas DeSalva was toying with her. "I'm sure you're wrong. Susan would never claim kinship if she didn't have to. Stepsisters we might be, but friends—no." She shifted farther away. "I would imagine she'd be more than willing to relate the story of how generous she's been toward her poor, struggling stepsister with a generous loan so I could finish graduate school. Then how magnanimous she's been to allow me to work off the loan on a pittance of a salary while she withholds the remainder to apply to my account." Jennifer gulped, appalled at what she had said and the venomous tone she'd used.

Well, well. Lucas grinned. Here was pure anger, something he could get his teeth into and deal with, instead of the phantoms of the past months. Were the thieves falling out?

Jennifer reached for her wineglass and took a swallow. Maybe the wine would make her forget her years of hurt and heartache over Susan's behavior. Glancing over the rim of her glass, she saw the cool green eyes watching her closely, and forced a bright smile. "Sorry, I guess my past is showing."

"You seem a little young to have a past," he teased as he leaned back in the chair, relaxing his tall frame by sheer willpower. "I've known Susan for more than two years and I find her extremely difficult to get along with."

Why was he so persistent in discussing Susan? "I find that hard to believe. Not with Susan's preference for male clients." She could have bitten off her catty tongue. What was wrong with her tonight?

Lucas relaxed farther back into his chair, congeniality and comradeship oozing from every pore. He grinned confidentially, his lips curling slyly at one corner. "Susan's not exactly my type. I seem to have fallen under the spell of violet eyes, magnolia skin and rose-petal lips. They should have named you 'Fleur' or something exotic, instead of 'Jennifer'."

Magnolia skin! Rose-petal lips! It was one of the corniest lines she'd ever heard. But for some reason, the smooth words that rolled off his lips had the sensuous feel of mink.

"Tell me, Jenny. Does Susan hire free-lance translators to work on her major accounts?"

"No," she breathed, still looking into his eyes, hypnotized by their changing depths.

"Do any of the employees ever take the translations home to work on?" He kept his voice low.

"No, just me." She withdrew her eyes from his.

This was too easy and the thought bothered him. Straightening in his chair, he gave a strained chuckle and reached for her hand. "Just you?" His thumb slid back and forth on the inside of her wrist. "Come on, everyone takes work home at sometime or other."

Confused at the sudden change in his questions she answered, "It's company policy. No work leaves the office. But because of the volume and complexity and the tight deadlines DeSalvas has demanded lately, Susan agreed that I could work on your account at home. Believe me, Lucas, those papers *never* leave my sight from the time I receive them till your messenger picks them up."

"How old are you?" he demanded, an edge of anger in his voice.

Jennifer was tired of his seesaw temperament and questions. "Twenty-five," she snapped. "Is there anything else you'd like to know? I have all my teeth." She grinned hugely, and despite himself he laughed. "My arches are good, my back's strong and I've been told I'm fairly intelligent."

"Admirable qualities," he murmured, "but I'm not in the market for a workhorse."

They stared at each other silently. "Honey, your eyes are an incredible color. I'll wager," he said, lowering his voice, "I'll wager they turn the same shade when you're making love."

Jennifer snatched up her purse and briefcase but a strong hand clamped around her wrist, stopping her upward movement and forcing her slowly back down into the chair. "I'd have credited you with a better sense of humor,'' Lucas stated, intrigued by the fleeting expression of fear that flashed across her features.

She did have a good sense of humor. The problem was the effect his words seemed to have on her. She watched him now as his eyelids drooped in a manner that filled her with thoughts of passion.

''Tell me about yourself, Jenny McCord.''

''There's not much to tell.''

''I can't believe that.'' Lucas studied her over the rim of his drink, his bottom lip barely touching the crystal.

Jennifer watched him as if mesmerized. ''My life story would only bore you.'' Her throat felt suddenly parched, and she picked up her wine and took a sip. ''Actually, I find it rather dull myself.''

''Try me.''

Try me? Jennifer felt her cheeks flush with heat, thankful Lucas couldn't read her thoughts. ''I was born in Georgia. My father was a diplomat, so I've lived all over the world. Maybe that's why I have a talent for languages,'' she mused. ''Early exposure. Anyway, I went to a variety of schools. My father died when I was thirteen and three months later my mother married Charles McCord.''

''That didn't bother you?''

Startled by the question, Jennifer immediately replied, ''No.'' The word came out harsher than she'd intended, and was softened with a smile.

''Go on.''

''This really is a bore, Lucas.''

''Go on.''

''I grew up, went to the University of Texas, majored in languages. I have a B.A. and my master's—attended graduate school and am now trying to find the time to complete my dissertation for my doctorate. End of story.''

She fidgeted uncomfortably under his hard, doubting stare.

"That's all?"

"Basically, yes. That's it."

Jennifer caught the blazing anger that flashed in Lucas's eyes and she jerked backward as if she'd been slapped. What was happening? She opened her mouth to demand an answer, but stopped, totally confused. Lucas was now smiling at her as if she were the only person in the room. The man was a chameleon, and his ability to alter his moods in a split second exhausted her. She leaned back, resting her head against the leather upholstery of the chair, needing time to compose her thoughts.

"Am I boring you, Miss McCord?"

Jolted back to reality by the sarcasm in his voice, Jennifer mumbled, "Sorry, what were you saying?"

"I asked if you'd like to join me for dinner?" He held up his hand to stop the refusal he saw on her lips. "We need to go over these translations, but quite frankly, I'm so hungry I couldn't think my way out of a wet paper bag." He smiled beguilingly. "Please, Jenny, have dinner with me." His voice dropped to a soft plea. "Don't make a lonely man eat an equally lonely meal."

How could she refuse—how could she refuse him anything? Lucas pulled back her chair and guided her through the maze of tables.

They walked around the back of the club, slowly making their way through the crowd toward the entrance. Jennifer walked before Lucas, his hand clamped around her elbow as he steered her forward. Almost within reach of their goal, Jennifer felt the pressure increase as Lucas pulled her to a stop, turning her to face the three occupants of a small, dimly lit table. As Lucas began to introduce her both men stood, leaving the woman between them to throw back her head to look up at the towering men.

"Jennifer, I'd like you to meet Shasta." Lucas stopped, reached around one of the men and pulled the tiny woman to her feet. "This pixie is Shasta Stone."

Jennifer exchanged polite hellos with her. Then Lucas continued the introductions. Why, she wondered, did she have the feeling she was being closely scrutinized by all?

"And this is Shasta's husband, Kane."

The man with the strange piercing eyes. Before she had time to comment, Lucas turned her to the other man.

"Jenny, my brother, Brandon."

She gave Brandon a dazzling smile. The family resemblance was remarkably strong. Both had the same features, but Brandon's were softer, his eyes a bright sapphire blue, sparkling with humor. Immediately she liked him.

"Well, hello there, pretty lady."

She felt Lucas's hand tighten on her arm at his brother's obvious flirting.

"How long have you been working for McCord's?" Brandon asked, wiping the friendly smiles from everyone gathered around the table.

"None of your business, brother," Lucas said, stepping into the awkward silence to stop what looked like a sudden flow of questions.

Jennifer frowned at the tension-filled atmosphere. Brandon's question seemed innocent enough, just as Lucas's had, but she detected the anger behind the words, and it confused her even more. Why? Why was so much animosity being directed at her? She'd never met these people before. Yet they all seemed to be accusing her of something. Her lips parted, forming a question, but she got no further than a surprised sigh as Lucas interrupted and quickly made their excuses. With a firm hand on her arm he guided her from the club. Only at the door, as he paid for their drinks, did she have the opportunity to look back over her shoulder. Her gaze met Kane's unusual eyes and she shivered. What had she done to deserve such cold contempt?

CHAPTER TWO

CURLED UP in an amber velvet wing chair in Lucas's hotel suite, Jennifer studied the man's bent head. Absorbed in checking the translations she'd given him earlier, Lucas had totally ignored her since their arrival. Her eyelids drooped pensively as she watched the play of lamplight on his blue-black hair. While the wine had flowed through dinner she'd faced some hard facts in her mellowed state. Now those facts had turned into a reckless fantasy that danced around in her head.

She shifted her attention to the room's furnishings, but not even the suite's understated elegance of dark, warm woods and contrasting silks and velvets in earthy tones of beige and brown could divert her thoughts from their disastrous course. Beyond an open set of carved doors lay the biggest bed she'd ever seen, its peach covers turned back invitingly, ready to wrap the occupants in silken luxury.

Jennifer pulled her gaze from the room and picked up the delicate china coffee cup, then immediately replaced it, rattling it in its saucer. Dammit! She was a grown woman and as normal as the next. Why was she berating herself for her wayward thoughts? The rustle of stiff paper caught her attention, and she glanced up to see Lucas absently playing with the corners of her work. What would it be like, she wondered, to be touched by those hands? Would they be tender or rough? She frowned and shook her head at the avenue her thoughts seemed intent on traveling.

All right, face it, she demanded in disgust. For the past three months Lucas had haunted her dreams and every waking hour. Just what was she going to do to be rid of him? Then, subtly and without warning, an idea began to take shape, an idea so outrageous that it was a long moment before she realized what she was planning.

A woman could have sex, she rationalized, then winced at the starkness of the word and amended her thoughts. A woman could *make love* these days without becoming emotionally involved. All she had to do was approach the idea rationally.

Jennifer slumped in the chair. She was old enough and intelligent enough to analyze her own problems, but recognition didn't always end in resolution. Suddenly, feeling unfulfilled and inadequate, she angrily rubbed her forehead with white knuckles and desperately tried to make excuses for her current state. But her needs, long suppressed, wouldn't disappear as easily as before. Now, for the first time, she faced the fact that her days and nights were empty not only of male companionship, but shared intimacy.

What had come over her? She'd never been attracted to a man before—not like this. Why not...why not follow her instincts just this once? She felt warm and relaxed inside, dreamy. Yet there was also a shakiness that warred with her serenity. Tonight was hers. She firmly pushed all problems from her mind. After all, she continued to argue with herself, it wasn't as if she'd ever have to see him after tonight. But there was one nagging question that plagued her crazy plan: how to seduce a seducer?

No! She couldn't do it. She jumped up and walked to the wide window that ran from floor to ceiling, looking out at the night lights of Houston with unseeing eyes. Resting her forehead against the cold surface to calm her agitation, she sucked in a deep breath of air. The idea was totally insane, a fanciful dream induced by too much wine and the presence of a very sexy man. She gnawed at her lower lip. Maybe just this once... She pushed aside the barrage of doubts and grinned. How to make the first move? What did she have to do?

"Jenny, would you come over here and explain this?"

Lucas's brow furrowed and his eyes narrowed a fraction as he watched Jennifer glide toward him. The barely perceptive sound of silk caressing silk as she walked all but shouted an invitation. He'd been attuned to her every move, every sigh, as he forced himself to concentrate on the papers lying in front of him. After reading and rereading sentences, he'd all but given up hope of understanding the documents.

"Which one are you working on?"

The elusive essence of roses tantalized his senses as she moved to stand beside him. He leaned back and inhaled deeply of the warm arousing fragrance. Then, grumbling a few unintelligible curse words, he answered her question. "French and Spanish I can manage, but checking the German translation is impossible."

In disgust he threw down the pencil he'd been twirling absently. "You've done such a superb job on the French, I'll simply take your word that this—" he tapped with an impatient finger "—has been thoroughly checked." As she leaned over his shoulder, her hand extended to flip through the papers, Lucas drew in a quick breath. The firm rounded breast brushing his arm branded him, and the knot in his belly tightened.

"You won't find any errors in these. When I do a final proofing, I check it backward word by word." She eased farther into his body and grinned as she heard the strangled sound he tried to cover with a cough. He wanted her!

She'd totally captured his attention. A heady triumph engulfed her in a warm flush.

"I usually don't pay much attention to the contents of my work," Jennifer said, "but I must admit that I became intrigued as to why an electronics firm would be ordering all that special steel from Germany." The question hung heavily in the air between them, and Jennifer was instantly alert to the stiffening of Lucas's shoulders and the shuttered expression that settled across his face. "Sorry," she breathed in his ear, trying to ward off the sudden chill in the air. "That was very unprofessional of me. It just struck me as odd." She felt him relax, and smiled. Men were so strange about their little business secrets.

What in the hell was she up to? Lucas twisted around in his chair to get a better look. He deliberately let his gaze trace her slim curves as she stepped back, gave an enticing wiggle and perched on the edge of the desk. A dull ache grew in him as her dress hitched up along one shapely thigh. Captivated despite himself, he watched as the other leg swung free in such a blatantly tantalizing movement he almost laughed aloud. Then he reminded himself there was absolutely nothing funny going on here and he frowned.

The lady was after something and though it fed his ego to think so, he didn't believe she was after his body. Or was she? Was she attempting to use the oldest trick in the book to get information? Aware that she was staring at him, he forced a smile, meeting the bewitching violet eyes.

He itched to loosen the thick, honey-gold braid and run his fingers through the silken mass. He wanted to bury himself deeply in her and hear her moan his name. Quickly he applied a mental brake to his thoughts. No, he'd play a waiting game, find out what her motive was and see how far she was willing to go to gain her objective. But, by

God, she'd better not tease him too much, or he'd give her exactly what she'd been asking for all evening.

Lucas smiled again, a crafty twist of his lips. Maybe he'd encourage her a little and see where it would lead. "Why do I have the feeling I'm about to be seduced?"

"Am I being that obvious?" Jennifer swallowed, surprised at the steadiness of her voice. Hearing his sharp intake of breath, she smiled to herself. In her mind, conflicting thoughts played a tug-of-war on the rights and wrongs of the course of action she was about to undertake. With a few simple words and provocative moves, she'd committed herself totally to this moment. Deep down she knew it was madness, but there was no backing out now. In a sudden panic she tried to interpret his expression, but all she saw was his desire and determination to finish what she'd begun. She shivered as though chilled, then felt his arms encircle her. Her pulse leapt crazily as she watched his lips slowly descend to hers. Then, closing her eyes, she gave herself up to the magic of his mouth.

The kiss became more pronounced as Lucas's arms tightened, drawing her into his body. She felt a wild impulse to laugh as she realized how well they fit. Her five feet six inches seemed designed to mold perfectly with Lucas's six-foot-two frame. She marveled at the sleek power of his body hidden beneath the tailored clothing.

Lucas gathered her closer as the kiss deepened. His arms pulled her tightly against him, igniting a response as she felt the heat of his body and the welcoming scent of him filled her nostrils. Imitating his actions, she delicately slid her tongue forward, diving into the dark moist cavern of his mouth. Her hands worked their way up from his shoulders and her fingers stroked the thick springy hair. With the same urgency her fingers hurried to outline the ear, then touched lightly over a high cheekbone and roughened cheek, stopping at the sides of their clinging mouths. The fusion of flesh and the thrust of tongues back and forth ignited a rush of heat and a spark of hungry expectancy.

His mouth released hers and moved slowly across her flushed face with small kisses. "You have the most marvelous hot little mouth, sweetheart," he whispered in her ear, sending another jolt through her as his tongue caressed the shell-like curves. "I'd like to feel it all over me, licking, biting, warming me with its sweetness." His hands slid up her back, firmly pressing her breasts into his chest.

At his words, Jennifer felt her bones begin to melt. She should have been shocked, embarrassed, but she could only wonder briefly what it would feel like to have his mouth on her body doing all the things he'd just described. His hands were in her hair, expertly pulling pins, letting the heavy braid slide down her back. With quick, deft movements he worked the braid loose, and her hair fell full and free, flowing and rippling down to her waist like poured honey. She looked up to see the wonder and reverence in Lucas's expression, then smiled before closing her eyes again.

Lucas gave a low moan and ran his fingers through the silken curtain, then buried his face in the shiny strands. "Never, ever cut your hair." He threaded a handful of sunshine through his fingers, then pulled her mouth to his, kissing her with an intensity that showed the teasing was over.

Jennifer stiffened slightly at the feel of his hand rubbing across her breast, cupping the firm mound. His thumb played upon an already-swollen nipple, making it stand erect. She tightened her hold on his shoulders, reminding herself fiercely that she'd wanted this.

She was being slowly sucked into a whirlpool of sensations, losing control of her body and her thoughts. Her hands seemed to have a mind of their own and though a little clumsy, they reacted with a natural instinct to touch and stroke. With a sinking feeling, she realized she'd have to be bolder. This business of being a seductress was more difficult than she'd imagined!

She lowered her eyes to the front of his shirt and decided it was the safest place to start. Carefully she worked the stubborn buttons loose one by one. Lucas had become very still, and when she looked up, she saw that his eyes were shadowy and cool. Forcing her stiff lips into a saucy smile, she touched his chest in fluttery movements and the rapid hammering of his heart vibrated under her fingers.

Looking deeply into his eyes, she ran the tips of her fingers across the hard pebbles of his nipples. Without any forethought to her action she lowered her lips to cover the hard peak. As her tongue strummed back and forth, she brazenly dropped her hand and lightly palmed the warm bulge below his belt.

Hands grasped her hair and pulled her head back. "Oh, love, don't. Don't do that, or I'll lose control here and now."

Jennifer grinned, complying with his request, then made matters worse as she traced the triangular mat of soft hair on his chest down to the waist of his pants with her butterfly touch. She watched his eyes close, then slid her arms upward and circled his neck, bringing his head down to hers with little nudges. But his lips wouldn't meet hers. Concerned she'd gone too far, she stepped backward and almost gasped out loud at the whispering swish of silk as her dress glided to the floor.

While she'd been absorbed in enjoying the feel of his body, Lucas had been expertly undressing her. Wearing only a cream-colored lace-and-satin full slip, bikini pants and panty hose, she stood before him, feeling totally naked. She didn't know what to do or say, so she said the most logical thing of all. "Kiss me, Lucas. Hold me. I'm cold and need to feel your arms around me."

"Woman, I'll do more than warm you. I'll make you burn." He groaned and pulled her into his arms, his hands riding the curves of her back, hips and buttocks. His fingers eased her slip up to her waist and became entangled in the band of panties and panty hose. "I hate these damn things." With an expert movement of both hands he flicked the irritating silk-and-lace barriers over her hips. His body dipped and he followed the garments downward, stopping only long enough to cover a satin-covered nipple with his hot breath. On his knees before her, he slowly unsheathed her thighs and leaned forward to kiss the tantalizing inner flesh as he pushed the flimsy material to the carpeted floor.

Before Jennifer could even choke out a sound his hands moved up her sides, from calf to thigh to waist, dragging her slip upward. She raised her arms without a protest and the slip continued its journey over her head, and was tossed onto the growing pile of discarded clothes.

"You are magnolias and rosebuds." His fingers wrapped around her shoulders and his head lowered to a dusky rose-tipped nipple. "And honey," he murmured between the valley of her breasts as his mouth moved to her other nipple.

Jennifer arched toward him, no longer cold or embarrassed but hot and wanton, wanting him to make the delicious tremors that shook her body go on forever.

Lucas gathered the firm cheeks of her buttocks and drew her against him. His mouth captured hers. This time the gentleness was gone replaced by a passion and desire that made Jennifer's ears ring and her legs weaken to the point of collapse. Sensing her complete surrender, Lucas quickly slipped an arm behind her knees and lifted Jennifer up, kissing her eyes closed as he walked to the bedroom.

In the shadowy room he stood her beside the king-size bed and stepped back. With wide, desire-haunted eyes she watched as he kicked off his shoes, stripped the shirt from his broad shoulders and began to remove his trousers.

There was so much she wanted to tell him, but she held back, knowing that if she so much as opened her mouth he would stop. And heaven help her, she wanted him in a way she'd dreamed of and imagined a shared passion should be. With shaking legs she sat on the edge of the big bed and lowered her eyes, following the movement of his beautiful hands as they completed the task of undressing.

Fascinated by the sight of him, she was aware of her shyness melting away. Tall, broad-shouldered, with long muscular legs and lean flanks, Lucas was a perfectly proportioned male. There was nothing frightening here, only the beauty of a thoroughly aroused male, and Jennifer wanted him. She needed to fill the aching emptiness of her life.

"Move over, Jenny, love, and make room for me."

She scooted across the bed but was stopped from going farther by strong fingers wrapping themselves around her thigh.

"Not that far," he said, chuckling softly. "Anyone would think you were trying to get away from me." His hand moved up along her thigh till his fingers came in contact with downy curls. "And we both know better, don't we? You do want me?" A long finger dipped and stroked, and all Jennifer could do was nod her head and close her eyes as her muscles tightened with each caress. "Don't you, love?"

"Yes." She opened her eyes, her breathing shallow as she reached for him and pulled his already-moving body up between her legs, till they lay face to face.

"Jenny, Jenny," he moaned, "you're so ready for me." Lucas levered himself slightly to one side, watching her as his fingers worked magic between her legs, sending an almost-numbing sensation through her body. "I've wanted you from the first moment I saw you sitting across from me." He shifted his weight, nudging her legs wide. "I want you *now*."

Jennifer realized what was coming and willed her body to become limp. She reached up, encircling his neck with one hand, the other flung across his smooth warm back, feeling the muscles under her fingers bunch. And when he slowly entered her, her eyes widened in surprise at how completely he filled her.

Though unfamiliar at first, the constant pressure urged her to respond to his moves. She wanted to close her eyes, shut out the world and only feel what was happening to her. But instinct made her look up, and immediately she froze. Lucas knew. His shocked expression said more to her than any words.

"You stupid little fool," he said, choking on the words, desperately trying to regain command of his body. But the staggering truth was that the woman in whom he was warmly embedded, the woman who'd seduced him with her sophisticated tricks and brought him begging, was a virgin.

His discipline for giving pleasure first whirled out of control. He groaned aloud in an effort to regain it and gasped, "You asked for this...you must have wanted it."

He tried to hold back on his final thrust but failed, then collapsed, gathering a bewildered and disappointed Jennifer in his arms.

Seconds ticked by with only the sounds of Lucas's ragged breathing filling the room, Jennifer continued to stare at the ceiling, wondering what had happened. There should have been more.

"Well, love, I don't think this was what you expected, was it?"

She flinched at the question.

"Easy, easy." His arms tightened their hold on her. "Don't go all stiff on me now. We're not through."

Lucas moved his hips slightly and Jennifer's eyes opened wider. She'd thought it was over, but as he started to move again, she realized just how wrong she was. Lucas certainly wasn't conforming to any rules she'd ever heard of.

Balanced above her on his elbows, Lucas gazed into her eyes, now dark with hunger and dilated with painful urgency. He smiled and watched the red moist mouth return the gesture. Then her lips parted as if to speak, and he touched a quick kiss to their softness. "There's no need for words, not now. I'll make it good for you, love."

He cradled her head in the crook of his arm, brushed away the damp strands of hair from her temple and moved his hips in a slow, steady movement. He had to fight back fiercely the urge to let go again. Dear God! He felt like a callow youth unable to control himself. She was so incredibly hot and tight, fitting him like an exquisite handmade glove. No one had ever felt this wonderful before.

Jennifer heard a low sobbing moan, realized it was coming from her throat, but couldn't seem to stop. She closed her eyes tightly and gave herself up to the moving force of his body.

"That's it, Jenny, wrap your legs around me."

She responded, moving in unison to his rhythm.

"Look up, Jenny. I want to see the desire in those incredible eyes." He groaned again, trying to control the explosion building in him. "You feel so damn good."

The luster in her eyes became an incandescent glow as she focused on the taut planes of his face. His breath disturbed a wisp of hair against her ear, and the simple movement sent a shaft of pure fire through her body. She could take no more. Light and sound seemed to merge. His tongue caressed the jumping pulse in her throat, then slipped into her mouth. Her own hands became embedded in his thick hair and she returned his wild kiss with unrestrained passion.

Yanking her mouth from his, Jennifer gulped in air, her heart pounding in loud drumbeats in her ears, her body aflame. "Lucas, make it stop," she cried out.

"Now, Jenny?"

"Yes," she breathed, "yes."

Gently Lucas slipped his hands under her hips and held her tightly against him as he began to increase the rhythm. Icy fingers played across her nerves like lightning across a black sky. Her eyes opened fully and for a second focused on Lucas's smiling face, before her world blew apart in a million shards of sensation. When she began to float down and feel the earth right itself, he refused to let go and sent her spiraling upward again, this time to the bright burning sun.

JENNIFER SNUGGLED DEEPER into the warm covers and drowsily sighed with contentment. All she wanted to do was sleep, but a persistent pain in her upper arm ceased to go away.

"Dammit, woman, don't you dare fall asleep."

Lucas's words shattered her serenity and he continued to shake her shoulder. "Stop it, Lucas." Half awake, she looked up at the man leaning over her and flinched at the anger stamped on his face.

"Get up." He tossed a walnut-brown terry shaving robe at her and strode toward the door. "You'd better be out of that bed and in the other room in two seconds or, lady, you'll regret it."

Lucas was dressed and Jennifer realized she hadn't even been aware that he had left the bed. A little smile lifted the corners of her mouth as she remembered the reason for her total exhaustion. From the living room came a bellowed, "Jennifer," and she jumped, shook her head to clear the cobwebs from her brain and tried to evaluate the situation. Hurriedly pulling on his robe, she sprinted through the door, only to be stopped by the sight of him pacing back and forth. One thing was sure, here was a man in a fine temper and his anger was all going to be directed at her.

Lucas halted, his expression full of self-disgust as he assessed her disheveled appearance. He steeled himself against the passion-reddened lips and sleepy look of fulfillment. Slowly he let his eyes travel to the gaping robe, which revealed a distracting amount of cleavage. Grasping the material in both hands, he held the lapels together and led her to a nearby chair, then gently pushed her backward. Jennifer attempted to stand, only to have Lucas push her down. "Stay put." Towering over her, he grabbed a matching chair for himself and positioned it before her. Elbows propped on his knees, he rested his chin on tightly clenched fists and his eyes bored into hers. "Now, damn you, talk."

She knew he was going to be a little upset. After all, no man wants to appear a fool, especially before a woman. Still, this anger was something she'd never expected.

"Look at me." He took a deep breath, striving hard to calm down. "I don't like seducing—"

"You didn't seduce me, Lucas." She smiled. "I seduced you."

"So you did." Caught up in his own memories, Lucas lost track of what he was about to say. His mind wrestled with conflicting pictures of the provocative, uninhibited woman he'd bedded and the innocent he knew her to be. He felt a traitorous warmth singing through his veins and shifted to a more comfortable position. "I don't know why or how this happened," he mumbled almost to himself. "We'll go into that later."

The tenderness in his gaze was replaced by a savage gleam. Suddenly all he could think about was the money DeSalvas had lost and that this woman was in some way part of the conspiracy. "Right now, lady, all I want to know is how much this night's work is going to cost me?"

Jennifer gasped at the crude statement and continued to stare at him in openmouthed, round-eyed stupefaction.

"You needn't give me that injured look, either. We both know that's an act." Lucas raked his fingers wildly through his hair. "Hell, you would have let me do anything to you and never have uttered a sound." He shook his head in disbelief and his eyes flashed momentarily with pain. "How much are you and Susan planning to try and fleece me for?"

"Susan? What does Susan have to do with us—with this?" Jennifer was thoroughly confused, and it suddenly became paramount that she make him understand the reason behind her actions. "Lucas, I don't want your money. I wanted you. It's that simple." She saw his mouth twist, cynically.

"No, honey, nothing's simple or easy. I'll repeat what I asked earlier—what's this going to cost me in dollars and cents?"

Jennifer leaned back and smiled. "And I'll repeat—I want nothing from you. If you must know, I never intended to see you again after tonight." That ought to take the wind out of his sails, she thought, and was shocked at his reaction.

Lucas jerked forward in a violent lunge that brought them nose to nose. "You mean I was nothing but a one-night stand?" he shouted. He had to get control of himself, he thought wildly, but the indignity of her words left him breathless. The absolute nerve of the woman, to sit there as bold as brass and tell him, Lucas DeSalva, that he was no more than her stud for one night.

The reversal of roles suddenly struck him, and he surged to his feet, turning his back on her before she could witness the laughter in his eyes. She'd checked every argument he'd been about to launch. Now he had to change tactics. He spun around. "Would you mind telling me how a woman of your age and supposed intelligence could still be a..." The word stuck in his throat.

"That's none of your business," she retorted without thinking. The menacing look he threw caused her grip to tighten on the arm of her chair. She bit down on her lip but couldn't seem to stop the next words as they came tumbling out of her mouth. "I don't know why you're so upset. After all, it wasn't *you* who lost anything."

Lucas took one quick step toward her, then stopped. Checkmate. She'd done it again. "Haven't I? You've yet to tell me what it's going to cost me." He threw back his head and closed his eyes. "Would it be too much to ask if you use any form of birth control? Because I sure as hell didn't hold back or take precautions.''

Jennifer felt her cheeks burn. ''No.'' She straightened her shoulders defensively. ''I don't make a practice of viewing every man as a prospective lover.'' She met his gaze serenely, but the horror of what he was suggesting began to sink in, and her stomach twisted with fear.

Lucas looked at her in awe and shook his head. ''Mad! Totally and irrevocably mad. How could you be so stupid as to pull a stunt like this? Did it ever enter your pretty head that you could get pregnant?'' He watched the color drain from her face with savage pleasure. ''Such things do happen, Jenny, even in this day and age.''

Dear heaven, no, she prayed silently. Surely life wouldn't be so cruel. She swallowed hard. Looking up, she watched the beautiful, warm green eyes frost over like an icy pond and braced herself for his next words. ''Or is that part of your and Susan's game? A pregnancy would tie everything up nice and tight, wouldn't it? Is that what you're hoping for, Jenny? Because if you are...'' He paused, then altered the threatening tone of his voice to one of cool restraint. ''Smarter, more sophisticated women than you have tried that trick, and, lady, it didn't work then and it won't work now.'' Calmer now, he sat down, satisfied that he'd made his point and absolved himself of any future problems.

''You poor deluded fool!'' Jennifer's eyes sparkled with anger. ''I feel sorry for you if you go through life thinking every woman wants something from you.'' She threw up her hands in disgust and bewilderment. ''And would you please tell me what Susan has to do with all this?'' She waited, but when he only continued to stare at her contemptuously she stood, proudly straightening the gaping robe around her, and began picking up various articles of strewn clothing en route to the bedroom. "What I did, I did for myself—not you or anyone else."

She slammed the bedroom door and hurriedly began to dress. Who would have thought a man of Lucas's worldliness would react in such a manner? With unsteady legs, Jennifer yanked open the door and marched out, primed to do battle again if necessary. But Lucas was nonchalantly standing at the antique bar, holding a large, half-filled glass of liquor. She marched to the door, grimacing as he lifted his drink in a silent mocking salute.

"Where do you think you're going?" He took a large swallow of the fiery, amber liquid, his eyes moving over her in derision, taking in her rumpled appearance. He slammed his glass down with such force that it shattered, spilling its contents and spraying the carpeted floor with shiny wet splinters of glass.

Hands on hips, Jennifer thrust her chin out determinedly. Her eyes dared him to make a move toward her, though heaven only knew what she'd do if he did—run, more than likely. "I'm going home. We've said all that needs to be said."

Lucas turned his back on her, plucked down another glass and poured himself a drink. "You're wrong there, Jenny. We're by no means finished." He spun around and leaned back against the bar in a relaxed confident manner that made Jennifer bristle. "I want some answers from you about your dealings with Susan, but you're right—not now. Tonight all I want to do is strangle you." He picked up the whiskey bottle, walked over to his recently vacated chair, sat down and carefully poured himself another drink. "We'll talk tomorrow."

"Goodbye, Lucas." Jennifer opened the door and walked out into the empty hallway.

"Not 'goodbye,' Jenny, love. Not by a long shot."

A cold shiver ran over her skin at his soft reply, more unnerving than all his previous rantings and ravings. As she pushed impatiently at the elevator indicator she smiled. After all, what could he do now?

Lucas stared hypnotically at the closed door as if his eyes could penetrate it and he could see Jennifer entering the elevator. He lifted the crystal tumbler to his mouth and tossed back the expensive liquor as if it were water. In one smooth, unhurried movement he stood, drew back his arm and threw the glass against the far wall. It struck with a resounding crash, followed by a string of curses. "Damn her lying, cheating soul to hell," he shouted, and stomped to the bar. But instead of replacing the smashed glass he reached for the telephone, punched out a series of numbers and waited for his brother's voice on the other end. "Get up here," he growled into the receiver, then hung up.

Within a short period of time, Brandon DeSalva was stalking the hotel suite like a sleek tomcat, sniffing out trouble and asking questions while a closemouthed Lucas helped himself once again to the liquor.

"Come on, brother, quit drinking yourself into a stupor." Brandon slipped up soundlessly behind Lucas and retrieved the glass. "If you want to get drunk, do it on your own time." He took a small sip, eyeing his brother's grim face over the rim. "I left a purring little kitten curled up sound asleep in her bed. The least I can do is be there when she wakes up, don't you agree?" All the while he was talking he'd been inching his way toward the closed bedroom door. Reaching his goal, he quickly twisted the knob and shoved it open. "Aha!" He started to laugh at the tumbled covers, the scattered robes, but Lucas pushed him out of the way, pulling the door shut with a solid thud.

"Well, well, well," Brandon murmured as he followed Lucas back to the center of the room. "Would it be too much to ask what you found out about Susan and Jennifer McCord?''

"Nothing."

"I see." Brandon eyed the bedroom door speculatively and frowned, not understanding. "Look, Lucas, I don't have all night." He held up his hand to stop his brother's retort. "No, there's no need to lie. I know you and your technique for getting information from women. Now—" he sat across from Lucas "—how are they passing our designs to the foreign manufacturers?"

"That's the hell of it, I don't know," Lucas mumbled into his drink, watching a skeptical expression cross Brandon's face. "I never got around to asking." His lips tightened as his brother threw back his head and laughed.

"That good, was she?"

"Shut up, Brandon!"

The smile on Brandon's face slowly faded to a look of bewilderment. "Well, what the hell did you do, then? The plan was—"

"I know the damn plan. Hell, it was my idea. So don't sit there and preach to me of plans." Lucas inhaled deeply and took a gulp of whiskey. "Dammit, man, she was a...uh, innocent," he muttered. Unable to say the word, he finished off his drink in one quick movement.

"What? Innocent of what? You said yourself she was involved up to her pretty eyes..." His words trailed off. "Innocent? You don't mean innocent as in *innocent*, do you?" But Lucas wasn't listening to his usually articulate brother stumble over his tongue. He was staring down into an empty glass. Brandon slumped in his chair, attempting to make some sense of their garbled conversation.

A queer feeling rumbled in Lucas's stomach, and he continued to concentrate on the bottom of his glass. For the last half-hour his mind had been having a field day with the ramifications of this night's activities, and not one of them had anything to do with stolen designs or the loss of corporate money. No, all his mind could grapple with was that he'd made love to a beautiful woman. A seductress who was a... The word was so alien to his vocabulary and experience he couldn't even whisper it. He didn't understand the heady feeling he got every time the word surfaced. When had the metamorphosis from metropolitan, liberated man to male chauvinist taken place? He didn't care if a woman had one lover or twenty in her past. The sophisticates of the world were appealing only because they were experienced and played by the rules. Hell, there had been so many women in his life he couldn't put faces to names he did remember, and vice versa.

Lucas swallowed, vaguely aware of Brandon's voice droning in the background. He'd ventured where no other man had. A warmth began to move through his veins, picking up speed and heat. He, Lucas DeSalva, had been given the most precious gift a woman could give and it confused him as to why he'd been the recipient of such a jewel. Slamming down his glass on the table, he surged to his feet. "And I'll be damned if I'll share this time," he yelled at Brandon, expecting him to fully understand his outburst. "Brandon, I want you to draw up the usual papers for Jennifer McCord to sign. We'll meet with her tomorrow and get her signature. Also, work up an employment contract. We'll see if I can steal her away from McCord's."

Brandon's mouth fell open. "Are you out of your mind? You want her to come to work at DeSalvas when it's possible—" his voice picked up volume and precision "—no, not possible, more like a foregone conclusion that she and that barracuda sister—"

"Stepsister," Lucas corrected.

"—have stolen our designs and sold them on the European market for no less than a million dollars in profits." Brandon gave a harsh laugh. "You want me to draw up the usual agreement," he snarled, "for that little thief to sign?"

"She's no thief, Brandon."

"No?"

"No!"

"How the hell would you know?" She has you so bewitched you're not even thinking straight."

Lucas smiled, and Brandon dropped back in his chair, shooting his brother a murderous look. "Listen, Brandon, she's too open, too easy with answers." He went on to explain how he'd kept the wine flowing and tried to trap her repeatedly. "She was telling the truth I'd bet the ranch on it."

"Okay, I'll go along with that till later, but how is she tied to Susan other than being her stepsister? Surely she can see what's going on?"

"I don't think so." Lucas shook his head, his expression distant and thoughtful. "One thing I do know, I plan to keep Jennifer McCord very close. Somehow she's the pawn in all this madness, and I want her as far away from Susan as possible when we close in." He continued relating the night's events with a marked hesitancy and carefully chosen words. Though Brandon was his brother, the corporate lawyer and his own personal attorney, Lucas still felt uneasy, vulnerable somehow. Lawyers always demanded to know everything, but he'd be damned if he'd fill him in on all the details. What little he'd related already made him feel a traitor to Jenny. He picked up the whiskey bottle and poured a generous amount in both their glasses. They sat quietly, each in his own thoughts, till Brandon broke the silence.

"Do you think Susan's working alone in this?"

Lucas frowned thoughtfully. "When I called her to check on the security and let it drop that we had a big project coming up, you could almost hear the wheels turning in her head. No, she's not alone in this. She doesn't have the contacts or the knowledge to sell in Europe. Either someone's working for her, or she's collaborating with somebody. He's the bastard I want." He took a quick drink and went on. "But that will take time, and right now the only thing that concerns me is that Jennifer said she took over our account three months ago." Lucas rubbed his forehead absently, as if to wipe away his nagging thoughts. Then he locked gazes with Brandon. "About that same time the designs for the computerized drilling valves showed up at U.S.A. Oil."

He took another hefty slug of liquor. "It's a damn good thing they didn't realize what they had, or we could be in real trouble." Lucas laughed, a sound devoid of amusement. "From what Kane's spy says, they couldn't make heads or tails of the design." He swirled the remainder of the liquid around in his glass, watching the myriad lights and colors play against the cut crystal. "Have Shasta do a thorough background check on Jennifer."

Brandon grinned. Here was the sly fox of old, back sniffing out his enemies. "Then you do think she's involved?"

"Oh, yes. But not the way you think. I have a feeling she's being set up. But why?"

"Lucas." Brandon studied his brother's pensive expression and bit his lip hard to keep from laughing out loud. "When you said 'innocent,' did you mean as *intactus*?" Lucas nodded, not meeting Brandon's probing sapphire eyes. There was a long, poignant pause. Then Brandon held out his glass. "I think I need another drink."

CHAPTER THREE

JENNIFER CLUNG TIGHTLY to the fine threads of sleep, dimly aware of a persistent ringing pulling her up from the security and comfort of oblivion. The irritating sound continued and her hand snaked out from the warm covers to grope along the top of the bedside table. Her fingers found the wood grain clock, and with clenched fist she thumped the top, hoping to shut off the alarm. But the harsh ringing went on and she opened one eye and glared at the telephone.

"Hello," she mumbled groggily into the instrument resting loosely on her shoulder.

"You just couldn't do as you were told. You had to go and screw up everything, didn't you?"

"Susan." Jennifer jerked upright at the venomous tones. Wide awake now, she asked, "What are you talking about?"

"I ought to fire you, *sister* dear."

"Susan..." Jennifer began, trying to offset the sarcastic tone that seemed to have become a permanent part of her stepsister's voice lately. "Calm down, Sue, and at least tell me what I'm supposed to have done."

"Don't call me 'Sue,'" the voice snarled over the phone.

Jennifer winced, realizing she'd unconsciously used the same nickname that Susan's father had. She should have remembered and tried to deflect the tirade she knew was coming. "I'm sorry, Susan, it just slipped out."

"You damn well should be, and you'll be even sorrier after Lucas DeSalva gets there. I have a feeling you'll wish you'd never been born."

Jennifer squeezed her eyes shut in a frantic effort to block out the memories of what she had done. Then her eyes popped open. How would Susan know? "What about Lucas—what are you talking about?" She flinched at the crudeness of the laugh that followed her question.

"Is he good, Jenny?"

"What?"

"Is he as good as he looks?" Susan purred. "Who would have thought it of our sweet Jenny?"

"Susan, I don't know what you're talking about," she lied, feeling a hollow sensation in her stomach.

"Don't you? Well, let me tell you a few things. Lucas DeSalva was at this office at a quarter to eight this morning to see you. When I told him you weren't due in till around nine-thirty or ten, he demanded your address."

"You didn't give it to him?" Jennifer cried, praying that just this once Susan would do her a good turn.

"Are you crazy? Of course I did. You don't turn down a man like Lucas. But, then, you of all people should realize that—after last night," Susan needled mockingly. "I'll have to hand it to you. Innocent you may have been, but you sure learned fast. You've got him panting for more. Though if I were you, I'd be very careful how I play my hand."

The mocking laughter came again, and Jennifer quickly hung up. She stared off into the distance, wondering how a man as gentle and loving as Charles McCord could have fathered a daughter like Susan.

She and Susan had been at odds from the moment he had married Jennifer's mother, and over the past twelve years, Jennifer had tried to make peace, Susan had never given her the chance. Nor would she let her forget that she held Jennifer responsible for the defection of Charles's love. It had been a catch-22 situation right from the start of her mother's remarriage. Jennifer was a shy, frightened child and Charles's compassionate nature responded to her need. When, after unlimited patience and much love from Charles, she began to trust him, Susan's resentment had broken the bounds of civility. But there was a deep guilt Jennifer experienced, too, a guilt that she had indeed taken Susan's father away from her and Susan played upon her feelings at every opportunity.

Jennifer closed her eyes and pulled the covers up to her chin. Thinking of the past hurt too much. She wondered if she would ever be able to put it behind her and live for the future. A humorless chuckle escaped her lips. At the rate she was going, her tomorrows looked as dismal as her yesterdays. She buried her face in her hands and groaned out loud. What had she done? Another pitiful moan escaped her lips. She was deeply shocked at her actions and tried to think of every excuse possible to account for her behavior. How had she allowed herself to be beguiled into committing that one disastrous act?

But no answers were forthcoming, and she clenched her teeth together so hard her jaws ached. Her only comfort was the knowledge that it would never, ever happen again. She threw back the covers in disgust and jumped from the bed. She could run away from the reality of her actions, but she couldn't hide from her thoughts. Sometime, one way or another, she knew she was going to have to face the consequences.

Jennifer studied her reflection in the bathroom mirror, searching for changes. Had her mouth always looked so vulnerable? "Stop it," she whispered, then shook her head. Now she was talking to herself. A sure sign, she thought unpleasantly, that she was slipping.

After a quick shower and a light application of makeup, Jennifer tugged on her favorite old, faded-blue terry robe, flicking her waist-length hair over her shoulders. In the living room she paused suddenly, quickly scanning the area, making sure everything was neatly in its place, loving the security of her mother's once-cherished possessions. Waterford-crystal lamps sat regally on antique Queen Anne end tables, catching the morning sunlight and showering the highly polished surface in a rainbow of colors. Old, white wicker furniture brightened the dark hardwood floors and the pale floral covers gave an airiness to the room. She sighed in satisfaction. At least here everything was as before, she thought, and marched into the kitchen to put on a pot of coffee. As the percolator happily bubbled away she dropped two slices of bread in the toaster and was just reaching into the cavernous depths of the refrigerator for the butter when the front doorbell rang.

Jennifer froze, her pulse suddenly pounding. Lucas! Surely not. The bell chimed again, and still she stood bent over, her eyes riveted to the small bulb at the back of the refrigerator. Susan said Lucas had asked for her address. His departing words came back in a hot rush. *"Not 'goodbye,' Jenny, love. Not by a long shot."* A shiver ran lightly over her skin, and rubbing her arms briskly, she doubted if the sudden chill had anything to do with the open refrigerator.

"Just a minute, please," she called out, then frowned at the shakiness in her voice. She straightened her spine, tightened the belt of her robe and smoothed back her long hair. If it was Lucas, what could he possibly do to her? As she approached the door her steps lagged a bit and her palms became damp from nervous tension. She tried to reassure herself she wasn't afraid of any man. Hadn't the past taught her there was nothing a man could do to ever emotionally hurt her again.

Jennifer yanked open the door and scowled at the two men on the threshold. "What do you want?" she demanded ungraciously, and then began to close the door a few inches. But her efforts were foiled as Lucas, followed by Brandon, pushed their way into her home. She twirled away, firmly planting her hands on her hips, unaware of the gaping front of her robe or the fact that in her haste her hair was spread around her shoulders like a silken veil, tantalizing the imagination of the uninvited guests.

Lucas stiffened as her husky voice licked at his senses. Her hair, a loose shining curtain of spun gold, seemed to beckon his touch. He knew she wasn't even aware of her sensuous appeal. He blinked as Brandon nudged his shoulder, then cleared his throat. "Good morning, Jenny. I believe we have some unfinished business."

"I can't imagine what," she fired back, acutely aware of Brandon DeSalva's steady gaze as he dissected her in slow measures. She glared at him and was surprised to see the twinkle in his bright blue eyes.

"This will clear up any questions, I think," Lucas held out a folded sheet of paper. As she reached for it, Lucas turned and walked over to the long white wicker couch and sat down, confident of his control of the situation.

Jennifer felt the normally long fuse of her temper begin to shorten at his show of arrogance. She dropped her outstretched hand to her side, feeling like an insect pinned up for inspection. "Excuse me, my coffee is ready." She spun around and was about to stomp off, when Brandon's voice stopped her.

"May I have a cup, too, Jennifer? My brother dragged me away from my warm bed at an ungodly hour this morning."

She nodded and quickly retreated to the kitchen. As the door banged closed behind her, she leaned back against the cool surface, doubled her hands into tight fists and waited till the urge to scream passed. Those green eyes! She'd been haunted by them all night as they mocked her, flashed with anger and darkened with desire. Wrapping her arms around her waist, she bent forward slightly. What was she going to do? Why hadn't she rid herself of her obsession with Lucas? Now, seeing him again, she realized how misguided her plan had been. She wanted him more than ever.

She felt within her a deep hunger to be held in his secure embrace and an aching hope that maybe he was different. But she didn't dare trust her feelings. Hadn't all her dreams and hopes been slapped down too many times already?

Jennifer straightened and hurriedly stacked cups and saucers on a tray. Suddenly she paused, her hands clutching a fine Wedgwood saucer as she fought to keep the memories of her father at bay. But Stuart Steel wasn't easily dismissed, even though he'd been in his grave for years. Nowadays society had a label for men like him: wife abuser. But Stuart had been far too intelligent and cultivated to ever lift a hand against his wife or child. He used his intellect, his sarcastic wit and the cruel edge of his tongue to batter his dependents. Jennifer struggled to suppress the memories and grabbing up the small urn of milk and sugar bowl, she slammed them down on the tray. It wasn't fair to remember, not now, after all the scars of her miserable childhood had healed. Or had they? At the door she took a deep breath to calm herself, then pushed it open with her hip.

The two men immediately stopped their low-voiced conversation and looked up as she entered the room. "Let me help you," Lucas offered and started to rise. Jennifer frowned at him, and he sat back down, unconsciously touching a piece of paper tucked away inside his coat.

The tension in the air set Jennifer's already-jagged nerves jumping, and the clanking sound of her spoon against the sides of the china cup rang out like the clear, sweet tinkling of a bell. She halted her movements, looked up and found both men watching her closely. "May I see that paper now?" she asked, her heart pounding against her chest in a sinking feeling that trouble was on its way with a vengeance.

Lucas hesitated a second, wondering if he was wrong in what he was doing. Was he pushing too fast, too hard, too soon? But God, she was a beauty and he wanted her again. Why wait and play the usual games when it was easier to get everything decided and out in the open. After all, he reassured himself, though she was sexy and lovely and he was drawn to her more than any other woman, she was just that—another woman to fill the nights. He extended the paper and sat back.

Reluctantly Jennifer accepted the folded sheet and flipped it open. She read the first few sentences then stopped, went back to the beginning and started over, puzzled at what she'd just read: "I, Jennifer McCord, do hereby agree and acknowledge the following." She swallowed, staring at each humiliating phrase as the words went on and on. Lucas was trying to force her to sign a paternity agreement that would release him from all responsibilities, including the use of his family name and any financial claims she might make on him or the DeSalva empire should she be pregnant. Her gaze lifted and shifted from one man to the other. "This is a sick joke, right?"

"Listen, Jenny. If there's anything in the document you don't understand..." He trailed off then began again. "That's why I brought Brandon. He's not just DeSalvas' corporate lawyer, he's also my personal attorney."

Jennifer felt as if the floor were about to open up and swallow her whole—she wished it would. Never in all her life had she been so embarrassed or insulted. It was bad enough having to face Lucas, but to realize that his brother knew the intimate details of their night together was intolerable. Her pale cheeks bloomed a bright red and her eyes darkened in fury. She opened her mouth to speak, but nothing came out, and she clamped her lips shut, trying to force herself to calm down. Losing her temper wasn't going to get her anywhere with these hardened businessmen. Her cool gaze swung to Brandon as he began to speak.

"I know this must make you a little uncomfortable." He met her direct look and a smile flickered around the edge of his mouth. "But you'll have to realize that my brother is a prime target for opportunists and fortune hunters. A paternity suit is hard to disprove. And after all, Miss McCord, you did proposition Lucas."

"She did not." Lucas looked at Brandon as if he wanted to hit him. "Jenny, believe me, I never told him anything like that."

Brandon picked up his coffee and grinned as his brother and Jennifer eyed each other silently for a long moment.

"I won't sign this," she said scornfully, and threw the document back at Lucas.

"You will."

"Do you take me for a fool? Don't mistake *me* for one of your dumb bimbos." Brandon almost choked and she shot him a dirty glance. "One indiscretion does not mean I'm pregnant. The odds must be a million to one of that occurring. Besides—'' she scowled at them ''—this agreement is all in DeSalvas' favor. What are my rights? Where does it say I'm to be protected from Lucas?''

"That's not necessary," Lucas all but shouted, fast losing patience. "I'd be the injured party."

"Would you?" she asked, her voice taunting. "Would you really? The way I see it, I sign away every right I have, even the legal power to keep my child if Lucas decides to claim him for his own someday. Where is all that DeSalva integrity?'' She paused, suddenly realizing just what they were arguing about. It was all pure conjecture, a hypothetical situation that wasn't likely ever to come about. But the desire to needle was irresistible, and she appealed to Brandon. "If I were your client, would you advise me to sign this?''

"No, in good conscience I would be forced to instruct you to tear it up and throw it in his face."

"Brandon! Stop playing games, dammit." Lucas ground out the words softly.

Brandon's next words stopped her from following his advice. "I'm not your lawyer, Jennifer, and I know my brother. If you don't sign, he'll make your life hell on earth." He leaned back and studied Jennifer with an air of endless patience. "I do agree that it is unfair to you and think that a revised agreement should be drawn up."

"Judas," Lucas grumbled.

"To protect you as well as Lucas. After all, we're only speculating on the future." He grinned. "Like trying to predict the commodities market, wouldn't you say?" Jennifer's frown deepened, and a strangled sound came from Lucas, but the warning noise didn't deter Brandon. "I know you didn't plan to sleep with my brother." His overbright gaze shifted from Lucas to Jennifer and he seemed to be thoroughly enjoying their discomfort. "And Lucas certainly wasn't aware of your—"

"Shut up, Brandon," Lucas roared.

Brandon stood slowly, straightened his jacket and inquired, "May I use your telephone, Jennifer?" She pointed toward the kitchen.

"How could you?"

Lucas's mouth tightened at the anger that flashed in the depths of her violet eyes. "What? Tell Brandon? He's my brother, Jenny, my right arm. There's nothing to be embarrassed about." He leaned forward and in a low voice asked, "I'd like to know just how the hell a woman could attain your age and remain a...so..." He still couldn't wrap his tongue around the word.

"Inexperienced," Jennifer offered helpfully.

"Yes."

"I didn't have time."

"Now that's the stupidest answer I've ever heard," he snapped.

"But the only one you're likely to get," she retorted, then closed her mouth on her next words as she heard Brandon's footsteps.

"I'm sorry to end this lovely morning visit, but something has come up at the office." He stared hard at Lucas. "Something that needs *both* our attention."

Reluctantly Lucas rose, and Jennifer followed, only too eager to be rid of the two men. Silently she escorted them to the door and didn't waste any time slamming it behind them. Good riddance, she thought and mentally dusted her hands of the entire situation.

Lucas scared her more than she was willing to admit, but there was still an attraction, a fascination—like that of a mongoose to a cobra. But now it was over and she thanked her stars that she'd never have to see him again. Walking over to the window, she eased back the curtains, watching as they reached their separate cars and stopped to talk.

Both were almost equal in height, but Lucas moved with an unusual, distinctive gait, a loose-limbed step that projected grace and harmony of muscle and bone, a poise that the younger man lacked. Lucas radiated a leashed power. Jennifer's hand tightened on the pale yellow curtains, wadding the sheer material in her damp palm. She was finished with him!

She spread her stiff fingers and let the curtains fall back into place. She had proved to herself that she was as much a woman as the next, hadn't she? There was no further need for Lucas. She spun around, her thoughts already jumping to the lateness of the hour and the bite of Susan's tongue when she came in late. But as she stepped away from the window she stopped. If she was through with Lucas, if she never planned to see him again, then why, she wondered, did she suddenly feel so empty—so betrayed?

LUCAS UNBUTTONED HIS COAT and slid his hands into his pants pocket. "Remind me to hire a new lawyer. With you on my side, I doubt I'll ever be short of enemies. What were you trying to pull in there?"

"Just testing the waters, Lucas." Brandon smiled and reached out, retrieving another set of papers from Lucas's inside breast pocket. He tapped them on Lucas's chest. "I don't believe you'll have the nerve to present these! He tore up the employment contract and the agreement for setting Jennifer up as his mistress.

Lucas growled and yanked the torn paper from his brother's hand, then threw them through the open window of the car.

"You should have seen the look on your face when she called your women 'dumb bimbos'—classic."

"Stop gloating, Brandon. It doesn't become you." But Lucas was smiling, too. He shoved his hands back into the pockets of his pleated trousers. "There's something not quite right here, though." He gazed thoughtfully back at the cheerful, yellow-trimmed brick duplex. "She was cool and sharp. Yet I sensed real fear under that serene surface. Am I crazy, or did you feel it too?"

Brandon followed his brother's gaze. "She's a contradiction, and yes, dammit, I had the same thought. Yes," he repeated, "under all that composure, she's scared to death of something."

"Jennifer is not a thief." Lucas slipped off the navy Armani sport coat, opened the door of the silver Maserati and hung the coat neatly on the hook behind the driver's seat. "I don't appreciate your dragging me out of there when I wasn't ready to leave."

Brandon's expression immediately sobered. "We've got problems." He tugged at the vest of his three-piece suit and stepping back into the shadow of a spreading oak tree, he loosened his tie. "Our courier was mugged in the men's restroom at Orly Airport." Brandon held up his hand to stop Lucas's question. "The French police say he's fine, just some bruises, but the company pouch was stolen."

Lucas cursed long and low. "The contracts for the three computer design engineers and their expenditures for the new project were in that pouch." He shook his head in disbelief, then laughed mirthlessly. "If I remember correctly, there was also a long letter enclosed ordering them to beef up security. Wonderful," he drawled sarcastically.

"That's not all," Brandon said. "Kane's spies at U.S.A. Oil have informed him that they've just purchased, from the European market, part of our plans for the computer.

They haven't figured out the use yet, but they've now been alerted to the fact that DeSalvas is doing design and research work in the oil-producing field. There's more." He paused, trying to read his brother's calm expression, then shrugged. "The specifications of the valve design were translated by McCord's for the German manufacture over a month ago."

Both men turned toward Jennifer's home, each deep in their own thoughts. "I want the leak stopped, Brandon." Lucas said calmly.

"Then fire McCord's, dammit!"

"No," Lucas shot back coldly. "I want to catch Susan and her accomplice. You tell Kane and Shasta they have a free hand." He slid onto the car's rich, black leather seat.

Brandon caught the door before Lucas could pull it shut. "What about Jennifer?"

Lucas squinted up at his brother through the blinding glare of the sun. "She's mine." He shoved a pair of dark sunglasses over the bridge of his nose. "I'll handle her when I get back from Paris." The Maserati's powerful engine purred loudly to life and Lucas tugged on the door, but Brandon refused to let go.

"I'll keep a close eye on her while you're gone." He winked, then slammed the door on Lucas's gathering frown. The car leapt forward, and Brandon stood watching till it sped around the corner. He turned his thoughtful gaze to the neatly kept lawn and the brick house and started up the sidewalk.

ON THE THIRD INSISTENT RING of the doorbell, Jennifer added the final twist to her long braid and held it firmly in place atop her head, hurriedly sticking in the long hair pins to anchor it securely. She stepped out of the bathroom, glanced at the bedside clock and sighed, resigned to the fact that she was already late for work. The bell chimed once more and she mumbled threats to her visitor around a mouthful of pins, she yanked it open.

Snatching the pins from her mouth, she glared at Brandon DeSalva. "I'm through with you DeSalvas. Go away!" A second later she found herself staring at empty space as Brandon, slippery as an eel, eased past her and made himself comfortable on one of the long wicker couches. She wheeled around, kicked the door shut with her foot and marched over to stand in front of him. "I want you out of here—now!"

"Ah, Jennifer, don't shout. I've got a terrible headache." He touched the tips of his fingers to his temples as if in excruciating pain, but his eyes were twinkling merrily. When Jennifer could no longer keep from smiling, he sighed extravagantly. "That's better. Contrary to what you think, I'm not an ogre."

"No, just a DeSalva. What do you want?" She sat down on the matching couch across from him and waited.

"I came back to explain a few things about Lucas. Maybe it will help you to be a little more forgiving about his strong-arm tactics."

Jennifer's lips tightened and her eyes flashed with renewed anger.

"Before you tear me to shreds, please listen to what I have to say."

"Does your brother always send you to do his dirty work?"

Brandon shrugged. "Occasionally, but he's not aware I've taken this one upon myself." He leaned back, crossed one leg over the other, unbuttoned his coat and stretched one arm along the top of the thick floral-print cushion. "Twice in Lucas's life he's been named in a paternity suit. The first time was while he was in his last year of high school—he became involved with a woman twelve years his senior.''

Jennifer's eyes widened in a mixture of astonishment and curiosity.

"Lucas was always a lot older than his age. I think most children raised on a ranch mature sooner because they see so much of life. Anyway, the woman was an opportunist and took full advantage of the situation. We were lucky to settle out of court.''

His hand slashed the air in a gesture to halt her questions. "Not because the child was his. After all, a blood test then could only prove the possibility of fatherhood. My family was agreeable to the settlement because of the damage the scandal could inflict on Lucas's future. And yes, to protect his ego and respectability in the eyes of his contemporaries. The child, a girl, was born blond and blue eyed, like her mother. As dark as we are, it was almost impossible for her to be a DeSalva.''

Fascinated despite herself, Jennifer poured them both a cup of lukewarm coffee. She handed Brandon his. "The second time?'' she questioned softly.

"Ah, now that was an all-out private fight.'' Brandon took a sip, thoughtfully trying to decide just how much to tell. His lips twitched at Jennifer's avid interest. "He became involved with a bankrupt Italian movie star just as DeSalvas was beginning to pull out of an economic slump, but the stock situtation was still shaky. A public scandal of the magnitude that the movie star was threatening…the damage would have been irreparable.''

He shrugged again and held his hands out in a defeated gesture. "We settled, and three months later the 'lady' had a miscarriage. Jennifer, Lucas has been used and his pride's been stomped on so much that I doubt even you could condemn him for being a little gun-shy. Like most people, he does whatever is necessary to protect himself. As far as women are concerned, Lucas feels safer with rules to follow and legal agreements to fall back on. So don't be too hard on him, please."

She sighed, feeling the hard knot of humiliation ease somewhat. Lucas had suffered, too. "Redraft an acceptable agreement and I'll sign it."

"Maybe I'll let Lucas bring it around himself when he returns from Paris." He threw out the tidbit of information to see her reaction.

"Oh!" she said, trying to appear disinterested. "How long will he be gone?"

Brandon stood, pulled his vest into place and unbuttoned his coat. "About two weeks. He told me to keep an eye on you."

Jennifer stiffened. "That won't be necessary. I said I would sign, didn't I?" She walked with him to the door and quickly opened it.

"You wouldn't consider dining with me tomorrow night, would you?"

"No. Absolutely not. One DeSalva causing me problems is quite enough, thank you."

"Not even if I promise to treat you like a sister? I miss that relationship."

"Are you kidding?"

"No, Jennifer. I loved my sister very much and though she was three years younger, we had great fun together. You remind me of her."

Jennifer softened under the entreating blue stare. Did all the DeSalva men possess such charming magnetism? Then she remembered fragments of her night with Lucas, and a red flush stained her cheeks. "No. I won't have dinner with you. Now go away. You've made me late enough for work."

"I'll take you anywhere you want to go—spare no expense—no place too far." He backed out, inch by inch. "French, Greek, Italian, even Chinese. Come on," he begged as her hand pushed at his chest, making him back up. "I just want a nice, quiet evening without some female trying to get at my bank account or trying to put a ring through my nose."

"What makes you think I'm any different?"

"Because you belong to Lucas."

"I, dear man, don't *belong* to anyone." She pushed again, this time harder, and forced him to back out of the doorway completely.

"I won't take no for an answer." She slammed the door on his words, but he yelled out, "I'll call you later at the office."

Jennifer sagged against the door and began to laugh. It had been a long time since she'd found anything amusing enough to laugh about and it suddenly felt good to be alive

CHAPTER FOUR

UNLIKE THE MAJORITY of business commuters who hated their daily flirtation with death on the never-ending concrete serpent that wound its way into downtown Houston, Jennifer loved the drive. There were those who claimed that the heart of the city had been surgically removed, divided and transplanted to the suburbs, in the Galleria, Greenway Plaza and other complexes. But she didn't believe it—not when you could walk the streets and feel the electricity of life permeate the very air around you.

This was a young city unbound by restrictions, a city filled with men who still made multimillion-dollar deals while eating a world-famous, sloppy hot dog at James Coney Island. A city with underground tunnels that spread beneath it like a river, the tributaries overflowing with shops and restaurants of every kind and description; any and everything to titillate the taste buds of even the most finicky.

At noon the lunch crowd could spend their hour of leisure at various places throughout the city or listen to a variety of entertainment sponsored by local organizations and businesses—opera, mimes, local rock musicians, even the Houston Symphony Orchestra. Jennifer simply loved to watch the people around her, feel the hustle and bustle, the heartbeat of the city. Excitement flowed along the busy streets in and around the mix of glass, brick and steel. There were critics aplenty who scored Houston's haremscarem skyline, but Jennifer reveled in the assortment of angles and never tired of looking up.

She swung her ancient Mustang into the parking lot around the corner from the towering structure of bronze glass that housed McCord's Translation Service and pulled to a stop. Jennifer was late, so late in fact that she managed to startle the usually overinquisitive young black attendant. She was halfway out of the car, when his high-pitched voice reached her.

"Three thousand, Miss McCord," he shouted as he loped along behind her, panting from exertion. "That's my last offer for that bucket of rusty bolts."

Jennifer stopped. Even in her rush to avoid Susan's sharp tongue, she couldn't ignore the eager appeal in those wide, innocent eyes. Of course, he was the biggest con man in the whole downtown area. She'd heard of his deals and had been duly warned by her coworkers. Her eyes traveled slowly to the diamond-bright, almost-classic, apple-red Mustang, then back to the deceptively bland gaze of her daily hustler. "Willie, you ought to be ashamed of yourself, making an offer like that. Why, just yesterday the traffic cop on Main Street stopped me and offered me twice that amount. When I told him of your offer, he said he'd have a talk with you."

"Never say you told Officer King that, Miss McCord," he squeaked. Then he flashed her a smile. "You're pulling my leg?"

She laughed and waved, stepping off the curb as the lights changed. But her good mood was shattered as she pushed through the doors of McCord's. She passed the huge computer room, crinkling her nose in distaste at the smell of hot electrical wiring coming from the rows of machines now being operated behind individual partitions. Modern electronics was wonderful; she just wished the machines didn't have to be kept at a temperature that made her lips turn blue from cold.

Jennifer entered her office, switched on her own unit, dropped her purse away in a desk drawer and picked up her work assignment for the day. Three familiar brown envelopes rested on her In box, and she quickly ripped them open. Someway she was going to have to convince Susan to take her off the DeSalva account. She flipped through the business letters to be translated into French, German and Italian, then scanned the English originals.

"I guess I'd be smiling, too, if I had two men sniffing at my heels. Brandon DeSalva has called twice." Susan pushed away from the open doorway and glided forward, her arctic-blue eyes full of malice. "You must tell me how you do it, Jennifer." She picked an invisible piece of lint off the sleeve of her two-piece, turquoise suede suit.

Jennifer eyed the expensive garment and the silver-and-turquoise Indian squash-blossom necklace appreciatively, admitting her stepsister certainly had a flair for clothes. She sometimes questioned Susan's high style of living. Granted, when Charles and her mother died in a plane crash five years ago, Susan had been left well provided for.

Jennifer remembered her own legacy from Charles and hid a tender smile. He had left her the home she now lived in. A duplex with one side her haven, her hideaway, and the other side rented at an exorbitant price because of its location and easy access to the network of freeways. She knew Susan had always resented the gift, and lately she'd been trying to talk Jennifer into selling it to her.

"Are you listening to me?" Susan demanded.

"Sorry, what did you say?"

Susan's thin, overglossed mouth twisted in a semblance of a smile. "I'd appreciate it if you'd get your mind out of the bedroom and off Lucas long enough to pay attention.

I asked you for the copies of the DeSalva translations. They need to go in the safe.''

A frown flickered quickly across Jennifer's brow in puzzlement. ''I was going to run them through the shredder now that they've been approved.''

''I'll do it.'' Susan held out her hand and Jennifer passed the copies over. It was company policy that all confidential work was to be stored for twenty-four hours after the client's acceptance, then fed into a shredder that turned the paper into confetti. She thought it strange that Susan wanted to withhold the DeSalva copies.

''If we lose this account because of your little escapade last night, you're fired!''

''Listen, Susan, what I do on my time is my business. Besides, I don't think a man in Lucas's position gives...'' She got no further as Susan's stony expression changed to fury.

''You might have been on your own time, Jenny, but you were conducting business—my business—and therefore representing my company.'' She slapped the papers across the palm of her hand and the cracking sound made Jennifer jump. Susan turned to leave, then stopped, her lips twisting slyly. ''If you don't like my rules, you can always leave.''

''You know the terms of our contract won't permit that, and I don't have the cash to pay off the balance of the loan.''

Susan was very still, her body taut. ''Yes, you do,'' she said quietly. ''Sell Dad's duplex to me.''

''It's not Charles's, Susan, but mine.'' Jennifer leaned forward, laying her hands down on the desk top and scowled. ''Why do you persist in wanting my home? Surely you're not thinking of selling that beautiful house where you were born and moving into the duplex? Besides, my house is worth five times what that contract is."

"Yes, but selling is the only way you're going to be able to get out of the contract, Jenny dear. Otherwise you work for me for the next two years." She let her eyes glide slowly, contemptuously, around the tiny office, taking in Jennifer's attempts to brighten up the drab decor with colorful pots of ferns. Her wandering gaze stopped at the picture on Jennifer's desk. It was a photo of a beautiful blonde with a shy smile and haunting sadness in the depths of her gray eyes—Caroline Steel McCord.

Susan tore her eyes away and glared at Jennifer. "Your mother was a cunning, scheming bitch who all but ruined my father with her cloying sweetness."

Jennifer gasped, but any retaliation she might have made would have been lost as Susan stormed out, slamming the door. She stared at the picture of her mother. It wasn't true. Caroline had made Charles ecstatically happy. What could Susan have possibly meant by accusing her mother of having ruined him?

How absurd and spiteful Susan could be. Caroline had been quiet and timid and used to come close to tears if you so much as used the wrong tone with her. In anyone else the vulnerability would have become tiresome, but her mother's angelic looks and fragility had everyone treating her as carefully as if she were a Dresden doll.

Jennifer heard the door open and looked up.

"I forgot to tell you," Susan said, barging in and throwing down several pink message slips on Jennifer's desk. "The consulate called and wanted you to confirm that you would be working the Egyptian embassy party in three weeks. I told them you'd return their call." She turned to leave, then halted at the door, her sulky expression adding years to her face. "Why the hell you take on those boring parties is a mystery to me."

"Is it, Susan?" Jennifer asked sarcastically. "You know very well that the added income supplements the meager salary you pay."

"You know the way to alleviate your problems. Or you could start charging Lucas for services rendered."

The door slammed shut, and Jennifer could have screamed in frustration. Susan always got the last word, the last dirty dig, and her barbs always hit their mark. It was bad enough having to endure her taunts about the past. Now, after last night, she'd given her stepsister a whole basketful of insults to throw at her.

She picked up the brown envelope holding the DeSalva files and began to read. But her eyes refused to focus on the words. In one night she'd found passion. Looking back, she couldn't believe she'd been so reckless and stupid, and yes, naive. Or was she so desperate for affection that she had deliberately pushed aside all her mother's preaching? Did that brief fling prove her womanhood?

She'd allowed Lucas to become an obsession. With her past, she should have known better. After all, hadn't her mother's fanatical obsession to make her independent of all men possessed both their lives? Her eyes were drawn to her mother's picture again and she flinched inwardly.

Guilt began to weigh her down. She'd put aside her principles, morals and promises for desire. She wondered if Lucas saw her as the fool she now saw herself as. Dear God! She was so confused and scared. Fear gnawed at her. She still wanted him—more than before. Damn, she didn't have time in her life for these problems, for the heartache a man could bring.

That familiar suffocating feeling was back—this time worse than before. If she saw him again, would she have the willpower to resist him? Could she honestly say she could turn him away? The answer when it came shocked her. No matter how hard she tried to recall all her mother had taught her, she knew that Lucas was the one man who could make her forget everything.

Jennifer cradled her head in her hands. One thing was sure. If there was the slightest chance of succumbing to Lucas again, she would have to protect herself. That meant an appointment with her gynecologist. She certainly didn't intend to repeat her mother's mistake.

LUCAS LOUNGED BACK in an overstuffed, leather executive chair, his expensively shod feet crossed comfortably on the corner of the ornately carved desk, a blue file lying open in his lap. He flipped the folder shut and absently ran the tip of his finger along the embossed letters of Masters Security. His eyes closed wearily and he sighed in frustration. The file on Jennifer McCord only gave him the facts of her past. There wasn't a line to help him understand the mystery of the woman herself, not a clue as to who helped form her life. He pitched the report on his desk and frowned as a small piece of paper fluttered out. A note from Shasta Masterson Stone. He smiled tiredly. Then as the words sunk in, his smile widened in appreciation of the woman's perverse sense of humor.

This is only a teaser to whet your appetite—do you want Masters to dig deeper? I thought you would! So I'm working on it. Call Kane when you get back. I think married life is beginning to make him feel hemmed in. Maybe you could take him off my hands for a few hours—take him out on the town—get him good and drunk—chase women—talk dirty, what-

ever you men do when you're out. But please do
something. He's driving me crazy!

Shasta

Lucas laughed out loud. The idea of Kane moving two
feet away from his wife was absurd. The unlikely couple
always puzzled people who didn't know them. Kane was
decadent and jaded, yet a breath-catching specimen of
manhood in the eyes of women. Shasta, in contrast, was
small, cute, a free spirit with a sharp tongue and a wicked
sense of humor. If any two people in this world were made
for each other, it was she and Kane. They roamed the
world getting into heaven only knew what.

Lucas had a feeling that the government was involved in
their activities, but no matter how hard he tried to find
out, both parties were as closemouthed as clams. He was
glad they had returned to Shasta's home in Houston, sup-
posedly for a rest and to visit family. He'd discussed his
problems with Shasta's brother at Masters, and the next
day a grinning Kane and Shasta had shown up at his office. They told him they were bored with resting and vis-
iting with family and needed some action.

He had had to admit that they looked considerably better than when he'd first seen them. That meeting, he recalled, had been strictly by chance. He'd boarded a jet in
London, headed for Houston and found the only other
first-class passengers were a bedraggled, pale and exhausted Kane and Shasta. Their explanation of lost luggage, passports and trouble with the Turkish government
hadn't carried the ring of truth.

"You're back early."

The voice startled Lucas and he looked up at the partially opened door, expecting to see Brandon. "Yes," he
called out.

"I thought you would be gone at least three weeks. What happened? Is everything okay?" Brandon still stood behind the door, out of his brother's view. "Is it safe to come in?" he inquired hesitantly.

Lucas suppressed a grin. "Yes. I'm not going to hit you—yet."

"Good." Brandon pushed the door open farther. "Because if you hit me I'll have to tell Jennifer, and she'll probably never speak to you again."

Lucas's good humor immediately vanished at the mention of Jennifer's name. "You son of a bitch, that was a dirty trick to pull, taking my woman out while I was away, then telling me all about it over the phone. Hell," he ground out disgustedly, "do you have any idea what was going through my head?" He tried to scowl fiercely at his smiling brother. "I told you to stay away from her."

Brandon's bright blue eyes began to twinkle and his eyebrows rose comically in faked surprise. "Ho-ho. Your woman, is it?"

"Stop being a jackass, Brandon. You know very well we've never gone after the same woman before. Hell's fire, we aren't even attracted to the same types."

"Don't try to categorize Jennifer McCord. That would be your second mistake."

"Oh, and what's the first?" Lucas leaned forward, his attention riveted on the man across from him.

"Don't push her. Not unless you want her to close you out completely." He saw the Masters report lying on the desk and inclined his head toward it. "That's not much help, either."

Lucas was quiet for a long moment, studying Brandon thoughtfully. "You're not going to stand in my way in this, are you?"

"Depends on what you have in mind for her." He held up his hand to stop the questions he saw coming. "Dammit, Lucas, I like her. She's as prickly as a porcupine, but she's intelligent and good company. I'm not sure if she's up to her pretty violet eyes with Susan's thievery or not. Something is not right in that relationship, either. There's no love between those two. Yet Jennifer can't leave Susan's employment. Why? I tried to get it out of her, but no go. She kept changing the subject every time, till it became a kind of game between us."

"Jennifer's under contract to Susan," Lucas said, remembering Jennifer's words the night they met.

"Okay, I'll buy that. What I won't buy is her reluctance to talk about the past." He pointed to the report. "Jennifer told me about her life, but with the same insignificant facts that are in that damn file, nothing more, nothing less." Brandon ran his hands through his thick black hair. "Hell, it's as if she didn't exist until her mother remarried and they moved to Houston."

Lucas studied his brother more closely and his frown deepened. A hard glint flashed in his dark green eyes and his full sensuous lips tightened. Unconsciously he clenched his fist.

Brandon caught the movement. "Don't look at me like that, Lucas." He grinned and held up his own hands in a gesture of surrender. "I'm not interested. I just took her out to dinner a few times and tried to get some information out of her."

"How many?"

"What?"

"How many times did you take her out?"

"A couple."

"Two? Three? More?"

"Six."

Lucas glared at his brother. "No good-night kisses?" Brandon shook his head and Lucas relaxed. "Brandon," he asked, "did it strike you as strange that Jennifer's father, as a diplomat, moved around a little too often?" Lucas rubbed his face wearily and was silent for a long moment. "I didn't think the government transferred diplomats around that often, especially if the envoy had his family with him?"

"Yeah, I noticed that. It seems that Stuart Steel and family only lasted about a year and a half at each post." Brandon flipped the file open. "Did you also catch the dates of Stuart and Caroline's wedding and the birth of Jennifer? Caroline was a good three months pregnant. Given the year and morals of the time, that little incident must have been an embarrassment to a man who had already attained some prominence in the foreign service. Did you also notice that Jennifer's mother remarried only four months after her husband's death?" He shrugged and shut the file. "Oh, well, I'm sure Shasta's next report will answer all our questions. How was Paris, by the way?"

Lucas was so lost in his own thoughts that it took a moment before Brandon's words penetrated. "Fine," he said absently. "The engineers were through with the computer-housing designs. I wanted to make damn sure they got here so I brought them back myself."

They discussed business and rehashed their problems, until the intercom buzzed and interrupted them. "Yes, Cleo." Lucas listened then smiled. "He's right here." His eyes glimmered with laughter, though his expression remained as serious as before. He glanced at Brandon and one corner of his mouth twitched. "I'll tell him. Thanks, Cleo."

"Tell me what?" Brandon inquired suspiciously.

"That JoBeth called to remind us that her handicapped children's fund-raising party is tonight, and she says if you're not there she's going to give your photograph to that gossip columnist."

Brandon cursed long and creatively, bringing a bark of laughter from Lucas. "That featherhead would do it, too. She knows damn well that I break out in a rash when I see a camera."

"It amazes me how you've escaped the professional snoops as long as you have."

"Finesse, dear brother, and running like a scalded cat at the mere sight of the paparazzi." He eased his long body off the edge of the desk and straightened his vest. "I've got work to do. I'll see you tonight at the Warwick." He halted his steps and turned to face Lucas again. A frown flickered across his brow. "Jennifer and I ran into JoBeth several times when we were out, and she was upset you didn't let her know you were going to Paris." He met Lucas's guarded gaze and demanded gruffly. "Why don't you just marry the poor child and put her out of her misery?"

Lucas kept his expression as bland as possible. "I've told you a hundred times we're just friends. Hell, Brandon, we've both known her all our lives. She's like a sister to me."

Brandon snorted disbelievingly and turned to leave, then stopped again at Lucas's next words.

"Tell JoBeth I won't be able to make it tonight, but I'll send a generous check later."

"Why aren't you going?" Brandon demanded.

"If it's any of your business, brother, which it's not, I'm going to Jennifer's to see if I can patch up some of the damage I've done."

"Listen, Lucas," Brandon began, then clamped his mouth shut tight. His shoulders, as broad as his brother's, slumped, and he forced himself to speak. "Go easy. I don't want to see her hurt, and I think you hold the weapons to inflict untold pain. She deserves better. Ah, hell." He raked the fingers of one hand through his hair in frustration. "To tell the truth, I don't know what to make of her."

"I'm not going to hurt her if I can help it, Brandon. But, my God, man, I have to have some answers. After all, I'm the one personally involved with her."

"That's what worries me, Lucas. I know your technique with women. Don't use her like the others."

"I can't make promises, Brandon. No," he growled, stopping the flood of accusations he saw coming, "this is a private affair between Jennifer and me. Stay out of it, Brandon, and from now on, stay away from Jennifer. No more dinners or visits to her home." Lucas accentuated his words with a fierce scowl.

Brandon's eyes began to sparkle at the not-so-subtle threat, and he couldn't suppress a grin. "Orders, big brother?"

"Damn right."

"I'll think about it." He swaggered toward the door once more. "I can't make you any promises," he said, throwing Lucas's own words back at him. "But I'll try to restrain myself just for your sake."

The door closed softly on Brandon's last words, and Lucas shook his head. He'd damn well meant the warning. He didn't relish competition from that quarter. Brandon's way with women had never been lost on him. There were very few females who could withstand his teasing charm.

The tightly held muscles along his jaw began to loosen and relax as he slumped down in his chair and closed his eyes. God, he was tired. Between the constant worry over the stolen designs, jet lag and Jennifer's continuous ghostly presence, he'd slept very little and his peace of mind was nonexistent.

He'd fantasized about her night after night. Wild dreams tormented his sleep. Erotic pictures drifted back and forth in his mind's eye of Jennifer straddling his body, her beautiful hair surrounding him in a silken curtain. In his fantasies he'd buried his fingers in the thick mass and pulled her eager mouth to his. The dreams only whetted his appetite for more.

What did it matter that no one believed him about her innocence? They'd never looked deeply into those eyes and seen the wanting and, yes, the aching need for love. He could easily recognize the feelings—he'd seen them in his own eyes. She might not realize it, but she needed him, and he was going to make damn sure that when the ax fell on Susan and her accomplice—whoever it was—Jennifer wasn't anywhere nearby.

Lucas opened his eyes. Their color was now a deep moss green, diffused with desire, confusion and wonder. How, after years of distrust, had he found so easy to trust a woman who had used him as a sex object, then discarded him as readily as he'd cast off women in the past.

The air seemed to crackle with his thoughts, and the ache in his gut persisted. He tried to close his eyes again in an effort to recapture the events of their night together. Sweet memories that had haunted him for the past weeks brought a look of pleasure to his face. She had been an untouched treasure. The smile that hovered over his lips slowly widened.

Why the hell was he sitting in his office when he could be with her?

He glanced at his watch and groaned. Time was suddenly his worst enemy. She wouldn't be home from work yet. He settled back comfortably in his chair to wait and nap and dream with the single-mindedness of a conquerer.

CHAPTER FIVE

JENNIFER STRUGGLED with the unwieldy grocery bags, shifting them in her arms as she tried to insert the key in her back door. After living in the same home for five years and unlocking the same door an uncountable number of times without difficulty, now, as she listened to the sixth ring of her telephone, why couldn't she get the key to fit? Finally, after another angry jab, brass coupled with brass and her door swung open—just as the telephone stopped its persistent ringing.

Life, she concluded, simply wasn't fair. Lucas DeSalva was to blame for all her newfound problems. She could lay all sorts of mishaps and troubles at his feet. Her absent-mindedness and tendency to drift off into an erotic dream world, her clumsiness and, worst of all, an embarrassing habit of calling people by his name. She cringed at the times she'd mistakenly called Brandon ''Lucas.'' Sometimes she wished he would phone her and she'd have the courage to see him again. Then maybe she could get him out of her system.

Jennifer uttered an unladylike expletive as she dumped the heavy bags on the kitchen counter. Who did she think she was fooling? Sex had reared its fascinating head, and she was adult enough to admit that the thought of repeating the experiment was appealing. Once was not enough to appease the hunger. But Lucas wasn't going to call. She'd made up her mind to that after the second week of silence. Even Brandon's explanations that his brother was still out of the country had begun to wear thin. After all, if Lucas was truly interested, wouldn't he have called, even from France?

The rest of the evening passed in unbroken monotony, and when the doorbell chimed, Jennifer jumped, ecstatic at the interruption and overjoyed at the thought of an end to her solitude. She took a couple of quick steps toward the door, then stopped as her gaze fell on the grandfather clock. Who would be ringing the front doorbell at ten o'clock at night? The chimes sounded again, but this time her headlong rush slowed to cautious steps.

Through the magnifying peephole she stared, dry mouthed, at Lucas's distorted features. In a nervous gesture she jerked her head, sending the long heavy braid flying over her shoulder. Her heart pounded in her throat, and she looked down at herself, then groaned in despair. Why did she have to be in her old robe again?

"Jennifer, are you all right?"

She realized that she had groaned again, louder this time, and instead of answering his muffled question, she quickly unlocked the door with fingers that trembled slightly.

He was standing there as casually as if they were old friends, and as hard as she tried to muster up resentment at his attitude, she could only stare at him. He looked so handsome with his coat off, the expensive tie undone and hanging loosely around his neck, the sleeves of the pearl-gray shirt rolled up to his elbows. Her eyes traveled slowly down the long length of him and just as boldly made a return journey.

"Do I meet with your approval?" he asked, laughter vibrating in his voice. "May I come in? It's damn hot out here."

She felt a fool and stepped back out of the way. "What are you doing here, Lucas?" she demanded, trying with little success to sound indifferent to his presence.

Lucas reached around and shoved the door shut, killing time as he tried to think up an explanation that wouldn't send her into a temper. "I've come to apologize for my behavior the last time I was here." He didn't wait for the questions he saw forming on her lips but turned away and made himself comfortable on the couch. When Jennifer moved to sit opposite him, he reached out and touched her wrist. "Sit here beside me, please."

She watched him closely searching for any hidden meaning in his words. She wasn't going to make it easy for him. Besides, she thought warily, she didn't know how to react to his presence or to his new gentleness. The situation was somewhat awkward for her, though obviously not for him.

Lucas took up her hand in his and held it firmly till she stopped trying to tug free. "Will you accept my apology, Jennifer? I was abominably rude and think I hurt your feelings with my boorish bulldozing."

"Yes," she snapped. His hand was warm and the massaging motion of his thumb along the inside of her wrist was making her pulse jump.

"I'd like to start over again." Lucas leaned forward, reducing the distance between them. "We got off all wrong, Jenny. An affair can't start in the middle."

Jennifer yanked her hand free of his disconcerting touch and swallowed the lump in her throat. "What affair?" she choked out. "I thought I made it clear—" She broke off, wincing as he reached for the long braid lying over her shoulder. He curled the ends around his hand and rubbed the strands between his fingers.

Lucas looked directly into her eyes. His own crinkled at the corners, though his mouth was held firm. Brandon was right. She was as prickly as a porcupine. "I won't lie to you, Jenny. I want you. No, don't move away from me." He held on to the braid, forcing her to remain his captive. "No matter what you say, there's much more between us than just sex. Why not give it and us a chance. If it works, fine. If not, we're both mature enough to walk away without hurting each other."

"Lucas." Jennifer realized he was being sincere and felt compelled to be the same. She held his gaze and her lips gave a slight mocking twist. "I don't know if I'm capable of a relationship, Lucas."

"Why? Why would you say that about yourself, Jenny?" he asked softly as he worked the rubber band off the end of the thick braid and his fingers began to loosen the interlocking strands. "Talk to me, Jenny. We can't go anywhere if we don't open up." When she frowned, he quickly went on. "I'll tell you anything you want to know about me." He smiled at the skeptical arch of her brows. "Anything—just ask."

"How does Brandon keep all his women straight, and who is JoBeth?"

The question took Lucas off guard and he quickly squashed his irritation. "I don't know how he does it. But one thing to always keep in mind about my charming brother is that he could talk a shark into becoming a vegetarian, so watch your step." His words came out gruffer than intended, and he flashed her a rare smile. "As to JoBeth, she and her father have the ranch neighboring ours and they've been friends of the family for years. JoBeth's like a sister to us."

"Have she and Brandon always snipped at each other?"

Lucas shifted closer to her in his agitation. He wished she'd quit talking about Brandon. It was definitely making him angry. "Yes," he ground out. "But I don't want to discuss their lifelong bickering. I want to hear about you."

Jennifer could feel the warmth of his body reaching out to her, beckoning her. He'd worked her braid completely loose and his fingers were stroking the long tresses where they fell across her arm and shoulder. The movement was almost hypnotic, and she licked her dry lips nervously. "There's not much to tell, Lucas. My father was a diplomat and we traveled around the world a lot."

She went on to relate her past as concisely as if she were reading a synopsis. Lucas realized that everything she was telling him was in the report he'd already read. But he was fascinated with what she wasn't telling him, and he tried probing deeper. She sidestepped his questions and shied away and after several useless attempts he realized that if he was going to keep from making her angry, he'd have to stop his line of questioning. He was mystified and intrigued by her guarded responses and her reluctance to reveal anything of herself or her past. What, he wondered, was she trying to run away from? He decided a different approach was needed.

"I guess the traveling around helped develop your ability for learning languages. But it must have been hard on you and your mother having to move every year or so?"

Jennifer didn't ask how he knew the details of her nomadic past as his fingers worked their way under the wide sleeve of her robe, caressing the inside of her arm in long strokes from wrist to elbow. She suddenly realized what was happening and tried to pull away. "Don't, Lucas," she whispered, but was too late as his mouth descended to claim hers. The kiss was long and slow and sweet, and after a few seconds her lips opened under the warm onslaught of his persistent tongue. "I've wanted to do that since the moment you opened the door." His arms slid around her and before she could protest or stop him he eased her onto his lap.

"Lucas, stop. Listen." She sucked in a ragged breath as his lips nipped gently along the column of her neck to her ear. "This can't happen again. I don't want..." She closed her eyes as his breath teased the curves of her ear. "You wanted to talk," she said desperately.

"I changed my mind."

"You said you wanted us to get to know each other." The tip of his tongue outlined her ear, sending the most wonderful sensations spiraling through her body.

"I think we know all that's necessary."

"No, no. You're wrong. I'm not looking for an affair."

"Hmm. You taste so good." His voice rumbled in the hollow of her neck and his fingers gently raked through her long hair.

Jennifer placed both hands on his shoulders, suddenly wanting to flee. "Oh, Lucas, don't do this to me," she pleaded.

There was fear in her voice and Lucas turned his head so he could read the expression in her dark violet eyes. "You don't really want me to stop, do you?"

"Yes—no." Her hands quickly captured his face, stopping its descent to the scented hollow of her neck once again. "Lucas, my life..." She stopped not knowing how to explain. "I've spent my life trying to avoid this very thing. I don't want to get involved with you or any man right now. It sounds trite, I know, but I need my freedom. Besides, you're making me crazy, damn you. I've begun to doubt everything I was taught." She laid her head on his shoulder, suddenly embarrassed by what she was reveal-

ing about herself, but still she went on. "I've always stri-
ven to get ahead and you come along and shatter
everything I've worked for. It's not fair." She sighed, then
mumbled, "My mother would roll over in her grave if she
knew what I was doing."

Lucas smiled tenderly. "You forget, Jenny—you seduced me." She nodded in defeat, and he briefly wondered at the lack of joy in his victory. He was making a
mistake; he knew it as sure as the sun rose in the east. He
was pushing too fast, taking advantage of her confusion.
But damn, she was here and willing, whether she would
admit it or not. "You do want me, don't you?" His hand
slid between the folds of her robe and began caressing the
firm round fullness of her breast. He spread the opening
and his head dipped so he could taste the honey warmth of
her flesh and inhale the fragrance of her skin. "Tell me to
stop, Jenny. Tell me to leave and I'll go."

She couldn't. Not now. Not with his hands and mouth
touching, stroking her in a way that she'd only allowed
herself to dream of. Before she knew what was happening
she was lying beside him on the narrow couch. The robe
twisted under her weight, and the tie at the waist slipped
loose, revealing the full length of her body.

"God, you're beautiful," he exhaled in a hoarse whisper. "The most beautiful woman I've ever seen." He
watched her lips turn up at the edges and the desire-filled
eyes darken to a dark plum. He reached out and threaded
his fingers through her hair. "Do you know I've dreamed
of your hair—of being draped in its softness." Before she
could say anything his mouth descended on hers and his
free hand slid from her hip to between her legs.

Jennifer moaned softly with pleasure. Her hands trembled as they stroked the expensive material covering his
broad back. She wondered why she was lying naked be-

neath him and he was still fully clothed. "Lucas, take your clothes off."

"Not yet, Jenny. I want you to think of nothing but me. No Brandon. No doubts, only you and me. No past to interfere with your happiness. Do you understand, Jenny? I want you to be just Jenny McCord, a woman who needs a man to make love to her."

"Yes, but..."

"No buts."

"Lucas...I—" Her words were cut off with a cry as a shaft of fire shot through her body, lighting her world with glorious colors. She arched against the hand that had set her aflame, and when the bright lights behind her eyelids stopped exploding and the wild pounding of her heart eased, she opened her eyes and gazed up at Lucas.

"You liked that, didn't you?" She snuggled closer like a contented cat, and he could almost hear her purr. Lucas smiled. "You try hard to deny it, Jenny, my love, but you're a passionate woman who loves to be touched. Now I want to make love to you." He quickly stood, then reached down and gathered her limp, willing body in his arms and headed for the bedroom.

THE MORNING SUN crept through the white eyelet curtains, throwing elongated shafts of light over the mound of rumpled covers. Jennifer felt the warming rays slanting across her face and rolled away from the unwanted intrusion. But like a determined despoiler, the light persisted in chasing away her dreams. Her eyelids opened. Then she hugged the pillow to her breast and squeezed her eyes shut, trying in vain to recapture the wonderful dream.

Snuggling farther down into her warm nest, she suddenly frowned. The scent of bacon frying and freshly brewed coffee wafted through the bedroom and her nose twitched. Food? Her stomach gave a loud rumble and she buried her face in the pillow, telling herself it was only wishful thinking. Then she remembered last night with Lucas and knew the dream was no fantasy. He was still there.

At the barrage of vivid memories, she pulled the sheet over her head. She didn't want to face Lucas this morning, or any other morning, she told herself fiercely. Maybe if she stayed in bed he'd eat then leave. But though she condemned herself for many things, she wasn't a coward. Admittedly her movements were slower than normal as she slid out of bed and rummaged through her closet for a decent robe to put on.

Her fingers trembled slightly as she shrugged into a mauve satin wrap trimmed with antique lace. She secured the wide sash snugly around her waist with a sharp tug. A few quick steps brought her before a mirror and she grimaced at her wild appearance. She ran her fingers through her hair, frantically trying to give it some semblance of order.

Jennifer lingered a few more minutes, gazing at her reflection yet seeing nothing but brief flashes of scenes from the previous night. Had she really made love to Lucas with such abandon? She shook herself out of her wanderings. Taking a deep breath, she straightened her shoulders. She'd have to face him sometime.

On feet that suddenly seemed to be weighted down, she quietly entered the kitchen. As noiselessly as possible, she eased into the nearest chair at the glass-topped table. The inviting aroma of food and the strange sight of Lucas standing with his back to her, busily cooking as though it were an everyday occurrence, was too much for her to take in at once. She frowned, thinking cynically that he'd probably done this so many times before, there was noth-

ing awkward about the situation for him. But this was all
new for her and she didn't like feeling uneasy in her own
home. Damn the man. Why couldn't he have gone home
last night?

"Don't frown so early in the morning. You'll get lines."

She jumped, then gazed up into green eyes, dancing with
suppressed laughter. Before she could think of a suitable
retort, he asked, "Do you take cream or sugar, or both?"

"Both."

"Fried or scrambled?"

"What?"

"Your eggs." He pushed a piece of notepaper across the
table and returned to the sizzling bacon.

Jennifer fought to keep her expression serious. After all,
there was nothing in the situation to laugh about, but as
Lucas turned back to the stove her tightly held lips blossomed into a wide smile. He looked so damn outrageous
and out of place in her small kitchen. She wouldn't have
had any room to maneuver even if she had wanted to help.
She noted once again his height and breadth, marveling at
how gracefully he moved for such a large man. Only a man
of Lucas's size and rugged good looks could get away with
wearing one of her frilly pink-and-white plaid aprons tied
around his waist. She had to bite her lip and give a fake
cough to keep from laughing. The colors of her apron
blended so nicely with his pearl-gray shirt. She sensed him
watching her from the corner of his eye, so she glanced
down, instead at the piece of paper he'd so proudly pushed
toward her.

The blood drained from her head so fast she felt dizzy
and she squeezed her eyes shut, fighting the feeling of
claustrophobia. "What's this?" she asked, her voice husky
with dread.

"I've made a list of things you'll need to do today if we want to have you out of here by tonight and into my place." Lucas expertly flipped a fried egg, happily disregarding the splattered grease.

"Out of here?" she questioned.

"And into my penthouse by tonight," he said, picking up his cup of coffee in one hand while wielding the spatula in the other like a sword.

Jennifer felt anger and humiliation building inside her. Her pale cheeks flushed bright red, and she bit her lip to check the spate of words threatening to pour forth. She inhaled a long, silent breath of air. The arrogant, high-handed, overbearing bastard. "Is this a—proposal?" she asked, a sarcastic edge to her question.

Lucas choked on the sip of hot coffee he'd just taken and sputtered, "I never said anything about marriage."

"I know." She smiled, but the smile didn't reach her eyes. "What you meant was 'mistress,' right?"

"No, not that, either. I'm asking you to come live with me, Jenny." He pulled out a white wrought-iron chair and sat down.

"We could try—"

But he didn't finish. Jennifer pushed back her chair and jumped to her feet, her breath coming fast and hard, like that of a trapped animal. He wanted to control her life. "No!"

Lucas surged to his feet, frustrated and angry. Smelling the scorched eggs, he yanked the smoking skillet from the burner. "What do you mean, 'no'? You haven't even heard me out." He dropped the mess in the sink and took a couple of steps forward, then stopped as he saw her retreating till she'd backed herself into a corner of the kitchen. There was real fear in her eyes and he froze, momentarily confused as to why she would be so afraid of him. "Now listen to me, Jenny," he said gently, as if he were trying to coax a startled deer.

"No. I don't want you." In her anguish she didn't see the look of puzzlement that played across his face. All she could see and think about was that he was trying to run her life, take over her future and force his standards on her. She could never accept a life like her mother's, and if it meant hurting Lucas in order to protect herself, it would be better in the long run if she did.

"You're not making any sense, Jenny. How can you stand there and say you don't want me after last night? Hell! From the first time we met you've done nothing but use sex to capture and hold my interest."

"You're wrong. I didn't use you." What could she tell him? That she'd become obsessed with him and had fought those feelings for months. She could never tell him that her emotions were out of control and that she'd been suffering an inner turmoil, a kind of tug-of-war between passion and the standards her mother had instilled in her. "Go away, Lucas...just go away," she murmured with a sigh of defeat.

"This is crazy, Jenny."

"That's tough," she shouted.

He was totally baffled by her vehemence, and wondered what had turned the purring kitten he'd held in his arms into the spitting tiger he now faced. Who the hell did she think she was to turn him down? After all, it wasn't as if he'd ever been attracted enough to ask another woman to live with him. His male ego suffered further bruising as he watched her uncompromising expression alter to one of contempt. "Bitch," he growled softly. "Tell me something, Miss McCord, do you find the thought of living with me distasteful?"

"Yes," she shouted, and the roaring in her ears increased. She could barely hear him now and shook her head sharply to clear away the voices from the past. Hurtful voices, cold and precise in anger—words that bit to the bone. Her father had scarred her life with his smooth cultured tone, so cool, so humiliating. She expected the same from Lucas and braced herself for the onslaught. "Get out, Lucas."

"Fine." Lucas yanked his coat from the back of the kitchen chair and slung it over his arm. "But let me tell you a few truths, lady. You're a tease of the worst kind. You lead a man to heaven, then pull the props out from under him and send him plunging to hell. Tell me, do you get a thrill from playing with men's emotions? You were willing to go to bed with me last night and probably any other night I'd have dropped by, so why the shock and outrage at my suggestion to move in with me?"

"I would not!" she yelled.

"Would not what? Go to bed with me whenever I wanted?" He laughed gratingly. "Honey, I could bed you anyplace, anytime I chose and eventually you'd willingly go along with it." He watched as she covered her ears with her hands and he smiled wolfishly. "Do you want to know why? Because you want me more than your damn scruples and it's killing you, isn't it?" His next words were like darts thrown over his shoulder. "When you grow up, give me a call."

The front door slammed with such force that the windows rattled in their frames, and the sound propelled Jennifer from her safe corner, sending her running to the living room. She halted in the center of the room and looked around, ashamed.

She'd really done it this time! Standing in the middle of a room that had suddenly grown unnaturally quiet and twice its size without Lucas, she wondered dazedly who was crying. Who would sob so wretchedly? Not her! Not Jennifer Steel McCord, who had promised that no male would ever reduce her to tears again. She quickly wiped her wet cheeks dry with the back of her hand. He'd called her a tease and a child in the same breath. She resented the first accusation bitterly. The second she was forced to agree with. But he didn't understand, couldn't know the reasons for her lack of experience with men. He was painfully correct; in some respects she was naive and immature.

Jennifer collapsed in the nearest chair. Once again she'd made a fool of herself, and worst of all, she'd made Lucas feel equally foolish. His ego was dented by her rude refusal of his offer. Leaning her aching back against the chair, she began to laugh, but all too quickly the laughter turned to a choked cry and fat tears snaked a shimmering path down her pale cheeks. At this point she hated everyone—her mother, father, Charles, Susan *and* Lucas. They were responsible for what was happening to her now.

All her values were slowly falling apart and she felt adrift in a sea of strange emotions. And Lucas—why had he become so important to her? One thing she was very sure of, she'd never see him again. Who could blame him? She had to face a harsh truth now. She could not blame Lucas for her erratic behavior lately. She had only herself to hold responsible, and suddenly she realized she must pull herself together.

The past was just that. Her mother and father were dead. They could no longer torment her with their preaching and teaching and constant demands. It was time for her to find her own way in life and forget what her family had tried to mold her into. There was a whole world out there to explore and she had to find her niche in life.

She would deal with her problems one by one till she was completely free. Then no one could stop her from doing what she wanted.

CHAPTER SIX

LUCAS REALIZED that the only piece of good luck he'd had in the past twenty-four hours was the fact that Jennifer's house was only ten minutes from DeSalvas and his penthouse apartment. Any farther distance and he would have been instrumental in causing an accident. His hands tightened on the steering wheel, squeezing so hard that the skin stretched to bone white across his knuckles.

"You stupid bastard." He spat the words out in self-disgust. Brandon had warned him. Hell! He'd warned himself to go easy. So what did he do? He pushed as hard as he could and pinned her into a corner. The anticipation and restraint he'd suffered for the past two weeks hadn't helped the situation, either. Now as he wheeled the car through the sparse early-morning traffic, he felt nothing but shame for what he'd done.

He drove up the ramp to the twelve-story, bronze-and-glass building that was DeSalvas. The lights from the underground parking lot glanced off the windshield, momentarily blinding him. With an angry jerk on the wheel he came to a screeching halt in his parking slot, directly in front of the private elevator that led to the penthouse suite. He rested his forehead against the top of the wheel and sighed out loud. Egotistically he'd taken advantage of her inexperience and in her confusion she'd retaliated in her own way.

Lucas shoved the car door open, slowly climbed out, then slammed it shut. The elevator doors opened with a whisper and he stepped inside, punched the button for the penthouse floor and leaned wearily against the dark wood paneling. Why did the vision of her cornered in the kitchen, fear shining hard and bright in her eyes, make his gut twist? And why the deep fear? He hadn't threatened her. Yelled a little, yes. But he'd said nothing that should have caused that wild, trapped animal look in her eyes.

The elevator door opened so quickly that Lucas, lost in thought, jumped as if he'd been shot when the warning bell sounded. Taking a few long-legged strides down the peach-covered hall, he fished in his pocket for his keys. He strolled into his apartment, his mind so wrapped up in his problems that when Brandon coughed he came to an abrupt stop. His keys dropped to the red marble floor and he shot his brother, Shasta and Kane a killing look.

"The boss man cometh," Brandon began, then broke off what he was about to say and started to laugh. Soon Kane and Shasta joined him and Lucas's scowl deepened ominously.

His eyebrows were almost touching as he watched his brother glide over to him in an effeminate, hip-swaying walk that brought an uncontrollable twitch to his lips.

"I must say, you savage, you," he lisped, "but that apron is absolutely adorable. Do you think I might borrow it the next time I wear my gray suit?"

Lucas yanked the offending piece of fluff from around his waist. He grinned, balled it up and threw it into Brandon's laughing face. "What's the reason for this Saturday meeting?" He helped himself to the coffee and picked up the remaining doughnut from the big box, noting that his three visitors must have been waiting for him for some time. He carried his meager breakfast to the conversation pit in the center of the living room and made himself comfortable on the overstuffed cream-colored leather sofa. He took in Shasta's impish grin and sent her a bland look in return.

Kicking off his shoes, Lucas propped his feet up on the long glass-and-brass table. No need to admit where he'd been all night or with whom. The fact that he'd neglected to obtain any information about Jennifer's involvement in the thefts would only make matters worse.

"Well," Brandon demanded.

"Well, what?"

"Did you find out anything useful from Jennifer?"

Lucas shot his brother a dirty look. "You have a big mouth, Brandon."

Brandon fought to retain his perplexed expression. "What are you talking about? That's the only reason you went to see her, to find out how deeply involved she was in the thefts, wasn't it?"

"How was JoBeth's party last night?" Lucas asked, rapidly changing the subject. He hid a smile as Brandon ignored his question.

"If you two are through digging at each other," Shasta grumbled, "I'd like to get on with this meeting. Kane and I have other plans for today."

Her superior tone didn't wash with Lucas and he glanced at his old friend, catching the grimace that flickered across his face. "Don't tell me, let me guess. You're going shopping?" Kane sighed wearily and Lucas chuckled. Shasta's lack of taste in fashion was common knowledge. It was also widely known that Kane had to drag her around to the stores and pick out her clothes.

Shasta frowned at both men. "If you think he doesn't enjoy himself, you're crazy." Her smile blossomed. "Did he tell you that he sits in the dressing room while I try everything on?'' She rummaged through her briefcase as she talked, and missed the discomfiture in Kane's usually blasé expression. ''Here it is!''

She slapped a familiar blue folder into Lucas's outstretched hand. Reluctantly he flipped it open, then lifted his gaze from Jennifer's typewritten name and watched as Brandon was handed an identical folder. ''How could you have done an in-depth report? I just read the preliminary draft yesterday.''

''Lucas, the file you saw was done a week and a half ago.'' He scowled and she went on. ''If you recall, I said I'd dig deeper. Where's your mind been lately?'' Her question met a poignant silence from all three men. ''I hate it when you gentlemen go all quiet and macho on me.'' She shot Kane a killing glance and flopped down in the nearest chair, oblivious to the damage to her pink silk dress. ''Men,'' she grumbled in total disgust.

Lucas clamped his teeth together and began to read. In a matter of minutes the muscles along his jaw were knotted in anger. Sometime later, and after two thorough readings of the fifteen-page report, he closed it. ''Kane, you've been the most critical of Jennifer. What do you think now after reading this?''

Kane took a long time in answering, and his lack of enthusiasm was as condemning as his next words. ''Sorry, Lucas, but I haven't changed my mind. I think Jennifer McCord and her stepsister are up to their eyeballs in stealing from DeSalvas.''

''You really dislike her, don't you? Why?''

''The fact is that I believe she's playing us all for a bunch of fools with a well-contrived act. She's a sham, a liar and a cheat.'' Both men ignored the long low whistle that came from Shasta's pursed lips.

"Goddammit it, man! How can you say that?" Lucas had to restrain himself from flying off the sofa at Kane. "She's worked for everything she has. How many women do you know who would make the sacrifice she's made to obtain an education—"

"And don't you find that strange?" Kane interrupted.

"Hell," Lucas went on, "from the minute she entered college till she completed graduate school she's attended classes year-round—full course loads, Kane. That means she couldn't possibly have had any time for an outside social life." The verbalizing of what he'd just read was like a revelation, a flash of truth, explaining Jennifer's inexperience. Lucas's dark green eyes locked with Kane's, and in that brief second he wanted to punch his friend.

"Also," Kane went on, ignoring the deadly look, "if you read the report thoroughly you'll see that I was acquainted with her father. Stuart Steel was a brilliant, cold son of a bitch who cared for nothing but his diplomatic position. He verbally belittled his wife publicly, and God only knows if he abused them physically in private."

Lucas opened his mouth to speak, but Kane stopped him with an angry slash of his hand. "Let me finish. Personally, Lucas, I think there's a possibility she hates men and is taking her vengeance out on the DeSalvas."

Lucas swung around to his brother. "What do you make of it?"

"I'm a lawyer, Lucas. I work with facts and hard evidence." His brilliant blue eyes, usually full of laughter, were dark with turmoil. He met Lucas's look squarely and flinched inwardly at the disappointment lurking in his brother's eyes. "My heart tells me one thing—my head tells me the opposite. Besides, there's more evidence that none of you is aware of."

"What!" three voices demanded.

Brandon began to pace back and forth. "I don't know whether you noticed it ot not when you were at Jennifer's house, but I did."

"Brandon," Lucas growled impatiently.

"Antiques, brother. Her home is filled with expensive items. Crystal, paintings, porcelain and furniture." He held up his hand to stop what he knew Lucas was about to say. "Granted, she could have inherited everything along with her home from Charles McCord. But, Lucas, it wasn't until last night that I realized she might be guilty. Believe it or not, it was JoBeth who brought it to my attention."

"What are you talking about?" Lucas asked, his voice soft and dangerously low.

"Oh, bloody hell." Brandon gave up trying to handle the situation diplomatically. "While you were in France, I took Jennifer to several rather dressy affairs and ran into JoBeth. Last night she made a strange remark to the effect that at least my date had some class. I asked her what she meant, thinking I was leaving myself wide open for another one of her insults. But surprisingly she only commented on the gowns Jennifer wore, described them as haute couture and named the designers. She remarked that only a woman with a very big bank account could afford them."

Lucas exploded. He roared and cursed and threw the report across the room. "I don't believe this. Can't any of you see that she's being used? I don't care what that damn report says or what any of you say. Jennifer is not a thief!"

"Of course she's not."

The room fell so silent that Lucas would have sworn he could hear everyone's heart skip a beat. "What did you say, Shasta?"

"You're right. I think Jennifer's being framed to take the fall for someone else." She smiled and sat back, enjoying the uproar she'd caused. When the spate of questions died down as to how she'd come up with her outrageous statement, she shrugged. "Call it woman's intuition, but I have this feeling she is. Anyway, what we need to do, Lucas, is to get hard evidence on the person behind the thefts, and quickly, before they make a bigger dent in DeSalvas's future earnings."

Lucas bestowed one of his rare smiles on Shasta. "I love you, pixie, and if you weren't married and I wasn't involved, I'd marry you myself." His smile disappeared as quickly as it had come and he scowled at the two men. "I want Susan McCord and whoever she's working with stopped." His gaze shifted from Kane to Brandon, daring them to contradict him. "I know just how to start the ball rolling to get Jennifer away from her stepsister." Lucas ignored the conversation around him, picked up the telephone and began to dial.

His life was about to change forever.

JENNIFER WEARILY LEANED HER SHOULDER against a green-veined, white marble column, eased an aching foot from her new shoe and sighed. She squeezed her eyes tightly shut for a brief second, desperately wishing for just one minute of peace and quiet. But it was not to be.

The Egyptian embassy party was in full swing as Houston's social elite moved around an art patron's River Oaks home. Muted orchestral music followed the milling, curious crowd as they progressed from room to room, scrutinizing the profusion of gold, jewels and precious works of art displayed for the benefit of the guests.

She looked around for her clients, forced her swollen foot once more into her shoe and ran her hands down the pale lilac taffeta cocktail dress. The shade complemented her violet eyes, and the off-the-shoulder design was accented with a wide ruffle—a ruffle that was the trademark of an original Oscar de la Renta gown.

Lovingly Jennifer caressed the material near her cheek. She had a closet full of designer gowns that once belonged to her mother. Until recently she'd seldom found any use for them. Now she was thankful she'd saved the priceless creations and that she and her mother were the same size. Admittedly the dresses were old, but they were classic Chanel, Dior, Givenchy, McFadden and Galanos. Their elegant, simplistic lines would never go out of style.

She sighed again. The Spanish ambassador's aides and their wives had proven more than a handful. Though she didn't regret her decision to expand her moonlighting translation work, she realized that spending an entire Saturday escorting four overenthusiastic Spanish women on a shopping spree, then attending the embassy party the same night, was a little much for her sanity. She began to weave her way reluctantly through the throngs.

Thinking about her day, she almost laughed. Who would have imagined the seemingly shy Spanish women turning into demons in their quest for prizes and treasures. The knowledge that Post Oak Boulevard is to Houston what Rodeo Drive and Fifth Avenue are to Beverly Hills and New York, spurred them into a frenzy of shopping. Jennifer shook her head in wonder. The Arab sheikh's five wives, whom she had taken shopping last week, seemed tame compared to these women. True, she had arranged for the ladies of the desert to do their shopping at Neiman-Marcus and Sakowitz after closing hours. Even then she had thought she'd met her match—till now.

"Excuse me." She slipped around a group of wildly gesturing Frenchmen and smiled brightly as one gave her a flowery compliment. As she turned away, her smile drooped slightly.

Damn, why did she have to think of Lucas now? It had been two weeks since he'd stomped out of her home. Fourteen days in which she'd forced herself to face some hard truths. Lucas was right in one respect: in some ways she was still a child. "Pardon me," she said, squeezing through a crowded doorway. No, not a child but a deprived teenager—deprived of the normal upbringing most children have been privileged to have by that age. Her mother had been wrong to force her values on her, and she'd been just as blind not to see what was happening. But now everything had changed. She was more in control of her life than ever. Even Susan had noticed the change in her.

Jennifer frowned. Now there was a real mystery. For the past two weeks Susan's moods had swung from uncharacteristic sweetness to a taunting viciousness that left Jennifer gasping. She didn't let Susan's eccentricities make much of an impression lately. All her senses were honed to a razor sharpness in her effort to forget Lucas and work the additional jobs so she could buy her way out of her contract with Susan. But two weeks just wasn't enough time to blank him out of her life. And there was that nagging little voice that kept asking her repeatedly if she truly wanted to dismiss him so readily.

She dodged around a group of people trying to balance plates of food in one hand, their drinks in the other, all the while speaking animatedly to each passing acquaintance. She was beginning to worry. Her clients seemed to have disappeared completely among the crowd. She checked her watch and quickened her search. The limousines would soon be waiting to whisk the Spanish entourage away to their hotels and she'd lost them.

Standing tensely on the threshold of the second ballroom, she quickly scanned the crowd, searching for a familiar face. But the subdued lighting from the row of chandeliers and the glow of candles made spotting her group difficult. Suddenly the tension between her shoulder blades relaxed as she glimpsed the women deep in conversation about a primitive gold mask on exhibit.

Her gaze traveled from the group to the grim-faced guards on either side of the display, and she deemed it time to encourage the women to move on. After a dozen false starts and stops as the women lagged behind, admiring some new object they'd missed, she finally shepherded them to the door.

Jennifer waved one last goodbye, a smile plastered to her lips. Then she froze. It felt as if each muscle had turned to ice and the fine hairs on the back of her neck stood upright. She knew as sure as she knew her name whose eyes were boring into her. Executing a graceful pivot, she turned as though pulled by an invisible string, her gaze colliding with a pair of forest-green eyes.

Her breath hung painfully in the back of her throat when she realized that Lucas's expression was as cold and foreboding as a river in wintertime. She quickly turned away, but not before she caught a brief glance of his date. Her lips tightened. JoBeth Huntley and Lucas, according to the current gossip columns, seemed to be quite an item. Lately Jennifer had found out more than she wanted about the gorgeous blonde. She was spoiled, wealthy and sophisticated and had a similar background to Lucas's. JoBeth's father was one of the richest oilmen in Texas and would like nothing better than an alliance between the two families.

Out of the corner of her eye she watched Lucas incline his head forward, say a few words to JoBeth, then begin walking directly toward Jennifer. In a rush she released her pent-up breath and started moving through the crowded room, away from Lucas, as fast as the milling people would allow. She was almost within reach of her goal and the open patio doors, when strong fingers clamped down on her bare shoulder.

"What the hell are you doing here?" he demanded as he spun her around.

His question had drawn attention from several surrounding groups. Jennifer glared at him, her eyes as cold as his. But in the back of her mind she wanted to jump for joy. He had left his date to come directly to her. Surely he had missed her. She shrugged off his hand. "I'm working," she answered quietly, then turned around, walking through the open glass doors onto the tiled patio.

"Where are you going? Come back here."

Jennifer ignored his questions and kept walking. For some reason Lucas was unreasonably angry and she wanted to get as far away from an audience as possible. Stepping along the brick path that wound through the elaborate garden, she inhaled deeply as the strong scent of gardenia enveloped her. The night was warm and moist, and the mingling fragrances of a variety of flowers hung heavily in the air. Silently she moved on, listening to Lucas's footsteps behind her. A smile lifted her lips, her eyes began to sparkle and suddenly she realized it was wonderful to be alive. Just as quickly as her smile began, it faded into a scowl. Why, she was actually enjoying his anger.

Jennifer stopped abruptly and turned around, almost colliding with Lucas's chest. She took a step back, her hand reaching for the rim of a cherub statue for support. "Now that we're away from a roomful of snoops, perhaps you'll be kind enough to tell me—" she glared at him stonily "—just who you think you are, storming at me, embarrassing me while I'm working?"

"Is that what you call it?" Lucas's temper was riding high, and he couldn't seem to get a tight rein on his emotions. He'd been fighting with himself all week over what he was about to do. Now anger justified his move. "How many of your clients expect the evening to end up in their hotel room?"

As hard as she tried, she couldn't restrain the flush of heat in her cheeks. He was right. More than once she'd been forced to explain that the translating service didn't include a night romp in her bed. She sighed and relaxed. "I can take care of myself, Lucas. Besides, what I do is none of your business."

An expressionless mask slipped over his features, and she waited for the ax she knew was about to fall.

"What you do is my business, Jenny. You see, I never allow my employees to moonlight."

"Your 'employees'?" She forced a laugh. "Your employee!" Her throat felt tight and her voice came out a hoarse whisper. "I think you've had too much to drink, Lucas. I don't work for you, not directly." Why was he staring at her? Then he spoke, and an earthquake seemed to rock the ground beneath her feet.

"I own you, Jenny. Susan sold your contract. As of Monday morning you work for me."

Jennifer wondered if a heart could actually stop beating, because hers felt as if it had. "No," she choked out. "Susan wouldn't—couldn't, not without telling me."

"Susan cares only about Susan and money, Jenny. Surely you know that?"

"This is a joke, isn't it?"

He shook his head, his eyes never leaving her bloodless face. "Come on, Jenny. It's not that bad. Believe me, I'll pay you what you're worth. At least four times what you're getting now."

"Money!" At her sides her hands clenched into tight fists. "You and Susan are just alike," she spit. "Money! What do I care for money when you're trying to run my life? Why, Lucas? Because I rejected your magnanimous offer to live with you? Revenge is a poor excuse for what you're doing to me. Don't do this, Lucas."

"Listen, Jenny." He reached out for her, but she backed away from his touch, and he dropped his hand.

"Damn you to hell and back, Lucas DeSalva." She spun around and started to walk away. His next words halted her frantic efforts to put as much distance as possible between them and she froze.

"Eight o'clock Monday morning, Jenny. Don't make me come after you."

She kept her back to him, her breathing shallow. "I promise you, you'll regret this, Lucas." The words released the invisible hold he had on her and she walked away into the shadow-filled garden.

Lucas's jaw clenched. He already regretted what he'd done, but it was the only way. He'd simply have to try harder to make her forgive him. Sighing heavily, he started after Jenny.

Jennifer's legs began to tremble and she picked up the pace of her steps. The night, once warm and welcoming, now took on a suffocating quality. How could this be happening to her? Just when she was beginning to get control of her life again.

One of her high heels sank into a crack in the brick walk, almost pitching her forward on her face. She regained her balance and with a sob yanked her foot a few times before she was free. Damn him—and Susan. How could Susan have done this to her? Jennifer didn't have any answers, but she intended to get some before the night was over.

Lucas called her name, and the sound of his voice kept her moving as swiftly as the poorly lighted path would allow. When she reached the edge of the patio and Lucas had failed to catch up with her, she relaxed. Then every nerve tingled as her route of escape was suddenly blocked by JoBeth.

"Can't you make up your mind which one you want, Brandon or Lucas?" Gray eyes, full of contempt, glared into hers. "I want you to stay away from the DeSalvas, Miss McCord. It seems that you're causing them nothing but trouble. Do you hear me?"

Sharp nails dug lightly into Jennifer's arm, and she glanced down, then slowly raised her eyes to meet Jo-Beth's. Silence hung between them till the restraining hand fell away. "I hear you, Miss Huntley, as I'm sure anyone else who is interested has." Before turning away, she added, "He's all yours." It was all she could think of to say, and she wanted to take the words back as soon as they left her mouth. Oh, no, by heaven, she wasn't through with the DeSalvas. But first she had to face another of her demons—a ruthless, greedy bitch named Susan McCord.

SUSAN SMILED SMUGLY into the full-length mirror and ran her hands down the sides of her body, loving the sensuous feel of the silk gown. She turned from side to side, admiring her trim curves, then ran her hands up over her full breasts, wondering if he would be able to tell she'd had breast implants six months ago to repair the damaging effects of time and gravity. She pulled the ivory lace-trimmed robe carefully around her, arranging the folds artfully so as to entice without being blatant. In a whirl of soft silk and trail of fragrant perfume, she left her bedroom.

He was in the same position she'd left him in only minutes earlier, sipping his drink and staring off into the distance. He caught the movement in the doorway and turned his head, his eyelids narrowing to slits.

Susan felt a shiver of anticipation run through her. Just thinking about the night ahead had been exciting. She glided across the room, her hips swinging suggestively, her lips parted and moist. Halting in front of him, she removed his glass from his hand and took a sip, making sure to place her glossed lips where his had been. She returned the drink and was mildly frustrated when he set it down on the table beside the couch with a loud thud.

"Expecting someone, Susan?" he asked, his voice as flat and emotionless as his eyes.

"Just you, love."

"I see. Well, I'm here, so why don't you tell me what the bloody hell was so urgent that I had to come to your house. You know how I feel about being seen together."

"Oh, I know all about you." Susan sank gracefully down beside him, arranging the robe around her before turning to him. His expression was mocking and her patience was wearing thin. Her mouth tightened at the knowledge that he was anxious to get away as quickly as possible. She wanted him and was tired of his games. Now she had a way to force his hand. "You can drop the phony British accent. I know who you are." A hush filled the room, and for the first time Susan felt uneasy about what she was doing. He finally broke the silence.

"Do you really? And just who am I, Susan?" He turned his head to look directly at her, and the tiny gold earring caught the lamplight and flashed out like a bright malevolent eye. There was a menacing look in his expression, as if her words had a physical effect on him. The light seemed to play eerily on the hollows and planes of his face and she sensed the evil lurking beneath the civilized veneer.

The evening wasn't turning out the way she'd planned. Nervous, she got up, walked over to the bar, poured herself a straight shot of gin and gulped it down. The liquor was like a breath of clean wind clearing her mind, and she realized she was making a mistake. This man was much more dangerous than she'd thought. She decided to try a different approach.

As she poured another drink with a trembling hand, she laughed huskily. "Do you remember when I called you two weeks ago, almost hysterical because Lucas was demanding that I sell him Jennifer's contract? He kept threatening to pull the entire DeSalva account if I didn't agree. You said it wouldn't matter to our operation and that we could work things out. You told me you had access to anything at DeSalvas you wanted, and that there wouldn't be any trouble obtaining the information for me to decipher. I did some checking around." She brought the glass to her lips and glanced at him over the rim. Her heart jumped painfully into her throat at his glazed stare. "I figured anyone with easy access had to be very close to the DeSalvas." She tried to smile, but felt only a sick dread. "I didn't realize just how close."

"You're a regular little detective, aren't you?" He rose slowly and walked over to stand before her. "I don't like people snooping into my business."

"Listen. I just wanted to know who you really were. Surely you can understand that. I mean, if you're who you are, then why have you involved me? You could have handled everything on your own."

"And be a suspect?" He clucked his tongue softly, and the sound reverberated through her. "No, the source of the thefts must remain a mystery. Now, what do you want,

Susan—more money? Haven't you gotten everything I promised, everything you asked for? Or is this little charade in demanding my visit for something else entirely?''

Susan gasped as his hand tangled roughly in her hair. She watched, mesmerized, as the black pupils of his eyes seemed to expand, taking all color away and leaving her staring into a dark merciless pit. His fingers tightened, bringing tears to her eyes as he forced her head back. "No," she whispered. Her denial came out shaky, her voice raspy with conflicting emotions. There was an overwhelming thrill in her fear, a waiting hunger in the way her body melted against his and in the hard glitter of her eyes.

"I once said we were just alike. Let's see how much.''

CHAPTER SEVEN

JENNIFER EXPECTED at any moment to feel the pressure of Lucas's hand on her shoulder. Her breath came shallow and labored like a marathon runner's, and her hands shook so hard she couldn't insert her car key in the ignition. After numerous jabs and curses, she finally gave a sharp twist to the key and the car roared to life. Within the familiar confines of her car and surrounded by locked doors, she calmed down and took one last desperate look around. There was no sign of Lucas. Good! She guessed JoBeth must have detained him long enough for her to make her escape.

She shoved the car into gear and began a series of back-and-forth maneuvers in an attempt to free herself from her sandwiched position between two much larger cars. When she finally succeeded, she almost cried out in relief as she swung her car onto River Oaks Boulevard, heading toward the first intersection. It was a blessing when the green light changed to red and she pulled to a stop. She closed her eyes and rested her hot forehead on the steering wheel. How could Susan do this to her? And Lucas—what was he up to?

A car's horn blasted behind her and she jumped, her heart hammering wildly in her breast. She was in no shape to face Susan, but face her she would. The dense traffic down Westheimer forced her total concentration until she reached the turnoff that would take her to the quiet, academic neighborhood near Rice University.

Two-story homes of brick and wood lined streets that still boasted wide thoroughfares, homes that were renovated and spruced up in the belief that older buildings had a sturdiness that modern structures lacked. The facelifts might have changed the homes, but the streets remained the same. They were still lined with huge old trees that spread an overlapping shade over the passing traffic below.

The motion of her car made strange patterns and the streetlights danced crazily across the hood. Time seemed to close in on her and warm memories of her life in the McCord house rushed back. Charles was the first man she'd learned to trust after her wretched childhood with her father. Granted, Susan made her days hell sometimes, but the memories of her life in this house only brought a smile now.

Jennifer turned into the driveway and cut the engine. She sat looking up at the big, two-story house and frowned. Surely what Lucas had told her was wrong, a misunderstanding of some sort. She knew she was only trying to fool herself. She just didn't want to believe that Susan would do something as hateful as sell her contract to Lucas without consulting her. Then Jennifer remembered Susan's strange behavior the past two weeks and her lips tightened. She shoved the car door open and marched up the sidewalk before she could change her mind.

After minutes of standing on the front porch in the humid night air, Jennifer felt her firmly held temper slip its moorings. She began pounding on the door and ringing the doorbell at the same time, calling out, "Open up, Susan. I know you're there." She kept on until she heard the sound of the metal lock being released.

The heavy carved door swung open and before Susan could stop her, Jennifer pushed past. For a second she was thrown off guard by Susan's appearance. Usually immaculate to a fault, Susan was in total disarray. Her over-bleached hair was a tangled mess, her lips looked puffy, her carefully applied makeup was smudged into dark circles under her eyes and there was a red rash over her lower face and neck.

"What in the name of hell are you doing pounding on my door at this time of night? Have you totally lost your mind?" Susan's voice was low and hoarse and her movements were sharp and stiff as she pulled the wrinkled silk robe around her.

"What am I doing here?" Jennifer laughed, surprising Susan with the harshness in her voice. "You never lose that incredible nerve of yours, do you, Susan? I came by to hear directly from you that you really sold my contract to Lucas without even telling me."

"Ah." Susan straightened, ignoring the aching protest of her body. "So you know? How does it feel, sweet Jenny, to be bought and sold? Where are all your fine morals now?" She walked over to stand face to face with Jennifer, her icy blue eyes as hard as diamonds, her tone sneering. "Wouldn't that self-righteous mother of yours roll over in her grave if she could see you now?"

Jennifer gasped. She couldn't believe the viciousness of Susan's attack. Had her stepsister always hated her so much? She refused to accept any responsibility for Susan's behavior. After all, it wasn't her fault that Charles had found the daughter he wanted in her and not Susan. "You needn't attack mother, Susan. She was always good to you and tried to help."

"Help!" Susan's hand shot out and struck Jennifer's cheek. "You stupid bitch. Your mother was an emotional leech who almost broke my father with her cunning sweetness, and you're just like her. You both make me sick and I swore that someday I'd get even with you for taking my father from me. I'm just sorry that your mother died without seeing what was happening to her precious daughter—and what you have in store when Lucas gets hold of you..." She trailed off, her voice high and piercing, filled with hate.

Something broke inside Jennifer. After years of restraint, her own emotions seemed to explode in her head sending flames of anger licking along every nerve of her body. She raised her hand and for the first time in her life struck another human. Not a stinging slap like the one she'd just received, but an openhanded blow that sent a totally unprepared and shocked Susan staggering backward. "You're a little old to be crying for your daddy now. After all, you're the very one who drove him away with your crude vulgarity. So don't dare try to blame my mother or me. You're sick, Susan—evil and so eaten up with hatred I doubt there's any hope for you."

She advanced a few steps in Susan's direction and was pleased to see the apprehension and uncertainty in her stepsister's expression. "Maybe I should thank you for selling my contract. I think you've unintentionally done the best thing you could possibly have done. At least I won't have to put up with you any longer." Susan opened her mouth and Jennifer took another step toward her. "Don't say it or I'll hit you again." She turned to leave, then stopped. "From now on, as far as I'm concerned, you don't even exist, Susan."

The door slammed and Susan jumped. "Well, well," a masculine voice mocked from the partially opened door of the living room. "Your little lamb seems to have turned into a tiger." Susan flinched at the laughter in the voice and tried to avoid looking at him. "Cheek hurt, darling? Come here and I'll kiss away the pain."

Susan shuddered with revulsion and wrapped the crushed folds of her silk robe protectively around her. She forced a confident smile and straightened her shoulders. "We're not through with that lamb yet...are we?"

JENNIFER TURNED onto a deserted side street not far from Susan's house. She pulled the car over to the curb under the darkness of a thick-limbed tree, folded her arms across the steering wheel and rested her head against them. She'd lost control, but God help her it felt wonderful. All her life she'd been taught to be a lady, quiet and unassuming. Study hard, forget about men, her mother had preached. Behave yourself, restrain yourself, stay in the background and get your education, and above all never publicly expose your true feelings.

Tonight she'd broken all the rules. First, her episode with Lucas, now this confrontation with Susan. She felt wonderful, cleansed, almost like a new person. So many things in her life had changed lately, and the one person she held responsible was Lucas.

She thought hard for a few minutes. There was a possibility that she'd been right when she told Susan that by selling her contract Susan had done her a favor. After all, hadn't Lucas said he would pay her four times as much as Susan had? Surely she could buy her contract from him. Besides, she thought, smiling into the darkness, working for DeSalvas might not be as bad as she'd first imagined. All she'd have to do would be to keep Lucas out of her personal life—but only after she'd made him pay for being so overbearing.

Jennifer put the car into gear and began driving away from her past. She started to chuckle, but it turned into a full-fledged laugh. Oh, she'd make him sorry, she thought. That little voice deep inside tried to warn her of the pitfalls of revenge, but she ignored it and continued to laugh. She had two days to form a plan—two days to decide how she was going to deal with Lucas.

WHEN MONDAY DAWNED hot and clear, Jennifer believed it was a bad omen. In her gloomy frame of mind the sky should have been ominously black and boiling with dark clouds. Instead there was a cheerfulness in the occasional gust of wind that tickled the trees and teased women's hemlines higher.

She sat stiffly on her sofa and gazed out the living-room window, only drawing her thoughtful stare away long enough to check the time. It wasn't as if she were looking forward to her coming meeting. She'd been up since four o'clock trying to decide what to wear, how to fix her hair— was her makeup too bright? She didn't want to impress Lucas. The fact that she changed her clothes six times before the sun rose was the fault of her headache and lack of sleep over the weekend.

Her eyes strayed for the hundredth time to the Queen Anne clock. Seven-fifteen. She figured she might as well leave. She'd rather be early than late.

Twenty minutes later she pulled into DeSalvas parking lot, turned off the engine and heaved a heavy sigh. She could have made it in ten minutes, but she had driven slowly and had sat through two lights, calmly ignoring the blowing horns behind her. Finally giving in to her impulse she gazed up, slowly inspecting the twelve-story building, floor by floor. All weekend she'd racked her brain for a plan and as yet nothing had come to mind. She was about to face Lucas with nothing more than her wits.

Her eyes shifted to the huge Galleria complex across the street. This morning she would have given anything to be walking through the mall doing nothing more time-consuming than window-shopping. Taking a deep breath for courage, she left the security of the car. There was a sudden militant sparkle in her eyes as she squared her shoulders, marched up the wide curving granite steps and through the bronze double doors.

She was startled and slightly taken aback when an elderly man in a guard's uniform spoke her name.

"Miss McCord?"

"Yes."

"Mr. DeSalva's waiting for you. If you'll sign in and follow me, I'll take you up to the executive floor."

He was a nice old gentleman who still practiced a Southern courtesy to women. She bristled at the idea of liking anyone connected with Lucas but found she couldn't resist the man's wide toothy grin or the twinkle in his black eyes.

"You have any problems finding your way around, you come to me. And if you're of a mind to work late, come get me before you leave and I'll walk you to your car." He touched the gun strapped to his hip. "This here ain't just for show. Always better to be safe."

Jennifer was touched by his concern and looked closely at the name tag pinned to his shirt pocket before she stepped into the elevator. "Thank you, Frank." When he spoke his next words, she realized he must have misinterpreted the white-knuckled grip she had on her purse.

"Here now," he said patting her arm. "There's no need to be nervous. Why, everyone around here is real friendly. Here we are." He held open the elevator door, craned his neck around and pointed to the double glass doors. "You go right through there and you'll see the boss's name on the door.''

A wan smile stretched Jennifer's stiff lips. She thanked him and began the longest few steps in her life. Dry-mouthed she pushed on the heavy glass doors. They parted smoothly as she stepped through. The letdown of facing a beautifully furnished reception area totally devoid of people was physical, and her shoulders sagged in disappointment. How, she wondered grimly, did she fight the lion in his den if she couldn't find him? It seemed a little masochistic and undignified to have to hunt Lucas down so he could devour her. The image made her laugh and she choked on the sound, fighting the feeling of hysteria. *Get hold of yourself,* she scolded.

With a few more hurried steps she stood before another set of double doors, thickly carved and highly polished. She slowly read the brass plate and scowled: Lucas M. DeSalva—President and Chairman of the Board. There wasn't a knob and she pushed experimentally. To her surprise the heavy doors opened easily under her touch and she slipped inside.

Lucas's outer office abounded with greenery. Lush baskets of ferns hung in profusion around a sand-colored suede couch. Louis XIV chairs and brass gooseneck lamps flanked an immense round coffee table. At the far corner of the room, near yet another set of doors, sat a wide semicircular desk and typewriter, unmistakably his secretary's.

She caught the sight of the nameplate on the desk and grimaced. Cleo. Of course he'd have some exotic creature with tastes that harked back to the jungle, she thought snidely. She turned her attention to the closed door in front of her. He must have a fetish for big doors.

Suddenly the thought of facing Lucas made her feel sick. Behind the door sat her enemy, her boss...her lover. She swallowed hard and nervously fingered the demure, Peter Pan collar of her dress. Now she wished she'd worn something more dramatic, something sexier. The dove-gray linen dress with its white collar and cuffs seemed totally wrong for her mood. She wasn't about to be subservient to anyone, especially Lucas. She quickly unpinned the pale pink rose from her throat and stuffed it inside her purse.

Aware that she couldn't stand there staring at the hated door all day, she squeezed her eyes shut, took a deep breath, tugged her skirt down in the back just to be sure her slip wasn't showing, exhaled and opened her eyes. Her hand shook slightly as she shoved open Lucas's office door, stepped hurriedly inside before she lost her courage and slammed the door shut behind her.

Lucas's head snapped around and met a pair of beautiful violet eyes shooting fire at him. He lounged back in his chair and smiled welcomingly. He didn't have time to utter his carefully planned speech before she was standing in front of him, her eyes all but shouting that she was about to lecture him on what she thought of his underhanded tactics. He tried to warn her, but she ignored his open mouth and the gathering frown across his brow.

"If you think that by buying my contract and forcing me to work here you can coerce me into becoming your mistress—" She slapped both hands flat on his desktop, gaining confidence, then leaned forward. "You make one pass at me—lay just one finger on me—and I'll...I'll file sexual harassment charges against you so fast it will not only make your head spin but will wipe that disgusting grin off your face."

An unexpected roar of male laughter from across the room abruptly ended her tirade. She wheeled around and could only stare in openmouthed embarrassment at the tall, slender man with the roguish grin and black eyes that danced with devilment. He gave her an apologetic shrug.

"Lucas, your manners are slipping. Introduce me to this charming lady who has the courage to put you in your place."

Lucas looked from Jean-Paul's interested gaze to Jennifer's flaming cheeks. "Jennifer McCord, meet a very old friend and business associate from France, Jean-Paul Arnaud."

Jennifer was floundering hopelessly, trying to think of something to say. Death would have been preferable to the humiliation she was experiencing. She shot Lucas a killing glance.

"Bonjour, mademoiselle."

Before Jennifer could reply, Jean-Paul captured her hands and lightly kissed the backs of each. He refused to release his hold as she tried to pull away. "Ah, Lucas, *mon ami*, what have you done to this beauty to make her so angry with you? Up to your old tricks, I see. Still corrupting the ladies. Why, I remember—"

"Jean-Paul," Lucas threatened.

"Oui, another time. I will leave you two to settle whatever problems you have." He raised Jennifer's hands once more, and this time she felt the warmth of his lips linger a brief second longer than the first polite salute. "Don't let him push you around, *chérie*."

Jennifer couldn't resist the wicked sparkle in the dark eyes and smiled in return. "I don't intend to be bullied, Monsieur Arnaud." She tugged her hands free from his hold this time.

"Non, non—Jean-Paul, please." He gazed at her soulfully. "We will become great friends, you and I." He

waved airily to a scowling Lucas and swaggered out of the now-silent room.

Jennifer watched the charming Frenchman leave and shut the door, then spun around and demanded angrily, "How could you let me say all those things with him sitting there? You could have stopped me."

"Could I really? How? You seemed very determined to me." His grin widened. "Though, now that I think of it, there was one sure way to shut you up. But I don't think you would have appreciated my methods." He looked pointedly at her mouth.

She struggled to contain the shudder of excitement that followed his words. He still wanted her. "You're right. I've had a taste of your methods."

"I get your message, Jenny. Sit down." He waved to the nearest chair and she sat, her expression composed and serious.

"Now listen, Lucas. We need to get some things straight between us."

"Yes, indeed," he agreed seriously, but the laugh lines around the corner of his eyes crinkled.

"Stop that."

"Stop what?" he teased.

"You know very well what I mean. You're placing a sexual connotation on my words."

Lucas held up his hands in surrender. "I beg your pardon. I wasn't aware. It must be your contradictory presence this morning."

"What do you mean?"

"That demure dress clashes drastically with the smoldering look in your eyes, Jenny, love. Why, I'd say you looked ready to eat me up when you walked in this office." His own eyes were twinkling merrily as she flushed.

Jennifer leapt up, glaring at him fiercely. "I knew it! I just knew the possibility of your acting like a civilized human being was too much to ask." She clutched her purse and was beginning to turn around, when his voice cracked like a whip.

"Sit." He waited till she was perched on the edge of her chair then lounged back in his own. "It seems as if I'm always apologizing to you, Jenny, but I am sorry. I was just teasing you a while ago. Surely you realized that." When she continued to stare at him, he shrugged. "I know you're suspicious and angry with me for the way I've handled your contract." He watched her body stiffen and rushed on with his prepared speech. No matter that half of what he had to say was a pack of lies. It was for her own good, even though he couldn't tell her. "DeSalvas is about to embark on the conclusion of a secret project that will revolutionize the oil-producing business. You've done a little work on the planning phase already, and I need a translator we can completely trust for this final phase."

He was satisfied with the eager interest in her expression and without hesitation at the deception he went on. "I approached Susan and tried to negotiate with her to loan us your services for nine months to a year, but she wouldn't hear of it. When I threatened to pull the entire DeSalva account, she began to hedge and talk price. Susan wasn't considering your gain with the outrageous amount she was asking. But she made me so damn mad that I demanded to buy your contract outright."

Lucas folded his arms on the desktop, picked up a paper clip and began pushing it around on the smooth wood surface. "You would have thought I was cutting off her right arm the way she squawked. Needless to say, after a couple of days we came to an agreement." Lucas sighed disgustedly, refusing to lift his gaze to hers. He went on, his voice tinged with regret. "I truly thought she had told you, Jenny. But at the embassy party I realized she hadn't, and I exploded and took it all out on you."

Slowly he lifted his eyes to meet hers hoping she couldn't detect the lie. "I'm afraid you got caught in the middle of Susan's greed and my determination to have you working for DeSalvas." He gave her a wary smile. "I apologize for my behavior at the party. But you see, Jenny, I really did need you to help me."

Jennifer listened in complete silence, taking in his every word, searching for a trap. She eyed him suspiciously as the little voice in her head reminded her to beware of Greeks bearing gifts, or, as in this case, of a shark with a wide, innocent smile. Yet her ears could only hear honesty in his words and tone, and sincerity shone in his eyes. "Why didn't you tell me all this the other night or at least call me the next morning to explain? I've spent a hellish weekend."

"I'd already made an ass of myself one too many times with you, Jenny, love," he admitted ruefully. "I figured your integrity would bring you here this morning and we'd clear everything up."

Jennifer blurted out the next question, her heart pounding faster. "And what about us, Lucas? I'm not foolish enough to try to ignore the fact that we've been lovers. Or the fact that the last time we were together you stormed out of my house mad as a cat with his tail caught in a closed door. But I just can't make myself believe you would go this far to get revenge."

"Thank you, I think, for the compliment." He chuckled, and the deep rich sound brought a smile to Jennifer's lips.

"You really need me?" She was beginning to feel excited at the prospect of working for a firm as prestigious as DeSalvas.

"More than you know," he murmured, and his gaze traveled from her bright honey-blond hair, neatly coiled, to the tip of her toes, which peeked out of the open-toed sandals. "You'll enjoy working here, Jenny."

She began to relax her guard and ask questions, till it hit her that he had cleverly sidestepped her question. "You didn't answer me, Lucas." There was no need to explain. She could tell by the tightening of his mouth that he knew just what she meant.

"If you want to know if I'll jump on your bones at every opportunity or chase you around the desk, the answer is no. But if you think my interest in you stops because you now work for me, the answer is again no. But I won't push you, Jenny. I need you too badly right now to have any friction between us. You'll also have to accept that there will be times when you'll have to accompany me to meetings."

He watched the renewed hostility return to her expression and frowned. "I'll need a translator with the German representatives, and my French is passable but not good enough for business negotiations." He quickly rose to his feet before she could protest at the new turn of events. "Don't worry, everything will work out. Give yourself time to settle in. Then we'll get down to work and I'll go over your duties."

Jennifer gathered up her purse and rose from her chair.

"I have a meeting in a couple of minutes, so I'll introduce you to Cleo and she'll show you your office and fill you in." He slipped around the desk and touched her arm. "Stop expecting the worst and smile, Jenny."

She did as she was told and forced a smile on her lips as she was ushered into the outer office and introduced to Cleopatra C. Jones. Her stiff smile curved crookedly in challenge as she met a pair of exquisite, expressive black eyes. Cleo Jones was of an indeterminate age—somewhere between forty-five and sixty-five, Jennifer guessed. But there was no mistaking the tall, stately beauty, the elegance of the thick, shortly cropped jet hair, the pale translucent skin and the full, luscious red lips.

Jennifer felt a sinking sensation as Lucas, having made the introductions, left the room. A tense silence settled between the two women. Jennifer continued to stare mutely, refusing to be intimidated by the glint in the dark eyes.

Cleo suddenly shrugged and grinned. "Good! You don't scare easily. That particular look usually turns Lucas and Brandon on their heels and sends them on their way." She sighed theatrically. "I guess I'm just out of sorts with the DeSalvas and taking my temper out on you." She gestured for Jennifer to follow her across the thick carpet. "I've been executive secretary here since I was twenty-five." Stopping before a closed door, she twisted around. "For thirty years I've known every move, every tiny morsel of gossip that goes on within this company. You, Miss Jennifer McCord, have been a closely guarded secret, and I don't like it." Cleo's hand hovered over the doorknob to Jennifer's office and she continued to stare. "I'd sure like to know why they've kept so quiet about you." Her eyes began to sparkle. "Those boys aren't going to put anything over on me. So be forewarned. I intend to find out everything there is to know about you."

"I'm no puzzle or secret, Cleo. And I'll be more than happy to tell you my boring life's story." She paused and took a shallow breath. "Say over lunch?" she asked tentatively. If she was going to work at DeSalvas, she was going to make an effort to fit in. Not the way it had been at McCords, where she felt she'd never belonged or been accepted. But, she reminded herself, that wasn't her fault. Susan had set the atmosphere, and everyone fell in line or got the sharp edge of her tongue.

It was strange, Jennifer reflected, but ever since she'd become involved with Lucas her life had begun to change—she was changing. The world seemed to take on a different appearance, and she felt happier, even light-headed, despite her confusion over Lucas. She thought of her mother and the past less and less as Lucas's presence continued to dominate her life. She just prayed that she wasn't giving up one obsession for another.

CHAPTER EIGHT

LUCAS LEANED CASUALLY against the doorframe of Jennifer's office, watching her as she studiously typed away. He smiled sightly, remembering Cleo recounting Jennifer's horror at finding her office equipped with typewriters instead of the expected computers. He couldn't blame her; she'd have to spend some readjustment time with the different equipment. Once she understood there was a chance a thief could obtain the access codes to the computers and tap into the system, draining all their secrets, she'd accepted the setup good-naturedly.

The tiny lines around his eyes deepened in pleasure as the overhead lights caught the golden head and highlighted the shining coiled mass. He could almost feel the strands running like warm silk through his fingers. She had the most disturbing effect on him, and until now he'd been too reluctant to put a name to the malaise.

He wasn't so cynical that he believed love was just a myth or a word used for the purpose of sex only. There had been far too many entanglements in his own life. The lonely years of disappointments and disillusionments he'd experienced had given him cause to doubt love, though he'd seen both deep love and strong marriages. But he'd never imagined he'd fall for anyone so quickly and so unexpectedly.

As he watched Jennifer, he thought of Shasta's report on her and knew that his new plan would work. Jennifer had

had an unconventional upbringing. As a child she'd been uprooted every year or so, and for one reason or another, she'd been used as a pawn by both her parents. After the death of her father she had gone through the traumatic experience of her mother's immediate remarriage. Caroline Steel McCord had wanted to live her life through Jennifer. She wanted to shape and mold her daughter to be everything she wasn't. Lucas was sure Caroline believed she was only preparing Jennifer for the future, but her teachings and her own insecurities had begun to destroy Jennifer's ability to grow as an individual.

It was hard for him to believe that a beautiful woman like Jennifer had had so little contact with men her own age. Now all he wanted to do was show her what she'd missed, how much fun it was to laugh and fall in love. He wanted to teach her to trust him and learn that sex wasn't all there was to a relationship. But first, all he wanted to be was her friend. The rest would come later.

"Why are you standing there staring at me as if I had a fly on the end of my nose?"

Jennifer's soft voice interrupted his wandering thoughts, and he gave her a wry smile. "How's it going?" He turned his attention from her face to her office, taking a sudden interest in the stark decor.

Not answering instantly, she watched him as he wandered around, examining the three typewriters, touching the keys and running his fingertips lightly over the foreign alphabet. Then he moved on to stand in front of the window, hands folded behind his back. She couldn't help smiling when he rocked back and forth on his heels and cleared his throat. If she hadn't known better she would have thought he was nervous and uncomfortable.

"Was there something—"

"I understand—"

They'd spoken simultaneously, and both laughed. Lucas swung around. "Go ahead."

"No, no. You're the boss, you first."

He'd never been this tongue-tied in all his life. "How do you like Jean-Paul?" His smile slipped a fraction of an inch. "I understand he's taken you to lunch several times."

"Twice, and I enjoyed it very much." She watched as he sauntered toward her and she marveled at the increased tempo of her heartbeat. This was silly, she reprimanded herself, a grown woman reacting like a giddy teenager. But no matter how hard she tried she couldn't seem to control the effect he had on her. Lucas pushed some papers from the edge of her desk and sat down.

"Jean-Paul could charm a cobra if he wanted to." His eyes bore into hers.

"That sounds like a warning." Her mouth quirked up as his eyebrows came together. "He's been nice to me, Lucas, and the only topic that seemed to interest him was relating tales of his long relationship with the DeSalvas." She didn't tell him that most of the stories Jean-Paul told were of his and Lucas's checkered past, mostly those involved with women. The stories were amusing, but there seemed to be a pattern to the conclusions of their escapades. Though Jean-Paul always rationalized his friend's motives, Lucas usually emerged as ruthless, thoughtless and sometimes even cruel.

"I'm not warning you against Jean-Paul, Jenny. Just be careful. He has a way of exaggerating situations. But he's fun, and a good man to have as a friend." He pushed the papers around on her desk till she removed them from his reach. "What I came in to tell you was that the owners of a German manufacturing company I do business with will be in town this week, and I've asked JoBeth to give a party for them and their wives." He paused for a moment, studying her puzzled expression. "I'll need you to help with the translations. Now, Jenny," he warned as she came quickly to her feet, "I told you this would be part of the job, and it's not as though you've never done it before."

Jennifer's frown deepened and her hands clenched at her sides. "I don't remember agreeing to spend my off-hours working for you."

"You did." Lucas smiled smugly. "Though I'll admit you were a little flustered at the time. Come on, Jenny. What are you afraid of?"

You, she wanted to yell, but she only continued to listen mutely.

"Have I chased you around the office? No! Have I leered at you?" His eyebrows wiggled suggestively at her. "Have I made any lewd remarks or tried to pinch your sweet bottom? I'm not a dirty old man, Jenny, and it's just a business meeting, after all."

Jennifer couldn't contain her laughter. She plopped back down in her chair, shaking her head at the ridiculous pictures he conjured up. He'd been exceptionally good, and she wasn't sure if she was disappointed or not. "Okay, you win. If I agreed, then I'll keep my word."

"Good. It's Friday night, so you have four days to think up all sorts of nasty things to do to get back at me." He hesitated, then stopped. "Oh, I forgot, the party is formal attire. Did Cleo tell you that you have an expense account? I wouldn't want you to have to buy clothes for these special occasions."

"I don't need your money."

Lucas sighed. "Jenny, stop misinterpreting everything I say. Dammit, it's business. I can write your clothes off as a business expense just as I do JoBeth's and the parties she sets up for me. So don't be so pigheaded. Take the money and enjoy spending it on something outrageous."

"No. I meant what I said, Lucas. I have a closet full of perfectly acceptable clothes. I don't need to buy anything." She regretted the harsh tone in her voice. "Honestly, Lucas, I won't embarrass you," she said, and smiled sweetly.

His eyes took in her luxirious golden hair. Then his gaze fell hungrily to the wide curved lips. Without another word he turned around on his heels and marched out of her office.

"What'd I say?" she quietly questioned the stiff retreating back. Then she shrugged. Men! What she knew about their habits would fill an index card and still have room on the back for a recipe. Strange creatures, she thought, and shook her head. But Lucas certainly was a handsome one. Forcing her wayward thoughts back, she began to reread the paper in her typewriter.

Deep in concentration, she heard a muffled cough and looked up. Her eyes immediately clashed with JoBeth Huntley's, and she refused to be the first to give way.

"Hello," JoBeth said unnecessarily, fiddling with the sleeve of her linen blouse.

"Is there something I can do for you, Miss Huntley?" Jennifer's voice was icy. She noticed the mint-green, Irish-handkerchief-linen dress and felt a surge of cattiness. She had several Irish-linen dresses herself. Suddenly she didn't feel like a peasant compared to this sophisticated woman.

"Yes, there is something. You could start by calling me 'JoBeth,' and secondly—" she looked up from her inspection of her cuff "—you could forgive me for the way I acted the night of the embassy party." JoBeth grinned at Jennifer's skeptical expression. "I'm really not the bitch I appear to be. It's just that I've known the DeSalvas all my life. They've been my world and I'm very protective where they're concerned." She saw Jennifer relax, and slipped into the only other chair in the office. "Both Brandon and Lucas speak highly of you, so I figured I'd better come make my apology." She seemed to realize how offhanded her explanation sounded and quickly amended it. "Oh, that sounds awful, doesn't it? As if I'd only apologized because Brandon likes you."

Through this stumbling explanation Jennifer began to smile. JoBeth Huntley, wealthy, beautiful, sophisticated, Houston's society darling, was somewhat of a bubble brain. She watched in fascination as JoBeth's shoulder-length hair shimmered with each movement of her head. Then she suddenly realized what it was that bothered her about the blending shades of gold-to-pale-blond hair. It wasn't possible for a natural color to have that many different highlights. JoBeth's beautician was a master at his art.

"If you don't forgive me, I'll never be able to explain why you hate me. And if I do explain, Brandon and Lucas will be furious with me for interfering again in their business." She leaned forward pleadingly. "Please say yes."

"Yes." Jennifer laughed.

"What's so funny and what are you agreeing to, Jennifer?" Brandon stood in the open doorway, taking in Jennifer and JoBeth's guilty start. "Hello, Bets," he greeted casually.

"I'd have thought you would have outgrown your childish habit of calling me names, Brandon. You know how I hate it."

Suddenly Jennifer noticed the air was thick with hostility. She was confused. Hadn't JoBeth just said how close she was to the DeSalvas? But the sparks flying between her and Brandon didn't create an air of congeniality. It was more like old warriors ready to square off and do battle once again. She leaned back comfortably in her chair and waited.

"It's just a nickname—Jo."

"Stop it!" She rose angrily and faced him. "I hate that name, too, and well you know it. What's the matter?" she sneered softly. "Did one of your many girlfriends turn you down last night and you're using me to relieve your frustrations?"

"Do you know, Bets, that's the most I've heard you say in the last month without mentioning my brother? Did you two have a fight?" His eyes were dark with anger and another emotion.

Jennifer looked from Brandon to JoBeth, suppressing the desire to smile.

"No, we did not have a fight. As a matter of fact, I have to see him now to go over some details of the party I'm helping him give Friday night." She sidled past him, then stopped. "I guess you won't be there, will you?"

Jennifer's amused gaze swung from one to the other, then back again.

"As a matter of fact I will." He shoved his hands into his pockets and hunched his shoulders. "But only if you promise there will be no press attending."

"Maybe." JoBeth threw the reply over her shoulder and stomped out, her high heels clicking like castinets on the tiled hallway.

Brandon laughed, but without the usual warmth. "God, what a butterfly. I don't understand how Lucas can put up with her so much."

Jennifer's grin widened.

"She'll drive you nuts with her endless social chatter. It amazes me that she can talk for hours and never say anything of importance." He ran his fingers roughly through his immaculately brushed hair, leaving it a ruffled mess. "She can get on my nerves more than anyone I know."

Jennifer's smile grew wider still. "My, my...she does seem to have quite the effect on you."

There was a long silence. Then Brandon shot out of the chair he'd just slipped into. "Are you out of your mind? JoBeth?" He began to laugh, a deep grating sound. "I've known her all my life—believe me, she's a walking disaster area."

"Oh, really? She's very beautiful, though."

"Yes," he agreed, dragging the word out slowly. "I'll grant you that, but then there's nothing upstairs." He tapped the side of his head. "Look," he said, interrupting her before she could say anything else. "I came by to see if you wanted to have lunch with me today. You know my feelings are hurt. I can't seem to get close to you since you've been here. If you're not at lunch with Cleo, it's Shasta or Jean-Paul. What happened to kindness to your old friends?"

Jennifer's eyes danced with mischief. "Oh, poor man, so mistreated. Who was that redhead I saw you with yesterday?" she teased. "Seriously, though, I can't today." She looked at her wristwatch. "Jean-Paul should be here any minute." She watched an expressionless mask shift across his face and he tugged his earlobe in a reflex action she'd seen before whenever the Frenchman's name was mentioned. "You don't like him, do you?" She blurted the question out, surprising herself with her insight.

"I never said anything against him. I just wish you wouldn't see so much of him, Jennifer."

"It's only a couple of lunches, Brandon. He's never asked me out or made a pass at me. Besides," she stated thoughtfully, "he and Lucas are best friends and business partners."

Brandon coughed. "Business partners? Did he tell you that?" She nodded, and he was quiet for a long moment before continuing. "I guess he is an associate in a round-about way. Did Jean-Paul tell you what business he's in with Lucas?"

"No. I assumed it was DeSalvas or some part of the computer side of the business."

"Jennifer, there are no partners in DeSalvas but De-Salvas," Brandon told her arrogantly, then grinned sheepishly. "Jean-Paul lost his family estate in France through some bad investments. Mind you, the man mort-gaged land and a castle that had been in his family for more than two hundred years on a crazy speculation." Brandon's dislike for Jean-Paul came through with every word. "When he realized he was about to lose everything, he came to Lucas and sold him his vineyards along with the land and winery. That probably was the only good thing Lucas will ever get out of their friendship—the best Na-poléon cognac ever produced."

Brandon paused a moment before going on. "But good cognac, the quality Lucas wants to produce, requires at least seven to twelve years of aging to be classified and la-beled as Nepoléon cognac. He and Jean-Paul have had some heated arguments about the quality. Jean-Paul wants to cut the aging and sell a cheaper product with a lower rating. Lucas won't hear of it. But as for Jean-Paul's partnership with DeSalvas—no way. He's strictly my brother's problem. Lucas hired him to promote the co-gnac around the world and gave him an interest in the profits."

"You really don't like him."

Brandon tugged at his earlobe. "Just be careful. I don't trust him." He turned to leave, a frown deeply etched across his brow.

Jennifer sighed. How strange. There seemed to be undercurrents everywhere. Cleo had explained that some of the tension was the natural excitement of nearing the completion of phase one of their new project. Only a select group of people were privileged to know what was happening with the secret project, and the very air seemed to have picked up the sharp crackle of intrigue and adventure. Several times at lunch with Shasta the question of security at McCord's and DeSalvas had come up, but Jenny had learned nothing significant from that quarter.

Her eyes brightened as she thought of Shasta Stone. For the first time in her life she had made friends, close friends with women—Cleo and Shasta. Cleo, shockingly outspoken, kept her highly entertained, and their shared love for old clothes cemented their interests.

And Shasta—how could she discern her feelings about Shasta, Jennifer wondered. Shasta had a quick wit and made her laugh at everything, most of all herself. On their first lunch together they hadn't driven more than a few blocks from the office, when Shasta had turned to Jennifer and suggested a lunch that catered to Jennifer's uncontrollable sweet tooth.

Twenty minutes later they were stuffing their faces with the biggest, gooiest banana split the nearest ice-cream parlor could make. She found herself telling Shasta things she'd never told anyone. Then she looked into big, dark, somber eyes, saw the sparkle in their depths, heard the outrageous remarks Shasta made and began giggling over the absurdity. Jennifer just couldn't believe this tiny lady was married to Kane Stone.

A hard shiver shook Jennifer. Kane Stone's eerie light gray eyes haunted her. They seemed to always be accusing, condemning and she didn't know why. What had she ever done to him? But she wasn't going to let her concerns about Kane destroy her newfound friendship with Shasta. She discovered there was a deep emotional commitment involved with having friends, and she was surprised at her own eagerness to accept the responsibility.

She propped her elbow on the top of her typewriter and cradled her chin in her hand. In less than two weeks she'd ventured a few more steps out of her shell. And the amazing thing was, instead of feeling scared at the commitment she was making, she felt alive and happy for the first time in a long time.

"*Chérie*, that lovely smile would melt the the most rocky hearts."

"Hardened hearts," she corrected automatically.

"*Oui*, hardened. But I cannot live on your smile. I must have sustenance." Jean-Paul stepped around her desk, clasped her elbow and helped her up. "Why don't you go put some lipstick on that pretty mouth. Then we will go to lunch."

Jennifer looked into his twinkling jet eyes and grinned. "On one condition—that we don't go to another French restaurant. I don't think my stomach can take any fancy sauces today."

"Are you ill, *chérie*?" he asked, in a concerned voice.

"Not sick, Jean-Paul. Just too much rich food lately. How about a good old American hamburger?"

"If you wish." His dark eyes gleamed with suppressed laughter. "I guess I shall have to suffer through your barbaric meal."

He smiled and motioned for her to speed up her trip to the ladies' room.

Five minutes later, Jennifer rushed back through the doorway of her office and jerked to an abrupt halt. Brandon and Jean-Paul confronted each other across her desk with barely concealed animosity. As they felt her presence she could see the forced relaxing of their shoulders, and a picture of two fighting cocks circling each other ran through her mind.

"You shouldn't leave your office unlocked, Jennifer," Brandon scolded, his gaze still riveted to Jean-Paul. "I found our friend here with his hands in your desk drawer."

"So! You're the culprit who's trying to make me gain weight?" She laughed gaily and moved around the desk to stand beside Jean-Paul. Placing both hands on his chest, she pushed the now-grinning Frenchman back a couple of steps and yanked open the drawer, retrieving four blue-and-silver foil-wrapped pieces of candy.

"Baci is my favorite. I became addicted to the delicacy when I lived in Italy." She babbled on to relieve the tension. "I must have told Jean-Paul how frustrating it was that I couldn't get them here." She opened her fist and held out the misshapened pieces. "Isn't he clever and sweet? He's found a place that imports them, and every day he's hidden some in the top drawer of my desk."

"Very clever," Brandon growled, and left the office without another word.

Jean-Paul watched Brandon's retreat, then turned his sad, dark eyes on Jennifer. He reached out and stroked the soft curve of her cheek. "Forgive me, but I must get things straightened out with Brandon. It pains me deeply to see him so filled with jealousy. Please *chérie*, may I have a rain bill on our lunch?"

"Rain check, and, yes, of course." She grabbed his hand and squeezed his fingers forgivingly. "Will you tell me what's between you and Brandon before you go?"

Jean-Paul turned his hands up and shrugged, his action conveying his unhappiness more than words. "What can I say? He dislikes me. But I think it goes deeper, and I'm only part of this anger he holds inside." He settled his long frame on the corner of her desk and stared out the window, swinging his foot back and forth absently.

"Years ago I made the big mistake of teasing Brandon, telling him he'd best hurry up with his law studies before Lucas became so deeply ensconced in DeSalvas that he'd never pry him loose from his presidency. Brandon didn't take my advice."

"I don't understand." Jennifer sat down, unwrapped a Baci and popped it into her mouth. "Why should Brandon be after the presidency? Lucas is the eldest. Shouldn't it go to him?"

"*Oui*. But that was not the way it was supposed to be. Lucas should have taken over the ranch, the cattle-and-horse breeding operation, the extensive real-estate holdings and investments, and the south Texas bank they own. Brandon, when he obtained his degree in international corporate law, would take over the presidency of De-Salvas and the worldwide operation with Matthew." He reached across the desk, plucked up the piece of candy she'd just unwrapped for him and quickly put it in his mouth, smiling at her fierce frown.

"As you know, everything changed, tragically. Matthew was seriously injured, Catherine Marie and Elizabeth, his mother and sister, were dead." Jean-Paul shook his head, his eyes closed tightly for a second in pain. "Lucas stepped in and took control. Later, when Brandon graduated, I believe he expected his brother to step down and return to ranching. But Lucas had come too far and worked too hard to back down to a wet-nosed kid fresh out of law school. There were hard, unforgivable words exchanged. I was there, *chérie,* and I don't think Brandon has truly accepted his brother's total rule. The DeSalvas are deeply emotional people even though they don't openly show their feelings. Mark my words, there's a volcano building in Brandon that's just waiting to erupt.''

Jennifer sat back in her chair, her face pale with shock. ''Are you telling me that Brandon hates Lucas?'' She couldn't believe what Jean-Paul was saying. Laughing, smiling Brandon with the twinkle of mischief and the teasing nature couldn't be filled with hatred.

''*Non, non,* he loves his brother, but he wants De-Salvas. Many a man has done unthinkable things for power. Always remember this, *chérie.*'' Jean-Paul reached out and clasped her hand. ''I don't want to hurt you, Jennifer, but there is something else between the brothers—or I should say someone. JoBeth.'' He glanced down at his watch and before she could question him further he jumped off the corner of the desk. ''I must go, or Brandon will leave before I can find him.''

Jennifer found herself sitting alone, as puzzled as before. She eyed the small package Jean-Paul had hurriedly pulled from his pocket and pitched on her desk before he rushed out of the office. All his explanations and she still hadn't found out why there was so much animosity between the two men. As she stared down at his gift, a small smile twitched her lips. He had whispered to her that the present was just a little something to make Lucas jealous.

Tentatively she touched the expensive gold-wrapped package, tracing the embossed label suspiciously. Why and what would Jean-Paul be buying her at Neiman-Marcus? Chocolate was one thing, but this... She couldn't stand the suspense any longer and tore the paper off with both hands.

''My, my. Who's sending you Joy?'' Lucas's frown belied his cheerful question. Without asking permission, he picked up the cream-colored card and read aloud: ''Because you remind me of a bouquet of spring flowers—

J.P.'' He dropped the small card as if it had burned his fingertips. "I need you in my office in five minutes.''

Jennifer watched Lucas's retreat with wide eyes. Jealous? Was it anger or jealousy she'd seen in his hard expression? Looking down at the ounce of outrageously expensive amber perfume, a smile began to curve her lips, a smile of pure mischief. *God bless you, Jean-Paul,* she thought, then jumped up and headed for Lucas's office.

"What did you say to Lucas to make him as mad as a hornet?''

"Nothing, Cleo. Honestly.'' She tried hard to keep a straight face, but her smile kept breaking through.

Cleo shook her head and waved Jennifer toward the inner sanctum. "Go softly. He can tear you to pieces if you push too hard.''

Jennifer nodded and stood before the closed doors. She tugged at the butter-yellow silk dress and tried once more to gain control of her expression. But she made the fatal mistake of looking over her shoulder at Cleo and her lips began to twitch and a bright sparkle deepened her violet eyes. "You're no help, you know.''

"I know, but if you could have seen his face when he stomped in here a few minutes ago you'd know why I'm grinning.'' The intercom buzzed, and Cleo held her finger to her lips and pressed the button down so Jennifer could hear.

"Where is she?'' Lucas's voice blared out.

"Right here.''

"Well,'' demanded the disembodied voice. "Why the hell is she standing out there when she's supposed to be in here?''

Jennifer reached across Cleo's desk and pressed the button down. "Because I'm scared of you when you're angry.''

There was a long pause. Then Lucas's husky voice said, "Please don't be afraid of me, Jenny. Come in."

"Well, I never." Cleo glanced at the intercom as if the object had suddenly sprouted horns. Then she turned to Jennifer. "Maybe you'll teach me that trick later?"

"Maybe." Jennifer pushed open the big double doors.

"YOU'RE NOT REALLY SCARED of me, are you, Jenny?"

"Sometimes." She shut the door and silently made her way to the nearest chair across from him. Why was it every time he was near she had trouble keeping her thoughts coherent. "Have you ever heard yourself when you're angry? Your voice holds a coldness that could freeze blood." He smiled, and she watched breathlessly as his mouth turned up and his green eyes took on a deeper hue.

"I would never hurt you, Jenny, love. Do you believe that?"

His question made her immediately uncomfortable, and her nervousness was evident in her clenched fist.

Lucas noticed the wariness, and could have kicked himself in the butt. Laughter and anger he could deal with, but when she closed up on him he wanted to shake her till she realized that he only wanted to help. He surged to his feet and made his way over to the drafting board tucked away in the far corner of his office. "Come over here, Jennifer. It's time you started work on this—it's one of the reasons I bought your contract from Susan." He waited, watching every move of her slim, graceful body as she stood and began walking toward him.

There was a familiar rush of heat in his groin and he fought to control his growing arousal. He turned and flipped the white cover sheet from a set of blueprints. Anger washed over him once more as he remembered Kane's words when he found out that Lucas was going to turn over the translations to Jennifer. He'd tried repeatedly to talk Lucas out of acting prematurely, but Lucas was adamant. There had been no leaks since she'd come to work for DeSalvas and he couldn't understand Kane's vehement protest to withhold the work any longer.

"Come around here where you can see this, Jenny." He moved the high stool out of the way and stepped back. When she was standing directly in front of him, he reached out and removed the first page, to show a black-and-white pen-and-ink drawing of an offshore drilling rig set in the middle of the ocean. "Looks ordinary, doesn't it?"

"I guess." What did she know of those metal monsters? Only that they drilled through the ocean floor for oil. She felt his breath tease the fine hairs on her nape and suppressed the shiver of pleasure. *This is important,* she scolded herself. *Pay attention!*

Lucas flipped to another page which depicted a massive control board with thousands of names and measurements. "Have you figured it out yet?"

"Nooo." She looked back over her shoulder, then wished she hadn't. He was much too close, and she could feel the warmth radiating from his body and smell the intoxicating scent of his after-shave. She quickly turned forward, forcing her eyes to remain on the papers in front of her.

"It's a completely computerized offshore drilling rig that will reduce the production cost of oil enough to show up in the consumer's pocketbook. Only one man is needed on the rig for minor maintenance, not the hundreds that rotate schedules every fourteen days or so. The oil company that buys this will save untold millions in salaries and supplies, to say nothing of insurance."

His excitement was becoming contagious, and she smiled, relaxing under the hypnotic sound of his smooth, deep voice. When he rested his hand on her shoulder, she covered it with her own. Before Jennifer knew what was happening he was standing beside her, his arm secured around her waist. She would have pulled away, but realized he was so absorbed in his explanation that she doubted he was aware of her presence.

"The only problem we came up against was the steel housing for the computers. They had to be thin, sturdy, airtight and, most important, rust-free. Saltwater and air are the worst corrosive elements there are. I found a German company that has invented a substance that can mix and coat steel. The treated slabs of metal could be molded into our designs and would provide virtually seamless housing for our computers. They're also totally rust-proof." Lucas folded the cover sheet down over the blueprints and rested his hands on her shoulders.

"This project is top secret, Jennifer, and no one is to know. I want you to rework the labeling of the blueprints from English to German."

The word *German* clicked in her head and she said, "Of course, the party Friday night."

"For the manufacturers of this baby." He patted the plans lovingly. "The party is a way of cementing the deal and a kickoff celebration for the operation." His grip tightened on her arms. Lucas gazed directly into her eyes. "There's only one or two problems. I don't want these plans worked on during regular office hours. They're too important for prying eyes to find. It's not that I don't trust you, Jenny. I don't trust what has been happening around here lately."

"I don't understand. What's been happening?"

Lucas smiled, wanting only to kiss her enticing lips. "I know you don't understand, and there's no need for you to worry. It doesn't concern you and everything is under control. The only thing I need is for you to say you're willing to work some long hours weeknights and weekends.''

"Yes, of course I'll be happy to do the work, Lucas." She didn't get any further. Her mouth was captured and opened to the warm insistent pressure of his tongue. Her arms snaked around his neck and he pulled her into the welcoming comfort of his body.

It was Lucas who broke away. He released his hold on her, turned around and began rolling up the blueprints, trying hard to conceal his heavy breathing with a casual conversation he neither wanted nor felt. "Fine, fine. We'll talk about this later."

Feeling let down, Jennifer wanted to put as much distance between them as possible. She headed for the door.

"Jenny, not a word of this project to anyone other than Kane, Shasta, Cleo or Brandon. No one else."

"I can be trusted, too, Lucas." She spun on her heel, offended at his remark. Her eyes flashed a warning, but the fire of indignation died as she met his warm gaze.

"I'll see you Friday night at eight, Jenny."

She closed the door softly. Totally absorbed in her own thoughts, she began walking across the office, when a voice filled with amusement interrupted her rather erotic thoughts.

"Hey, kid. Come down off that cloud before you bump into something dangerous."

Jennifer shot a wide smile over her shoulder and simply shook her head, continuing on her way.

"Your lipstick is smeared and you'd better fix it before someone puts two and two together and comes up with you and Lucas instead of four."

Jennifer rounded the corner of the office, trying hard to keep from laughing. Like a thief she glanced furtively both ways down the hall, then pulled a tissue from her pocket and wiped her mouth. She started to walk away, then stopped as Cleo's next words reached her.

"Smart girl!"

She grinned, then frowned fiercely. "Smart girl"? She certainly hoped so. Despite her fears, despite the past, she still wanted him. Where her desires would lead she was afraid to question too closely. For now she had to have confidence in herself and trust her newfound emotions, because she realized she couldn't give him up.

CHAPTER NINE

JENNIFER'S FEET HURT and her stomach began to respond in an embarrassing way as the aroma of food drifted across her path. The fixed smile she wore made her face feel as if it were about to crack, and the fingers on her right hand were stiff from the overenthusiastic grips of some of the gentlemen. She hated reception lines with a passion. Endless streams of chatty, sparkling guests she'd never see again, let alone remember their names for more than a second after they had passed through the line. And try as she might, she couldn't convince Lucas that there was no reason for her to be at his side.

She glanced at him out of the corner of her eye and had to admit how handsome he looked tonight. In all her fantasies she'd never pictured him in a black tie and tuxedo. And for all his stature he carried himself with an elegance that turned entirely too many female heads. Not many men his size could get away with the dapper tailoring of a black dinner jacket with grosgrain lapels, a dress waistcoat of cotton piqué and a tiny pleated shirt studded with brilliant emeralds. Looking down, she grinned. The dress boots she'd expected had been replaced by a pair of black patent-leather evening pumps.

Jennifer let her eyes travel up his height and whispered between lips that scarcely moved, "Liar." She pressed her shoulder against his arm to make sure she had his attention. "Cheat," she mumbled under her breath, then immediately straightened as he introduced her to the mayor.

"Now, what was that you were saying?" he asked, once the mayor had been dispensed with.

"Cheat!"

"No before that." They were interrupted by someone who was obviously a business associate of DeSalvas, and as Lucas turned slightly to introduce the old gentleman to the German guest of honor, Jennifer let her gaze once again roam the rooms in awed fascination.

The minute they had arrived at the home of JoBeth's father she'd nearly choked. Deeply buried amid opulent River Oaks homes, the Huntley estate of sand-colored brick rose majestically like a castle, complete with twin turrets. They had been met at the door by an arrogant majordomo, then ushered into a world she'd only read about. It was like entering a palace, replete with white-and-gold patterned marble floors, a monstrous curved stairway, tall columns and Persian rugs scattered everywhere.

White-gloved waiters circled mutely among the milling throng of guests with ornate silver trays laden with fluted champagne glasses filled with pale honey liquid. At the far end of the long room an orchestra played an old favorite.

"Overpowering, isn't it?"

"Yes."

"Now that we have a few seconds, shall we continue our previous conversation?"

"I don't remember what we were saying."

Lucas leaned down, and she felt the wisp of his breath caress her bare shoulder. "Think, Jenny, and I'm sure it will come back to you."

She glanced up, then wished she hadn't. He was studying her with a strange, intent expression.

"You were calling me names, I believe."

"Oh, yes. Charlatan."

His lips twisted. "I missed that one."

"Pity—it rather fits. How about 'liar'?"

"Ah, yes. Now that sounds familiar."

Jennifer tore her eyes away from his and bit the inside of her cheek to stop herself from erupting in an unladylike laugh.

"I'm crushed to the bone that you'd think of me in those terms. But you know, I suspect they're nice compared to what you're really thinking."

Although she'd been listening carefully to what he was saying, she still glanced around the crowded room, trying hard to appear as unmoved by his teasing as possible. Irritating man. How was she supposed to stay mad at him if he kept her laughing? Jennifer's blasé demeanor fell away quickly as she spotted Shasta and her husband. Kane Stone looked ready to kill.

Lucas followed the direction of her gaze and murmured, "What's wrong?"

"Do you think Shasta's okay?"

Lucas chuckled. "Yes, she'll be fine. It's just that he has once again hoisted himself on his own petard. He picks out her clothes and makes her wear them, forgetting how fabulous she can look. Then when he sees the interest of the other men he grumbles and threatens to take her home and make her change. A fitting punishment, don't you think? After all, she's usually the one to put up with women falling all over him."

"You'll have to admit that her dress is cut outrageously low. I hope she doesn't make any sudden moves."

"I'm sure Kane's praying for the same thing. And speaking of dresses, have I told you how lovely you look? That gown is a knockout. If you're not careful, I'll end up being a bear like Kane for the rest of the evening."

"You have..." she trailed off as another couple made their way down the line. The flow had slowed and Jennifer waited impatiently for JoBeth to call a halt. As Lucas talked to the elderly gentleman she couldn't help but grin, remembering the stunned look on his face when she'd opened her door for him earlier. The Galanos gown was a masterpiece of beads, sequins and flowing chiffon. The high-necked halter-top dress fitted snugly to her breast, waist and hips, then flared out slightly in a cloud of yards and yards of royal-purple chiffon shot through with shimmering tiny silver threads. But it was the top that drew attention. As the lights caught the beads and sequins the gown almost seemed to come to life, flashing, moving, winking in shades of the darkest damson to the palest violet. Jennifer realized from the envious looks that no one had guessed the gown was at least ten years old.

"Come on, Jenny, love. JoBeth has seen fit to release us from this hell."

Lucas's hand touched her back and she almost jumped with shock at the feeling of warm flesh sliding slowly down her spine. She'd forgotten the most intriguing part of the gown—it was completely backless.

Lucas hadn't forgotten as his fingers caressed her velvety skin. He wondered if he'd make it through the night without making an ungentlemanly grab for her. *Control, old man—and keep it light.*

"Lucas, I want to talk to you before we go in there." She held back, digging her heels in as he tugged on her elbow. "You lied to me," she accused in dulcet tones.

He didn't need an explanation. "Not now, Jenny." He tightened his grip on her arm, smiling at the people who passed them on their way to the ballroom.

"Your German business associates speak better English than we do," she hissed softly.

"I didn't lie." He pulled her close and whispered gruffly, "How was I to know that their wives would speak English, also?"

"Ask!"

He shook his head. "You know how correct the Germans are. The opportunity never presented itself where I felt comfortable enough to ask, so I took precautions."

"Me?"

"Right."

It was plausible, though she still felt uneasy about the hasty explanation. But Lucas didn't give her time to question him further. In a few seconds she found herself firmly anchored at his side and surrounded by his German friends and their wives. By the time everyone had a cold glass of champagne, the orchestra began another number. Lucas squeezed her hand.

"Come dance with me." began to edge their way from the circle of people who hand firmly clasped his shoulder.

"Evening, brother. Jennifer, re the most beautiful woman here tonight." Brandon sed her cheek, ignoring Lucas's scowl.

JoBeth was right behind him and her sulky voice floated up. "You've told every woman you've run into the same thing. When are you going to come up with a new line, Brandon?"

Brandon wheeled around to face JoBeth. "Did it ever occur to you, Bets, that I meant what I said? Maybe I think every woman is gorgeous in her own inimitable fashion."

Lucas tried to inch Jennifer away from Brandon and JoBeth, who were now glaring silently at each other. But once again they were stopped, this time by JoBeth.

"No, you don't, Lucas DeSalva. The first dance is supposed to be with me." She shot Jennifer a malicious glance. "After all, I am your hostess and I come first."

Lucas mumbled a few choice words under his breath that only Brandon could make out.

"As much as I hate to admit it, brother, she's right. But don't worry about Jennifer." Brandon hooked his arm around her waist, pulled her into his embrace and began dancing across the white marble floor. "I'll take good care of her." He laughed. "Don't scowl, Jennifer," he admonished as he spun her around again, then settled her more comfortably in his arms.

"JoBeth's been nagging me about one thing or another since I arrived." His sapphire eyes glimmered with amusement. "I mean, really, what's so awful about coming in through the kitchen and avoiding all that hoopla? Hell, I know everyone here. But will she leave it at that? No. What's really bothering the little pest is that I won't allow her to drag me through the society columns the way she enjoys doing with my brother." His rattling conversation dwindled away as he met her knowing eyes. "We will not discuss JoBeth, right?"

"If you say so."

"I do." He began whistling softly along with the orchestra, trying to ignore the stubborn light in her eyes and the thrust of her chin. "Okay," he said. "Out with it before you burst."

Jennifer swallowed hard. Now that she had her chance, she didn't know if she wanted to ask her question or not. But the thought of more sleepless nights won her over. "Are Lucas and JoBeth having an affair?"

He was quiet for so long, whirling her slowly around the dance floor, that she thought he wasn't going to answer her. When he began to speak she would only look up as far as his black silk bow tie.

"I honestly don't know, Jennifer. And it's not a question I can ask Lucas outright. For some odd reason known only to him he admires the featherhead, and though he's said many times that they're only friends and she's like a sister, they do manage to spend a lot of time together. I don't want to see you hurt, so maybe it would be best to believe him till we see otherwise." He spun her around, his eyes staring over the top of her head into the distance. "By the way, what brought on that question? Did he say something to make you think they were lovers?"

"No. Actually, it was Jean-Paul who hinted at the possibility. He also said he didn't want to see me hurt."

Brandon muttered a word not meant for Jennifer's ears. "I'm sorry. But you don't know how I'd like nothing better than to tear that bastard's throat out."

Jennifer was aware that the pressure on her hand had slackened, and she almost laughed when she realized that Brandon was fighting the urge to tug at his earlobe, an action he had done previously whenever Jean-Paul's name was mentioned. She let the direction of her eyes drift to the object of her thoughts and almost stumbled over his well-shined shoe. "Brandon DeSalva—your ear is pierced!"

He missed a few beats, then swung her around sharply, almost angrily. "Yes, and isn't it a nice point of conversation?" he asked sarcastically. "Can you imagine how an ultraconservative Texas judge would take to a lawyer entering his courtroom sporting a flashy earring? I'll tell you," he growled. "He'd kick the man right out of his court."

Jennifer was confused. Surely all this anger and bitterness wasn't over a barely noticeable hole in his ear. "If you feel that way then why did you have it done?"

"Ah, that's the crux of the matter, Jennifer. I didn't have any say." They danced in silence for a few minutes. Then Brandon sighed deeply, his chest heaving with suppressed anger and frustration. "I busted my buns to get out of law school, almost to the point of exhaustion. So, after my law exam, I took an extended vacation in Europe. I finally ended up in France."

The strangest sensation washed over her, as if she knew what was coming without being told. She braced herself for another confusing story about the friendship between Jean-Paul and the DeSalvas.

"Somehow Jean-Paul found out I was in Paris and took me under his wing." Brandon guided her around the crowded dance floor expertly, dodging other couples automatically. "You must understand that up until then Jean-Paul had been someone I looked up to and admired. He appeared to be rich, was close friends with Lucas and my father, and I thought he could do no wrong. Well, I soon learned. He got me so blind drunk one night that I passed out cold."

His hand tightened on hers. "When I woke the next afternoon I had a gold loop hanging from my ear. Don't say it! I've heard all the arguments from my brother and father that it was only a practical joke. The thing is, Jennifer, Jean-Paul knew how conservative and stuffy the Texas judicial system can be. We discussed it many times." The muscles along his jaw tensed. "I'm sorry, but no one can convince me that he didn't do it deliberately—no one but me heard his gloating laugh." After a few quiet seconds he gave a snort of disgust that brought Jennifer's head up. "Would you just look at her? How the hell does she move in that damn dress? It's skin tight."

Jennifer turned her head and spotted JoBeth and Lucas. Brandon was right, and she'd wondered the same thing herself. The white sequined gown looked as if it had been sewn on her tall, curvy figure. She glanced up, her eyes sparkling with amusement.

"Don't say it," he warned, "because you couldn't be more wrong!"

THE NIGHT WORE ON and Jennifer danced with the gentlemen from Germany and Lucas did his duty dance with their wives. They passed each other occasionally and she would catch his gaze and return his smile.

Jean-Paul, a late arriver, tapped her partner on the shoulder and quickly cut in. She was a little surprised at his preoccupation.

"Is something wrong, Jean-Paul?" Twice she'd tried to make conversation, only to be ignored.

"*Non*, there is nothing wrong. I was admiring how beautiful JoBeth is tonight and how right she and Lucas look together." He squeezed Jennifer tighter. "Oh, *chérie*, how thoughtless of me. Please forgive my wayward tongue. I know how much you love Lucas..."

"You're wrong, Jean-Paul," she said, her soft voice cutting him off. "I'm Lucas's employee—nothing more."

"But, *non*—" he broke off suddenly as Lucas dropped his hand heavily on his shoulder.

Without a word Lucas gently but firmly pulled Jennifer from Jean-Paul's arms. He threw his friend a grateful glance, took only a few steps and the music ended. "Well, damn. Just my luck."

The orchestra struck up a Strauss waltz and he groaned. "I haven't waltzed in years." He glanced at Jennifer's dreamy expression. "I'll bet with your diplomatic background your mother had you in dance lessons as soon as you could walk. Shall we?"

She hesitated just a moment, but as the beautiful notes of "A Thousand and One Nights" began, she found she couldn't resist. "It's been years and years for me, too, but if you're willing to look a fool, so am I."

He took her lightly into his arms, and started moving around the floor, circling, twirling and swaying. They were quiet as they danced, each gaining confidence as their lessons came back to them.

Lucas inhaled deeply and a half smile twisted his sculptured mouth. The fragrance she was wearing filled his senses, unfamiliar and exciting, a mixture of floral and something totally exotic. One thing, though, she wasn't wearing Jean-Paul's gift of Joy. He felt a hot rush of desire flow through him. This wouldn't do at all, not in front of fifty or so people.

Jennifer finally looked up. Feeling alive and free, she laughed as they glided across the floor. Then she sobered as his words sunk in. "How did you know about my diplomatic background? I don't believe I've ever told you about my parents."

He guided them through a tricky turn and grinned lopsidedly. "I had a check run on you. Now don't go all stiff on me, dammit, or we'll do more than disgrace ourselves." His hand moved slowly up and down her bare back, loving the texture of her skin. He was intoxicated with her essence, and vivid pictures of her naked and welcoming, her glorious long hair surrounding him like a silken curtain, filled his mind. He ground his teeth together. All he wanted to do was go on touching her. He cleared his throat. "We run a security check on everyone. No one is exempt."

The air seemed suddenly to have thinned, washing away any arguments she might have had as she twirled around the floor. She'd always loved Struass and had never considered his music sensuous or sexy. But as Lucas stroked her bare flesh her pulse began to throb with the beat, building with the music's every note. She looked up and her eyes meshed with his. A hollow feeling spread through her insides, and the beat of the music became like a lovers' chant for release.

They swayed together, in and out, back and forth, and her breasts touched and rubbed against his chest. His eyes darkened to the deepest forest green and she watched, fascinated, as the heavy lids half closed. The two of them parted, then came together again and the movement, the rhythm became more than the steps of a dance.

"Do you have any idea how inviting your mouth looks? God, I wish I could kiss you right here and now." Lucas stroked her with each move as they drifted across the floor. He whirled her around, and the breeze teased her damp flesh and sent a shock of fire through her veins.

"And your skin. How I'd love to touch you, make you catch your breath in that funny way of yours when you like what I'm doing."

Each word resounded in her head, each a little more painfully tempting than the previous. The room and every living soul vanished, leaving only the two of them in an embrace as old as time.

"Close your eyes, Jenny, and let it happen."

Hypnotized by the caress of his voice, she felt her eyelids flutter closed. He swept her back and forth, to and fro, to the steady beat of the music, till her pulse beat in time. She felt like a bird—free and wild. In and out she soared among the clouds.

The music was coming to an end, but she couldn't seem to get control of her emotions. She moaned, a low sound in the back of her throat. She tightened her grip on his shoulder and squeezed the other hand she was holding for support.

"Easy, love. I'm going to swing us around to the edge of the dance floor before the music ends." With a flourish he whirled her around, dropped her hand and stopped.

Dizzily, Jennifer realized she was facing the empty dance floor with Lucas now at her back. His hands were clasping her arms to hold her upright as the crowded room burst into applause. Mortified, she could feel her cheeks burn with embarrassment. She tried to turn and leave the room as inconspicuously as possible, but Lucas's hands tightened on her arms almost painfully.

"Don't move, and smile, Jenny. No one knows what happened out there but you and me."

She tried to shrug off his hold on her. Couldn't he tell she was going to collapse? Couldn't he feel her trembling in every muscle? She ducked her head, horrified to feel tears filling her eyes. What was he doing to her? And what was happening to her?

"If you move, we're both going to be in a fix, love. I'm in the same condition you are. The only difference is you're able to hide yours. I'm not."

After a long silence his meaning sunk in and she sagged against his chest with a moan.

"Smile at the pretty people dancing by," he commanded. His arm reached past her shoulder and caught a passing waiter. "Grab two champagnes, Jenny."

She passed a cold glass back to him and said in a strangled whisper, "I wish I were home—anywhere but here."

"I'm with you." Lucas shifted her slightly to one side, but he still used her body as a shield to hide his obvious arousal. He felt like a love-starved teenager ready to burst his britches. A chuckle escaped his lips.

"I don't find this at all amusing." The music had begun again and the floor was soon crowded once more. "I want to get out of here—now." She quickly drained the champagne, then wished she hadn't as she felt her head reel. Swaying, she leaned closer for support. His fingers swept lightly up her arms to her shoulder, then farther, till his thumbs caressed her collarbone.

"Don't touch me, Lucas...please." She was aware of curious eyes watching their every move and forced herself to calm down. She jerked her head up and felt herself sway. The wine she'd gulped down was churning uncomfortably in her stomach, and her legs ached from her effort to keep them from giving way. "How could you do this to me?" she muttered through a fixed smile.

"Lady, I've got some shocking news for you. This was not intentional. I'm certainly not enjoying getting caught like this."

Blood rushed to Jennifer's already-pink cheeks. "If I had any backbone at all I'd walk off right now and leave you."

Lucas leaned down and whispered in her hair. "Tit for tat. They'd see my condition and blame you. Why, I can just hear them—'Hussy...getting that poor, poor man all excited, then walking off and leaving him in that condition.'"

Jennifer quickly covered her mouth with her hand. How could he joke at a time like this? A strangled giggle escaped her lips. How could she laugh?

"There, you see, there is a funny side to all this. Buck up, Jenny, love, here comes our first and second test, Cleo and Kane."

A cornered animal at least had the choice of fighting or running, she thought bitterly, but she was forced to stand there, feeling humiliated and ashamed for what had happened to her. She didn't have the courage to face Kane's knowing eyes, so she focused all her attention on Cleo and the young man on her arm.

"Is that her son with her?" she asked, anything to relieve the silence that had sprung up between them.

Lucas chuckled under his breath, a sound of real amusement. "I'm afraid you're in for another eye-opener tonight. That young man is Mark Colby, Cleo's fiancé."

Hoping to cover her reaction, Jennifer stared down into her empty champagne glass. A poke in the back from Lucas reluctantly brought her head up. She met Kane's scrutiny and lifted her chin proudly. She was not going to be intimidated by any man.

Her head high, she turned to Cleo. Introductions were made and she quickly judged the young man to be at least fifteen years younger than her friend. Mark Colby took her hand warmly and she melted under his twinkling brown eyes. He was, in her estimation, a hunk. Tall, broad, with curly black hair and a smile meant to turn a woman's knees to jelly.

Lucas jabbed her in the back once more, this time with a little more force than before. "Didn't you say you needed to find the ladies' room?" His glance reassured her that it was safe to give up her protective stance. "Cleo, why don't you show Jennifer the way. And don't worry about Mark. I'm sure someone will keep him busy till you get back." A few good-natured insults were exchanged among them before Cleo motioned for Jennifer to follow her.

"Why is it, Kane, that every time I see you I get the feeling you're about to drop the ceiling on me? I dread the sight of you more and more." Lucas smiled to take the sting out of his words, though it wasn't necessary. Kane understood exactly what he was saying. "You've become synonymous with bad news."

Kane grinned, an expression that didn't go unnoticed by at least a dozen women. "I know. Shasta's starting calling me Mr. Doom-and-Gloom."

"Where is your better half, by the way? Incidently, that dress she's wearing is dangerous."

Kane ignored the needling. Gray eyes, pale and compelling, scanned the ballroom, missing nothing in their search. "She's trotting along behind Cleo and Jennifer, heading out of the room." He laughed as his tiny wife almost broke into a run to keep up with her friends. "I've got some news."

"Of course—what else." Lucas caught Kane's look and swore under his breath. "Goddammit, Kane, don't ruin my evening." He set his glass down on the nearest table and frowned at Kane, then sighed heavily. "Right, out with it. But first I need something stronger than wine." He motioned to a passing waiter and retrieved two Scotch-and-waters from the silver tray. "Here, you might as well join me."

Kane tipped his glass toward Lucas and took a hefty sip. "I got a couple of interesting calls right before we left the house tonight. It seems Jennifer's stepsister is beginning to liquidate some of her assets." He felt Lucas's tension. "She'd had her house up for sale with one of those discreet realtors who don't bother putting up a sign in the front yard. The house sold two weeks ago, and she rushed through the closing. One of my informants also tells me she's been selling off some of her office computers."

For a second Kane studied the glass in his hand, rotated the clear cubes of ice in the amber liquid, then looked up, watching Lucas's expression change from polite interest to a stony mask that even caused him pause. "I'll agree that all this information isn't earth shaking in itself. But the fact that she ran nearly three hundred thousand dollars through her bank, then in a matter of hours it disappeared and her balance dropped to a respectable couple of thousand is suspicious. She didn't redeposit that money into another American bank, either, at least not as of an hour ago.''

"Switzerland?'' Lucas suggested, a muscle twitching along his jaw.

''Yes, it looks as if she's funneled the money to a Swiss account. The three hundred thousand was strictly for the sale of her house and the computers, so there's no payoff on your stolen goods there, but...''

He trailed off and Lucas picked up the threads of his thoughts as easily as if they were on the same wavelength. ''It looks as if she's selling out and planning to skip the country. Now I wonder why and when this move is planned?'' Lucas leaned closer, and his voice dropped to a harsh growl. ''I don't want her stepping one foot out of this country and leaving any doubts as to Jennifer's innocence. What can you do?

Kane steeled himself for what he knew was coming next. ''You don't think Jennifer might be ready to take a trip with her stepsister?''

''No, dammit, Kane. Why can't you just admit you're wrong? There hasn't been a theft since she started to work for DeSalvas. Doesn't that tell you something?''

''Maybe there's been nothing important to steal? Okay, okay. To tell you the truth, Lucas, I just don't know. Shasta says I've become more cynical than ever and that I can't see my nose in front of my face because of it. Maybe she's right.'' He raked his fingers through his blue-black hair. ''Hell! I'm so used to expecting the worst of people. Why don't we just keep a closer watch on Susan and see what her next move is?''

Lucas agreed. ''I want Susan's ass, Kane. Somehow, someway, she'll slip up.'' He clasped his friend on the shoulder in a gesture of thanks. "I see some of my German guests looking a little lost. I'd better go lead them to the food." He started off, then stopped. "Tell me something. How did you get the bank to give you access to Susan's account?"

Kane regarded him steadily for a long moment. "I didn't ask and they don't know."

The two men studied each other silently. Then Lucas nodded and left. He was brimming with curiosity. He'd give a goodly sum of money to know who Kane and Shasta worked for, or better still, what kind of work they did that took them all over the world and gave them access to information no one else could obtain. He shook his head. His real concern was Jennifer, and he was suddenly scared for her.

Susan and her partner, whoever he or she was, were out for more than money. They wanted to bring the DeSalvas to their knees. For weeks he'd wracked his brain trying to come up with a person who hated him or his family enough to want to destroy them totally. The fact that they were vicious enough to use an innocent woman like Jennifer made his blood run cold. He'd be damned if he'd calmly wait around and see her hurt. But it was like shadowboxing. Just when he thought he might have a lead the trail would end abruptly at Jennifer's door. Someone out there was not only smart enough to steal from him, but malevolent in the way they did it. The bitter taste of fear filled his throat, and he experienced a sinking sensation in the pit of his stomach. His troubles weren't over—not by a long shot.

CHAPTER TEN

SOMEWHERE IN THE TWILIGHT between deep sleep and consciousness, Jennifer drifted in an erotic haze. Her arm tightened on the warm shape next to her and she burrowed closer. A distant noise tried to pull her out of the darkness, but she fought wakefulness. A tiny smile of pleasure curved her lips.

She could get addicted to this sense of security.

Her lips pursed silently, inviting a kiss, wanting only to feel Lucas's mouth on hers. There was eager anticipation in her soft lips, but the awaited fulfillment didn't come, and she stepped another level toward consciousness. Tiny lines of frustration furrowed her brow, and her frown rapidly deepened as the sound of bells became louder.

"Answer the phone, Lucas," Jennifer mumbled drowsily, the words sliding together. Forcing one eye open, she glared balefully at him. Suddenly her sleepiness vanished, and both eyes popped wide open. Lucas wasn't in her bed! He wasn't holding her in a loving embrace. She was alone except for the down pillow crushed to her chest—and her dreams.

Disgusted she threw her feather friend across the room. Her giggles filled the air, drowning the persistent ringing of the telephone. She yanked her own pillow from under her head, glared at the phone and yelled, "Oh, shut up for heaven's sake." Then she laughed disbelievingly as the squat instrument immediately fell silent. "Hell's fire," she groaned, then pulled the pillow over her head, trying to relax and return to the land of sweet dreams.

It was not to be. The ringing started again. Jennifer peeked out from under the pillow, glanced at the bedside clock and almost screamed. Eight o'clock! Who could be cruel enough to call this early on a Saturday morning? She glared, telling herself she definitely wasn't going to answer the damn thing, not at this hour. Besides, it was probably someone wanting to sell something. Solicitors had become very sneaky lately in their efforts to catch their quarry. She stiffened her backbone in determination. No, she wasn't going to answer it.

"Hello," she barked into the instrument hanging limply from her fingers. No willpower, she cursed herself.

"Good morning, Jenny, love."

"You!"

"Beg pardon?"

"You have a nerve, waking me up after you kept me out till three o'clock this morning."

"But, Jenny—" Lucas's husky voice sent a delicious shiver through her body "—it's a beautiful morning. The sun's shining and there's a good strong Gulf breeze—"

She wondered why his voice had suddenly become wheedling.

"The air smells of the sea and a new day and I need you to come to the office and begin the translations on the blueprints."

"Absolutely not."

"Jenny."

The wounded tone didn't fool her. "I'm not even awake." She refused to be manipulated by this man. "It's too early, Lucas." What could she possibly wear to the office on a Saturday? "When I agreed to work on this secret project, I assumed I'd have some advance notice." Her white chinos and the red, white and blue print silk blouse would do nicely, she thought. "Besides—" she pushed herself up into a sitting position "—what about Herman and the rest of the German entourage? Don't you need to entertain them today?" There was a long pause and for a moment she thought he might have hung up. But, no, she could just discern a noise that sounded like muffled laughter. "Lucas."

"My guests decided they'd spend today catching up on their rest."

"Smart people," she replied.

"I need you, Jenny."

He was using that persuasive tone again, and she marveled at what a patsy she'd become lately. Then she smiled as she remembered what had happened last night. Patsy, she might be, but one Lucas wanted. "I'll come, but not too early, Lucas—I'm still sleepy and tired."

"Anytime after lunch is fine. You could even join me for lunch if you want to. It's up to you."

He said goodbye and Jennifer returned the receiver to its cradle, her thoughts drifting back to a previous leave-taking. Her satisfied smile immediately slipped to a look of confusion. Lucas had managed to round up his group around eleven-thirty, by which time his German friends had had enough to drink to loosen up, and they'd wanted to see Houston's nightlife.

Much later, Lucas had escorted her to her door. At the time she had been too tired to worry whether he wanted to come in, and she had a vague remembrance of feeling excitement when he had taken her limp body into his embrace. She'd gone willingly, eagerly. He'd chuckled at her lack of resistance, teasingly suggesting it would have been a perfect time to carry her to bed and ravish her. Jennifer could only smile feebly. He'd taken her key from her loose grip, opened the door and given her a warm kiss on the forehead before gently pushing her into her house.

Jennifer jumped out of bed, grabbed her robe and headed for the kitchen. Just as she was rounding the corner to the living room she stopped and cocked her head. Was she destined to hear bells all day? She hadn't drunk more than two glasses of champagne so a hangover was highly unlikely. The bell chimed again. Surely Lucas hadn't misunderstood and come to pick her up? The doorbell rang again, longer this time.

Her faltering steps lagged to a stop as she passed the wide ornate mirror behind the dining table. Who was that bright-eyed woman with life coursing through her veins? It was more than a new day; it was a new beginning. She grinned at her reflection.

During the night she had admitted that the impossible had happened. She was in love with Lucas. Just a little in love, she scolded herself. A thousand problems came with such an admittance. If she loved him and wanted him, shouldn't she want to marry him? A chill ran over her skin. Marriage meant losing her independence, her freedom and possibly her sanity. She could never accept being ruled by another.

"So," she asked the thoughtful lady looking back at her with eyes that were now sad and certain. "What's the answer, kid? You want him, but what will you do once you get him— If you get him?" Maybe living together wasn't such a bad idea, after all. There'd be no legal ties to hold her, nothing to restrain her if she wished to leave. Jennifer nodded. It was something to think about.

The doorbell sounded, more insistent than ever. "Okay, okay," she grumbled, "I'm coming, dammit." She quickly undid the heavy locks and swung the door wide. "Susan!" Besides astonishment her voice held a mixture of anger, hurt and a fleeting hope that, just maybe, her step-sister had come to her senses and wanted to apologize for her behavior.

Stepping back, she allowed Susan to enter. Her stomach revolted at the overpowering musky scent that seemed to hover around her head. She quickly backed away from the invisible cloud of perfume and watched Susan as she sauntered into the living room. Always dressed to perfection, Susan nonchalantly removed the expensive wide-brimmed, brown straw hat. The combination of olive-green raw-silk slacks, tobacco-brown coat plus matching leather belt and shoes was stunning. The distinctively colored striping and tailoring of the outfit fairly shouted Gucci.

Susan yanked off her dark sunglasses and Jennifer stiffened, her welcoming smile frozen as she met the malice in the heavily made-up eyes. Susan tossed a folded section of the morning newspaper onto the polished surface of the dining table.

"You're coming up in the world, Jennifer. One day a nondescript translator, now the publicized mistress of Lucas DeSalva. Be careful, darling, or you'll soon become so notorious that when Lucas kicks your skinny butt out you'll have an impossible time getting work."

Only half listening to Susan's malicious conversation, Jennifer picked up the paper and began to read. "There's nothing scandalous here. Just a picture of Lucas and me caught laughing at something JoBeth said." She glanced up from studying the article and returned Susan's look. "Your jealousy is showing, Susan."

"Of you?" She snorted in distaste, her glacial stare running insultingly over Jennifer's disheveled appearance. "I think not. But I didn't come here to trade barbs with you."

"You could have fooled me."

Lines of irritation marred her carefully applied makeup as she went on. "I came to retrieve my father's wedding ring, which you've had these past years."

"I don't think—"

"Don't think, dear. You're liable to hurt yourself." Susan grinned, pleased with her joke.

"Stop digging, Susan, or you might just find it thrown back in your face." She watched, satisfied at the wariness in her stepsister's blue eyes. Without another word she turned and left the room. Susan would never change and she finally realized it would be best for her to completely sever the relationship. She was amazed that she'd put up with her vindictiveness as long as she had.

After a careful search of her jewelry box, Jennifer returned to the living room. "I found the ring—" She trailed off, surprised to find herself talking to an empty room. Confused, she glanced around. Then she heard a noise and called, "Susan." She stepped quickly around the corner and stopped in the open doorway of her office. "What do you think you're doing? Get out of my desk."

Susan immediately took the offensive. "Why, Jennifer, you know you're not supposed to retain files of any of our clients." She slapped a manila folder down with a loud crack on the desktop.

With bright red cheeks, Jennifer made a quick lunge and snatched the file from the desk. "That's personal and has nothing to do with the work I did for you."

"But it's all about Lucas, isn't it?" She sneered, her voice dripping sarcasm. "I wonder what Lucas would think if he knew you kept a file on him, especially now that he's so jumpy." She murmured the last part softly to herself. "Tell me something, do you write in your diary how he makes love?"

"Stop it, Susan."

"Do you savor all the dirty little details?"

"Get out...now!"

Susan laughed coarsely, grabbed the gold-and-diamond ring from Jennifer's hand and marched from the room and out the front door.

Jennifer stood still, watching her stepsister leave, feeling such a deep relief she was almost ashamed. The time ticked by, and she remained standing as the past came flashing back. Remembering some of Susan's cruelties, she shivered, then shrugged and shook her head as if to clear away the last distasteful residue of her past with Susan.

Jennifer quickly checked the surface of her desk, as well as each drawer, but she couldn't find anything missing. She wondered what Susan could have been looking for. Before leaving her office, she turned once more, scanning the room to see if anything else had been disturbed. She noticed that her typewriter cover was slightly askew, and returned to her desk and ripped the nylon protector off. She couldn't believe her eyes. The typewriter cartridge was gone. Now why would Susan take a used ribbon? Or had she herself simply forgotten to put another one on? The unanswered question plagued her the rest of the morning.

TWO HOURS LATER Jennifer pulled her car into her reserved parking space at DeSalvas. So she was early, she scolded herself. She tried to rationalize that she was awake and dressed, her house was clean and she was bored. Quickly she jumped out, slammed the car door shut and sprinted for the front steps. At the entrance she stopped and looked back. It was indeed a beautiful day. Inhaling deeply, she turned and pushed open the glass door.

The sound of women's voices reached her, and she walked through the reception area. Cleo and Shasta were laughing and the sound brought a smile to her lips and she quickened her steps. At the open door to Cleo's office she stopped and asked, "What's so funny?"

Shasta, her back to the door, squealed and jumped off the edge of Cleo's desk. "Don't do that," she cried, placing her hand over her heart, waiting for the pounding to subside to a normal beat once again.

Jennifer clicked her tongue, making little sounds of mocking sympathy. "Why so nervous? Anyone would think you had a guilty conscience." She shifted her sparkling gaze to Cleo and missed the way Shasta's wide smile slipped a fraction.

Cleo saw the flash of pain in Shasta's eyes and immediately launched into a question. "What are you doing here on a Saturday?"

"Lucas called and asked me to begin—" she hesitated as she remembered his warning, and even though Cleo and Shasta were aware of the project she couldn't bring herself to voice the words. "He wanted me to help him with some work," she mumbled.

Both women visibly brightened. "Aha!"

Jennifer fought to keep the flush from her cheeks. "Work, ladies."

"Oh, yeah." Shasta's big brown eyes glimmered wickedly. "Be careful. He's a sly devil."

"Now how would you know?" Cleo demanded. "And you'd better watch what you say. Kane Stone's still not above taking a punch at Lucas if he heard you and thought you were telling the truth."

"I'll have you know, Cleopatra Jones, that I had a very active love life before Kane Stone."

"But not with Lucas!"

There was a long pregnant pause as Shasta, her nose in the air, began to laugh. "No," she agreed. "Never with Lucas."

Jennifer felt herself relax, not realizing till that moment that she'd tensed at Shasta's bragging. Her eyes strayed to Lucas's closed door before she returned her attention to her watchful friends. "Is he here? I think I should be working."

Cleo and Shasta glanced at each other, then at Jennifer. "You won't be working in the office," Cleo informed her.

"He's transferred the blueprints to his penthouse apartment." Shasta tried to hide the grin that threatened to split her elfin face at Jennifer's worried frown. "Didn't he tell you?" she asked innocently.

Too innocently, Jennifer thought. "No, he neglected that tidbit of information." She could feel the blood pumping rapidly through her veins and tried to calm herself. "How do I get there?" she asked, suddenly remembering only twelve buttons on the elevator.

"There are three private elevators that go only to the penthouse," Cleo explained. "One is in the underground parking area, one in the lobby and the last is in Lucas's office." She pulled a key from her desk drawer. "You need this to work them."

The brass key lay heavily in Jennifer's damp palm and she wrapped her fingers tightly together. She took a few steps toward the office, then stopped at Cleo's next words.

"Jennifer, before you go, settle a little argument Shasta and I are having. I told her the dress you wore last night was a Galanos gown." Cleo shot Shasta a superior look. "She swears it was an Emanuel. But, then, what can you expect from a woman who hates to shop and makes her husband pick out all her clothes?"

"You were—" Jennifer began, when Shasta cut in.

"Just because I hate to shop and don't have any taste does not make me an imbecile where clothes are concerned. The dress was an Emanuel. Right, Jennifer?"

"Well actually..."

"That's not possible, Shasta. The Emanuels are entirely too young to have designed that dress. It's at least ten years old. Right, Jennifer?"

Both women fell silent and stared at her, and she fleetingly wondered why she had the suspicion this was a well-rehearsed act. But for whose benefit? She shook off the uneasiness and smiled. "Sorry, Shasta, but Cleo's right. The dress is a Galanos, and it's probably over ten years old." There was a sudden tension in the room and she couldn't shake the feeling that she was being set up for something. "What are you two up to?" She shifted her puzzled gaze from one woman to the other.

"You'll have to tell Kane where you pick up old designer gowns. He grumbles about the high prices every time he has to shop for something special for me."

Jennifer glanced at Cleo, knowing she knew her secret. "I didn't buy the gown, Shasta. It was my mother's." The key in her hand seemed to grow hotter, as if it had a life of its own and was beckoning for her to hurry. "I'd better go."

SHE WAS NUMB from the waist down, her back ached and her eyes felt as if they were ready to fall out of their sockets.

Jennifer straightened on the high stool, placed her hands on the small of her back and arched, stretching out the tight muscles. She sighed and relaxed, studying the progress she'd made in the past two weeks. Time seemed to have flown by, and she wasn't sure if she was happy or not that in another week or so she'd be through.

Four evenings a week she'd come to Lucas's penthouse apartment to work. Four evenings a week, after she'd finished, she'd been fed, pampered and catered to. At first she'd been uneasy with all the attention. Then she weakened and began to enjoy herself—or, almost. She kept expecting Lucas to "put the make on her." Instead, at the end of each evening, all she received was his witty conversation and a few good-night kisses. Her emotions were completely jumbled. After all, hadn't she made up her mind that she wanted him? The problem was that his ardor seemed to have cooled down and he treated her like a trusted friend or, heaven forbid, a sister. She stoutly refused to let him see how crushed she was by the sudden switch, and she couldn't figure out a way to reverse the situation.

Her body sagged dejectedly and she dropped her chin into her cupped hands, her elbows leaning against the drafting table. She let her eyes wander and as before, the room afforded the distraction she needed. In awe she inspected the large open area for the hundredth time, amazed to find some new object of interest she'd previously missed.

She grinned as she remembered those first steps from the elevator onto the red Verona marble, a soft speckled rust color so rich and muted it defied description. She let her gaze drift over the marble columns topped with brass moldings, cleverly concealed lights and brass urns with illuminated bases.

The long, Italian kid leather couch was invitingly comfortable and the silk-covered walls radiated warmth. The living room was decorated in lush sensual materials and soft colors. The penthouse was like a pleasure boat moored in the Texas sky, with floor-to-ceiling windows that looked out over the panorama of a Houston skyline.

Entranced, Jennifer let her eyes quickly scan the room. As on many other occasions, her gaze rested on the one object that held her totally enthralled—a floor-to-ceiling divider of etched glass that separated the living room from the dining room. The clear glass and white-frosted etching depicted an African jungle, with all the marvelous animals in various stages of their journey to a remote water hole. She chuckled suddenly as she spotted something she'd missed earlier—a lion cub peaking around a leafy bush, his eyes round with wonder and playful mischief.

"I believe you like my etching more than I do," Lucas spoke quietly from behind her.

Though he moved as soundlessly as an animal, his presence didn't surprise her. Lately she'd been able to sense his nearness whenever he entered a room. "I keep finding little details I've missed." She turned her head and felt her heart stop at the sight of him. He casually rubbed the towel through his wet hair, his chest gleaming damply, attesting to a recent shower. Her eyes wandered lower to the worn, faded jeans. Jennifer gulped. They hung so enticingly low on his narrow hips that she expected any minute to see them slip around his bare feet. She twisted back around and let her breath out as slowly as possible.

Lucas hadn't missed the hungry look in her eyes and the same expression was mirrored in his own. He reached out automatically to snatch her off the stool, then reluctantly stopped. Dropping his hands on her shoulders, he began to slowly massage the tight muscles. "You've been working too long. Why don't you take my advice and come in late on the mornings after you've been up here?"

Jennifer closed her eyes and sighed in ecstasy as his fingers worked their magic along her neck and back. "And who will type up the instructions and specifications? Oh, that feels wonderful," she murmured huskily as her head rolled limply from side to side. "You need both ready at the same time, don't you?"

Lucas remained silent, his eyes glued intently on the wispy strands of hair and the downy skin at her nape. It amazed him how the light caught the golden tentacles and made them come to life with a sparkle as bright as sunshine. He stifled a groan as he remembered how her hair moved and shimmered around him like a curtain of light. And the feel—warm silk slipping along his body, tickling, teasing and driving him crazy. He swallowed the lump in his throat and tried to tell himself denial was good for the soul. He moved a whisper closer. His soul be damned. Her warmth and scent were hypnotic and he eased closer still as a desire too strong to resist drew him into a deep, dark pool.

Get hold of yourself, he cautioned with a determined resolve, remembering his promise to win her trust first. He closed his eyes for a second, letting the heat of passion subside, and reminded himself that his victory, when it came, would be even sweeter. He dropped his hands from her shoulders and turned around. "I'm going to get dressed. Then we'll have dinner."

Jennifer could only nod her agreement, knowing that if she tried to talk her voice would give away her tightly held emotions. She listened to the sound of retreating steps, of bare flesh slapping on marble and grinned. He wasn't as unaffected as he wanted her to believe. Maybe in the next week or so she could push that control over the edge and bring out the lover in him. She certainly intended to give it her best. After all, she had no intention of being just a friend. She'd come too far to turn back, given up too much of herself to stop. There had been so many dark years and now she wanted to fill her life with only sunshine.

CHAPTER ELEVEN

"YOU LOOK WORSE than death warmed over." Brandon lounged against Lucas's closed office door. "I'd say you've lost about ten pounds and from the shadows under your eyes, you've had more than a few sleepless nights. If this is love, then I want it about as much as the plague." He moved across the thickly carpeted floor, his twinkling gaze riveted on his brother's tired face.

Lucas grunted without bothering to open his eyes. He slouched farther down into the big leather chair, shifted his feet on the desktop and sighed long and loud, a sound of pure frustration. "Go away, Brandon. I'm in no mood for your brand of humor this morning." Opening one red-rimmed eye, he glared at the grinning idiot making himself comfortable in the chair opposite him.

Brandon couldn't contain the short burst of laughter. "She's driving you to drink!"

Lucas's mouth quirked in a disdainful grimace. "I lifted a few last night. So what?"

"I'm worried about you, brother mine. Lately you've turned into a regular homebody. You've been so good I expect you to sprout wings any minute."

"You know very well what's going on," Lucas growled. "For heaven's sake, Brandon, shut up and go away. My head is killing me." He pressed his fingertips to his pounding temples and massaged slowly, then dropped his hands heavily to his lap. A fierce frown pleated his brow at his brother's laughter. "What do you want that's so important it can't wait till later?"

Brandon slipped out of his coat, folded it neatly and pitched it over the back of the other chair. He unbuttoned his vest, leaned back, propped his feet on the edge of Lucas's desk and flipped open the file he carried.

Lucas watched his movements with hostility. "Brandon!" he snarled through clenched teeth. Then he flinched and closed his eyes in pain.

"Dad tried to reach you last night and finally called me when he had the operator check your phone and was told it was off the hook." He shuffled some papers as loudly as possible, bit the inside of his cheek and waited for Lucas's explosion. When none came, he cautioned. "The Triple Bar Ranch delivered the bull you bought and I had my secretary cut a check for nine hundred ninety-nine thousand dollars from the ranch account."

Lucas murmured an acknowledgment.

"Why couldn't you have just gone ahead and paid them the million they originally asked for?"

Lucas sighed. "A matter of principle. Really, Brandon, can't this wait? I have a beast of a headache this morning."

"Have you seen Jean-Paul lately?"

"Ah, hell," Lucas grumbled, but the abrupt change of subject and the violence behind the question brought his eyes open a fraction so he could study his brother. "No, why?"

"I saw him hanging around Jennifer's office earlier."

"So?" demanded Lucas menacingly. "He's always underfoot somewhere. Besides, she's not there. I ordered her to take the morning off. She's been working just as hard as I have—harder actually. She's the one bent over the drafting board for hours. But what does this have to do with anything?"

"You don't care that he's making a play for Jennifer right under your nose?"

Lucas forced himself to relax, knowing his brother well enough to realize that, hungover or not, he wasn't about to get any peace till he'd answered all Brandon's questions. "I'm aware of your dislike for Jean-Paul. I, personally, have never seen him as a threat either to my business or my personal life."

"More fool you!"

"What's eating you, dammit?"

Brandon slapped shut the file in his lap and pitched it on the desk. "I don't know, but I think he's up to something."

Forcing his eyes wide open, Lucas stared glassily at the ceiling. "Heaven help me, everyone is seeing phantoms these days. Next you'll try to convince me that JoBeth is the mastermind behind the theft."

Brandon burst out laughing at the absurdity and Lucas winced. "Now that is hilarious. The only secrets she knows is whose wife is cheating on whom and believe me, she'll tell if you ask."

Lucas grinned. "I heard you escorted her to the hospital charity ball. How did that come about?" He watched, fascinated, as a rosy flush tipped Brandon's ears.

"I felt sorry for her. Well, damn! You were supposed to take her and then abandoned her to your project and Jennifer."

Lucas reluctantly smiled at his brother's sudden discomfort. "You can do better than that. I..." He trailed off as the intercom buzzed. Lucas lunged forward so quickly he almost upturned his chair. He grabbed the edge of the desk to steady himself and slammed his fist down on the blinking light. "What!" he shouted, then held his breath till the pain in his head subsided.

"Shasta and Kane are here, Mr. DeSalva. They'd like to see you right away if you have time."

Cleo's sarcastic tone could penetrate steel.

Lucas and Brandon flinched. "Sorry, Cleo," Lucas said. "Send them in."

"Of course, Mr. DeSalva."

"I said I was sorry. Don't push your luck today, Cleo."

"Yes, sir," the disembodied voice purred. Then there was a distinctive click as he was cut off.

"Women," he grumbled, grinning at Brandon. But any amusement he might have allowed himself died immediately as Kane and Shasta entered his office. His gaze switched from her sickly attempts at a smile to Kane's blank expression. Something sharp knifed through him with lightning speed, leaving him breathless.

Without a word of greeting Kane strode over to Lucas and handed him a buff-blue folder. "You better take a look at this."

"What is it?" Brandon's voice died away as he watched Lucas open the file and begin to read. "Lucas." He started to stand when he saw Lucas blanch, his skin draining to an ashen white. His brother's feeble gesture sent him back into his chair to wait.

Lucas braced his elbows on the desk and held his head in his hands as he read. Each damning word seemed to take the life from his face, making him look like a cadaver. He reeled under the impact of what was before him.

"There's no question now, Lucas," Kane said.

"No—no question." His voice was hoarse.

"What the hell is going on?" Brandon demanded.

"You tell him, Kane. I haven't the stomach for it." Lucas shoved his chair back, walked over to the wall of windows and stared out at the busy street traffic below.

Kane cleared his throat. "My contact in Vienna sent these." He leaned over and tapped the open file on Lucas's desk. "There are the first few pages of instructions and written specifications for your new computer housing design. He wasn't able to buy all copies. It wouldn't take long before some creative minds work it out. But that's not the worst of it," he said grimly. "This report was done here two weeks ago and only Lucas and Jennifer had access."

Hearing the words was far worse than reading them. Lucas flinched and laid his hand on the wide window frame to support his weak knees. Somewhere in the distance he could hear Brandon yell, curse and begin to pace the floor. Beads of perspiration dotted Lucas's forehead, and he reached up to wipe them away. He jumped suddenly as a small hand touched his arm.

"What are you going to do, Lucas?" Shasta asked. She glanced over her shoulder, then lowered her voice to a whisper. "She didn't do it, you know. I don't understand how, but someone's getting those documents from this office." Her slim fingers tightened on his arm, strong fingers that pinched him into awareness. "I've just realized how dangerous all this is. Till now it was just a game, but there is someone out there who hates you and is using Jennifer as a pawn—a way to get to you. How far are they willing to go?"

Lucas studied the big brown eyes staring up at him, telling him more than her words that she believed in Jennifer and was genuinely concerned for her safety. "Thanks, Shasta. Do you think you can convince Kane of the danger she's in?"

Waving an airy hand, Shasta dismissed her husband. "Forget Kane. He'll come around. Besides, I can handle him."

"Forget Kane, like hell!" Kane had come up behind them and stood glaring at them, his light gray eyes even paler with anger. "If the two of you still believe she's innocent despite the evidence to the contrary, I'll help." He turned to Brandon. "I guess you go along with them?" Brandon nodded. "Okay. I'll help you prove it, if I can." He pried his wife's fingers from Lucas's arm. "But you'll do it my way." Shasta made a squealing noise and he amended his words. "You'll do it *our* way."

"She's not guilty." Lucas's eyes met Kane's squarely. "And I believe she's in more danger than we're aware of." Suddenly he could feel the anger building inside him, and he stalked back to the desk, picked up the report and tore it into halves. "Who! Who the hell knows how I feel about her? I haven't told anyone."

Brandon made a disgusted sound in the back of his throat. "You didn't have to tell anyone, because the two of you practically shouted it to fifty people at JoBeth's party. That was one hot waltz, brother."

"But why?" Lucas frowned and pounded his fist on the desk. "I feel so damn helpless," he shouted, then snarled, "Who would benefit the most? Forget the money angle. This goes beyond simple greed. Susan's in this for what she can get, but whoever she's working for doesn't care. They want more."

They all fell silent. Then Shasta piped up. "What would happen to the company if you were to be hurt or killed? Who would take over?"

"Brandon," Lucas answered softly.

"Hey! Surely you don't think I'd do anything like this. I'm family, for Pete's sake. The loving brother, remember?" When they all remained quiet, Brandon remarked hotly, "This is *not* funny, people."

Shasta's giggle broke the strained silence. "He's right. Brandon would never do anything to hurt the company."

"Well, thanks a lot, pixie. I wouldn't do anything to hurt Lucas, either."

They began to talk all at once, sharing opinions, offering suggestions of some way to expose the thief. Shasta shook her head disgustedly, brought her two fingers to her lips and whistled a long shrill sound that made Lucas stagger back to his chair, Brandon cover his ears and Kane smile.

"Always a little lady, Shasta?" Kane asked sarcastically, but he couldn't hide the twinkle in his eyes.

"We need a solid plan," she said.

Lucas's hand shook as he reached for his coffee cup. He brought it to his lips, tasted the cold brew and grimaced. With a loud thump he commanded their full attention. "You people go work it out." He looked at Kane. "But as of now I want someone to follow Jennifer everywhere she goes—night and day. I don't want any surprises. No matter what you think, Kane, I want her protected. If anything happens to Jennifer—" He let the threat lie heavily in the room.

Kane nodded his understanding. He'd do the same if the situation were reversed. "I have something in mind, but I'll need Jennifer out of her office for about three or four days."

"What plan?" Lucas and Shasta demanded together.

"I want to plant some surveillance equipment in her office—cameras, bugs, that sort of thing. But it will take some cosmetic work to hide the equipment."

"I don't know." Lucas massaged his temples, his headache ten times worse than before.

Shasta leaned forward eagerly. "Didn't you say something to Cleo about the starkness of Jennifer's office? Tell her you're going to have it decorated."

"Wouldn't she want to be involved in that?" He lifted his shoulders, admitting his helplessness when it came to women and their peculiarities.

"You'll have to get her out of town," Kane said. "We can't take the chance she'll walk in on us. Can you send her somewhere?"

Brandon coughed loudly to draw their attention.

"Lucas, why don't you take Jennifer to the ranch? Tell her you need to check on something, but you don't want to stop work on the project, so you need her with you. Besides, Dad wants to meet her." He grinned at the three people frowning at him in varying degrees of disgust. "It just takes the brilliance of a lawyer's mind to work out all the important details in a delicate operation like this."

"You mean you're better at lying than we are?" Shasta suggested in dulcet tones.

"Something like that, yes," he grinned. "But it will work if Lucas will play his part and sweet-talk the lady. Right, brother?"

Lucas nodded and watched them file out of his office. When the doors shut quietly behind Brandon he raked his fingers through his hair and closed his eyes. He prayed he could talk her into coming to the ranch. There was a bitter taste in his mouth that had nothing to do with his hangover. The thought of one more lie piled onto the growing stack began to eat at his insides. If she ever found out how she'd been manipulated... The possibility didn't bear thinking about, not now, not today, when his guts were twisted with the fear that she might get hurt and never know the reason till it was too late. But heaven help the person who tried to harm her.

JENNIFER SHOT A FURTIVE GLANCE around the lobby of DeSalvas before she stepped into the elevator. The heavy doors slid smoothly shut, and she gave a limp wave to the security guard before the doors closed completely. She felt light-headed, even dizzy, and grabbed the brass railing that circled the burnished walls of the steel cage. What had she done? She swallowed. What was happening to her? She punched the twelfth-floor button, slumped back against the cold wall and hung her head.

When the elevator came to a stop she stuck her head through the opening and checked to see if anyone was around. The hall was empty, and muted voices floated from the offices beyond. As quietly and quickly as possible she sprinted toward the women's rest room at the end of the long hallway.

Once inside she forced herself to stand before the long wall of mirrors above the lavatory. Slowly she raised her head and looked at the stranger staring back at her with wide, tear-filled violet eyes. Panic gleamed from their depths.

She gulped, then blinked at the new hairstyle. Her beautiful long hair, which she'd only trimmed to keep in condition, now hung in a shoulder-length page boy. Smooth and sleek, it rippled whenever she moved her head. Tentatively, she touched the shining strands. It wasn't so bad now that the first shock had worn off.

Jennifer leaned closer to the mirror, pleased to see the highlights that sprang to life under the bright overhead lights. How could she have let Jean-Paul talk her into this? She leaned back and shook her head wildly, watching as the thick silky mass fell neatly back into place.

Maybe she should seriously consider strangling Jean-Paul. He'd come into her office late yesterday, just before she was to leave for the penthouse. His sympathetic concern for her tired, washed-out appearance had sent her digging for her compact.

She remembered his solicitousness and his advice that perhaps it was time for a change, time to be daring, time to shock Lucas out of his complacency. Give the man a run for his money, he'd whispered in her ear as she contemplated the thick braid twisted atop her head. Make him stand up and take notice the way other men were going to, he'd cajoled. And like Eve listening to the serpent whispering sweet promises, she'd been more than receptive. Like a lamb being led astray.

Making that one appointment had reminded her of another appointment she should make. Since she had the morning off, she had dialed her doctor to reserve a time for her annual checkup.

As she moved closer to the mirror, Jennifer watched her eyes fill with tears. Her hands clenched the sink till her knuckles turned a bloodless white. She was worse than stupid! How could a woman her age not have seen the signs? How could she have lain there in that impersonal sterile room and related all her symptoms as if she were talking about the flu?

She should have realized what she was saying, but she hadn't. When the doctor asked what the chances were that she was pregnant, she'd almost become hysterical. It had taken a nurse to calm her down and the doctor's reassurance that they had to wait for the lab results to be sure.

The doctor was wrong, of course. She couldn't possibly be pregnant. Life wouldn't be so cruel as to let her repeat her mother's mistake. There was only one thought that kept her sane, and she kept those words locked in her mind. "There are alternatives," he'd told her compassionately.

Jennifer inhaled deeply. She wouldn't need to think about "alternatives." All she had to worry about, she reminded her mirror image, was either getting used to her short hair or deciding if she was going to let it grow back long.

She managed to get to her office unseen, and hurriedly unlocked her desk and began to work. Ten minutes later she was immersed in the German translation, when she heard a familiar footfall. Her head shot up like a cornered animal sensing danger.

Lucas froze in midstride, his eyes locked on Jennifer's short hair. "How could you?" he bellowed.

Her chair crashed over as she jumped up and took a step backward. She thrust her chin out, but it trembled noticeably, and she clenched her jaw to keep it from quivering even more. There was a painful sting behind her eyes and she blinked hard a couple of times.

People were beginning to gather at the open doorway, curious at the commotion. She caught a glimpse of Cleo and sent her a pleading look. But there was no help from that or any corner. As the staff caught a good look at their boss's expression they slowly crept away. Their retreating steps picked up speed when Lucas's voice sounded again, and though softer than the first time, it sent them scurrying.

"How *could* you?" he yelled, then spun around and marched out of her office, his furious expression forever imprinted on her mind.

But there were other emotions behind the sparkling green eyes that she hadn't missed—pain and sadness. Dazed, she uprighted her chair and sat down. Her knees trembled and her hands shook. She'd really done it now. Damn, who did he think he was, anyway? It was her hair after all.

"Don't worry. He won't kill you." Cleo appeared in the doorway. "Personally, I love it. Turn your head. Yes, it's lovely."

"You think the style's right for me?" she asked, then burst into tears.

"Hey." Cleo quickly shut the door and put her arm around Jennifer's heaving shoulders. "Hey, it's not that bad. He'll come around. It was just the shock. Or is it more than Lucas that's troubling you? What's wrong, Jennifer? You can talk to me."

"I've never cut my hair before," she blubbered, and covered her face with her hands, knowing she'd told only half the truth. "This is silly, but I guess it's all tied in with my childhood...." The word "childhood" brought on another deluge of tears. "A symbol or something." She hiccuped through her fingers. "Nothing has been working out right lately."

Self-pity was setting in and Jennifer tried to get hold of her emotions before she broke down completely and found herself telling the tenderhearted Cleo her real problem. She accepted the tissue being forced on her, wiped her eyes and blew her nose loudly. "I'm sorry I fell apart like that."

"You're tired and a bundle of nerves. Why don't you go home and rest?"

Jennifer shook her head, and her newly cut hair flew in a honey-colored ripple. She didn't want to be alone, not now. "Where's Lucas? I guess I'd better go talk to him."

Cleo patted the trembling shoulder and handed Jennifer another tissue from her jacket pocket. "I wouldn't if I were you. Wait till the smoke clears. Besides, he stomped out of here a few minutes ago." She brushed a few displaced strands of Jennifer's hair into place. "I don't know if he will be back or not."

As soon as Cleo left Jennifer tried to bury herself once more in her work, but what little concentration she'd had previously now seemed to have melted away. All she could think about was the look in Lucas's eyes.

She buried her face in her hands once more and a million questions buzzed in her head.

"Chérie, your hair!"

A deep anger rose against Jean-Paul, as if he were the cause of all her problems. "Go away."

"But, *non.* I have skulked around these hallowed halls all morning waiting to see if you took your good friend's advice." His black eyes shone with pride as he admired her new hairdo. "Enchanting, adorable." He kissed the tips of his fingers in appreciation. "How irresistible you are."

"Lucas hates it—and me."

"Non!"

"Yes." Her cheeks burned as she remembered Lucas's reaction. "He yelled at me."

Jean-Paul snapped his fingers in the air as if to totally dismiss Lucas's feelings. "He will forgive you when he sees how the men stop and stare. *Oui?* You are more beautiful than JoBeth, and that he will see, also. But wait." He stepped out of her office and leaned down.

Jennifer followed his movements, then frowned as he returned carrying a tall frosted glass filled with a dozen long-stemmed roses. "I tell you, Jean-Paul, Lucas hates my hair, and it's all your fault." She sniffed appreciatively and swallowed.

"These roses are for you for being so brave." He set the lovely arrangement of red buds surrounded by delicate fern and tiny baby's breath on her desk.

A bitter taste filled her throat and she swallowed again, harder this time. Her skin grew damp and clammy. "They're gorgeous." A distant buzz filled her head and she turned pale. "Please, Jean-Paul, take them away." Jennifer placed her hand over her mouth and leaned back, rolling her chair as far away from the cloying fragrance as possible.

Jean-Paul yanked up the vase and placed it outside her office door. When he returned he pulled up a chair and sat down. "Are you better, *chérie*?"

"Yes." Jennifer took a deep breath. "I'm fine now. It's been a rough day. Jean-Paul, I'm sorry." She rested her elbows on the top of her typewriter and laid her chin on her folded arms. Silence fell between them. She felt uneasy under the sharp scrutiny of those jet-black eyes and recalled Brandon's conversation concerning his pierced ear and his accusation of Jean-Paul's involvement. Without realizing what she was doing, her eyes were drawn to Jean-Paul's ear, and she laughed. His eyebrows rose in question. "Your ear is pierced!"

"Oui." He touched the lobe. "Since I was a young man I've had this. A constant reminder of a very special lady. She thought we should share everything, including pain." His shoulders lifted in a gesture far more explicit than words. "How could I refuse? It wasn't till later that I learned she'd also tried to talk Lucas into joining her in the game. He, of course, was too wise to fall for her tricks. I was the fool."

"Did she mean so much?"

He shrugged, again his gaze intent on Jennifer's face. "When are you going to tell Lucas of the happy event?"

His question caught her completely off guard. Her cheeks blanched, making her dark violet eyes seem too large for her face. "What are you talking about? What happy event?"

"Non, chérie." He shook his head, disappointed at her attempt to deceive him. "You are trying to convince a man

who has two children. I can tell, you understand? The skin becomes translucent, a softness enters the eyes. It cannot be hidden, not from an aware man. Besides, you reacted to the flowers just as I suspected you would.''

Jennifer had to force her mouth closed. ''It's not true,'' she whispered frantically. ''You're not married.''

''What does this have to do with children? I tell you I have two, a boy and a girl.''

She couldn't stand it anymore and jumped up, scooped the papers from her desk into a drawer and locked it. The walls were closing in on her, squeezing the air from her lungs, and her breathing came in short laborious gasps. She had to get away.

''Chérie!''

As if from a distance, Jennifer heard the concern in Jean-Paul's voice. Grabbing her purse, she pushed past him.

''Jennifer. *Mon Dieu, chérie.* What is it?''

She didn't bother to answer his frantic inquiry. Once free of her office, she sprinted down the hall, his voice spurring her on. Thankfully the elevator was before her, its door slowly shutting. She lunged forward and managed to squeeze through before the doors closed. Jean-Paul shouted and banged on the door as she sagged against the back wall.

THE MINUTE she stepped into her living room she knew she'd made a mistake. The past was everywhere. She swung around in a circle, her eyes taking in every object, and suddenly it dawned on her that she no longer had a life of her own. A sob rose from deep in her chest and she fought for control. There was nothing of herself in this house. It was as if she existed only through her mother's treasures. Was she about to repeat her mother's most disastrous mistake?

The thought shocked her into motion. She took a deep breath and walked over to the white wicker couch. Calmly she sat down, reached for the telephone and dialed. Three tries later she spoke softly to the nurse, then clamped her eyes shut as she heard the dreaded words.

"Positive," the twangy voice said. "Would you like to set up your next appointment with—"

With marked precision, Jennifer carefully lowered the receiver back in its cradle and clutched the purse resting in her lap. She shuddered. Flashes of her father's cruelty and her mother's tears seemed to play through her mind like a horror movie. She could hear her father's biting sarcasm, the constant reminders that he'd been forced to marry and lose the chance for a brilliant career because of her birth. The memory of her mother's valiant acceptance tore at her heart.

Jennifer sat in a trance, her fingers squeezing the fine leather of her purse. The telephone rang constantly, a never-ending sound that she did not even acknowledge. The caller continued persistently for an hour, then finally stopped. Jennifer blinked at the lack of noise, then fought to slip back into the black void. But reality forced itself on her.

Pregnant! She didn't want a baby. What would she do? The thought of what her mother's life had been like made Jennifer feel physically ill. She pressed the purse into her stomach and leaned over till the nausea passed. How could she raise another human being when her own life was such a disaster area? A baby would be someone to love and love her in return but she didn't need the restriction. The doctor said she had options and she had to decide.

The doorbell rang, a long, loud burst that she ignored. With it came a pounding on the front and back doors and the muffled sound of her name being called. Lucas would ask her to marry him; of that she was sure. The sick feeling was back—worse this time. She moaned and began to rock back and forth. Trapped in a marriage; trapped in the past. God help her! Was she living her life or reliving that of her mother's?

She stopped rocking and sat upright as a ray of light began to fill the darkness in her mind. A baby—another human being—helpless and soft. Her thoughts became jumbled and incoherent. If she was repeating her mother's life, maybe she could at least do some things differently. After all, when she asked herself the one question she'd avoided till now—could she have an abortion and take a tiny life—the answer was irrevocably no.

Once the decision was made, the vice around her heart loosened its grip. Ideas began to take form. She was so lost in her plans that she didn't hear the sound of glass shattering on the kitchen floor; nor did she catch the low growls of a male swearing, or the thud of a body hitting a hard floor.

All Jennifer could think about was how she could keep her job and if not, could she support herself doing freelance work. Suddenly her plans came to an abrupt halt and she was scared. Was she doing the right thing?

"Jennifer. Jennifer. Honey, are you all right?" Brandon squatted before her, taking her icy hands in his and studying her blank eyes as they stared off into space. She was white as a ghost, and the lack of expression on her face made his heart skip a beat. "Jennifer, have you taken anything? Jennifer!" He tapped her cheek, and was relieved to see her eyes focus on him.

"Brandon, what are you doing here?" She looked around, dazed. "How did you get in?"

"Never mind that." His hand sliced the air impatiently. "Are you okay? Have you taken anything?"

"What are you going on about?" She sucked in a deep breath as she looked at him and finally realized that what she'd hoped to keep a secret was out. "You know. How?"

"That you're pregnant? Yes. Jean-Paul called me when he couldn't reach Lucas."

"But he didn't know, not for sure." She frowned. "I didn't know then, either."

"It doesn't matter. Jennifer, have you taken anything?"

"No. Why do you keep asking me that?"

Brandon heaved a sigh of relief and eased onto the couch beside her. "Jean-Paul said you were so upset, hysterical. He was sure you were suicidal."

"Never," Jennifer gasped, highly offended. "And I wasn't hysterical. How could he tell you something like that?" She was suddenly angry, and Brandon smiled. But her anger quickly died, along with Brandon's smile. "You said Jean-Paul contacted you—not Lucas?"

Brandon shook his head. "Lucas received an urgent call and had to fly to Dallas on business."

"Oh. You won't tell him, will you, Brandon?" she pleaded, her cold hands squeezing his fingers. "I can take care of this myself."

"What do you mean, 'take care'?"

"Not what you think. Please don't tell Lucas."

Brandon pulled his hands free. "I can't do that, Jennifer. He has a right to know."

She knew it was wrong of her to ask him to go against his brother. "Sorry."

"Listen, Jennifer, you don't have to worry about anything. If Lucas won't take care of you, I'm always here. I'll do anything but offer marriage." He shuddered theatrically and laughed when she did.

But her shaking had nothing to do with amusement. Her skin took on a sickly cast and moisture covered her face in a fine sheen. "Brandon, I don't feel so good." She clamped her hand over her mouth, jumped up and ran to the bathroom.

Fifteen minutes later she opened the door, held the frame for support and stared at Brandon. He was standing before her with one of her nightgowns dangling from his hand. If she hadn't felt as if she were going to die she would have laughed. He'd found "Old Faithful," the ankle-length flannel nightgown that was her security blanket whenever she was sick.

"Here." He handed her the gown, then tossed her her beloved knee socks. "Put these on and get into bed." She opened her mouth to protest. "Hush, you don't have the strength to argue. I'll stay with you tonight." Or, he thought, until he could reach Lucas and be relieved of his duty by his brother.

"You don't—"

"Bed!" He shouted, then gently pushed her backward and shut the bathroom door.

Well, maybe she'd allow this one concession, since she didn't have the energy to fight back. She opened the door and padded out in her faded pink gown and her green-and-white wool Christmas socks. Ignoring Brandon's laughter, she slipped into her turned-back bed, pulled the covers to her chin and frowned. "You're pretty smart for a bachelor."

"I know. Now go to sleep. You're exhausted." He leaned over, planted a loud wet kiss on her forehead and chuckled at her snort of disgust. "By the way, your hair looks great."

He stood up and turned to leave, but Jennifer caught his hand and pulled him back. "Are you going to call Lucas tonight?"

"I have to, Jennifer. Don't ask me not to."

For the first time in hours she felt warm, and her eyelids began to droop sleepily. "It won't make any difference, you know?" she murmured.

"Go to sleep," Brandon said gently. At the door he turned and looked at her. If he'd had a mustache he would have twirled the ends in glee. His brother was in for some interesting times.

CHAPTER TWELVE

THE RICH AROMA of brewing coffee coaxed Jennifer awake—that and the low rumble of bass voices. She snuggled deeper into her warm nest and sighed softly, dismissing the intruding sounds. Men in her house? Ridiculous! There was something amusing in the thought and she chuckled sleepily as she burrowed farther under the covers.

When a loud burst of muffled male laughter penetrated her dreams, her eyes popped open in questioning horror. Everything that had happened yesterday rushed back at her with the delicacy of a herd of elephants. She squeezed her eyes shut and pulled the covers over her mouth to stifle a loud groan. No one had to tell her that one of those voices coming from her kitchen belonged to Lucas. Maybe if she continued to stay in bed he'd leave. Fat chance, she thought grimly. He'd come for his pound of flesh.

Jennifer groaned again, but this time the sound came out as a whimper. She didn't want to have to argue about her decisions to anyone, especially Lucas. Besides, how could she intelligently discuss the arrangement, when she'd only thought of it hours ago. Her doubts at the crazy turn her life had taken rushed back full force, and she swallowed a rising fear that ate at her insides like acid. Maybe she should review her options once more before she faced Lucas.

The weakening of her resolve made her angry. Was she a coward? After these past weeks of changes was she going to scurry back into her shell?

Kicking the covers off, Jennifer struggled out of the tangle of sheets and blankets and marched to the bathroom. She quickly brushed her teeth, washed her face and ran a hurried brush through her hair, stopping only long enough to admire the new style, which fell instantly into place with barely a touch. She leaned closer to her reflection, meeting her gaze squarely, and whispered, "You're wasting time. Might as well face him now."

Before her courage dropped to the zero level she yanked a robe from the back of the door, pulled it on and walked out of the room. She didn't let her steps lag or her backbone lose its starch as she kept up the momentum from her bedroom to the kitchen.

Lucas was aware of her entrance even before Brandon greeted her. He kept his eyes on his work and carefully turned the strip of frying bacon. There was an awkward pause and he grinned in sympathy. This wasn't going to be easy for either of them, but he fully intended to take advantage of his good fortune. Granted, his timetable had been speeded up considerably, but—he shrugged philosophically—that was life, always playing tricks on the unsuspecting.

Jennifer eased quickly into a chair and managed a nod at Brandon's cheery good-morning. Her careful contemplation of the table's surface was interrupted as a cup of hot coffee was pushed beneath her nose. She raised her head. "Thanks, Brandon."

Looking around was a mistake. She took in the two men, casual in their rolled-up shirt sleeves, comfortably at home in her kitchen—too comfortable. The place was a wreck. Dirty dishes were everywhere—plates, cups, glasses. Her eyes widened in bewilderment. Had there been a party here last night while she'd slept? Surely two men couldn't have made this big a mess?

Brandon noticed her shocked expression. "I'm certainly glad you're awake. Lucas has been a little nervous, so while we waited he cooked—everything in sight." He reared back in his chair and patted his stomach. "I don't think I could have eaten another bite."

Deliberately, Jennifer kept her attention focused on Brandon. When her clasped hands resting on the tabletop were surroundeed by Lucas's warm grip, she jumped.

"Jenny, we have a lot to discuss. I know this isn't what you wanted. I know you—"

"No, Lucas. You don't know anything about me at all."

His green eyes glowed warmly, and an indulgent smile turned up one corner of his mouth. "That's where you're wrong. I know everything there is to know, from the moment you were born till the evening I first met you. I know that when you were a toddler you fell down the steps in the main entrance of the Hotel Ritz in Paris and Ernest Hemingway picked you up and dried your tears. You learned to ski in Cervinia when you were six and broke your arm in the same spot at Gstaad two years later." He could see comprehension dawning in her eyes. She tried to pull her hands free, but he cupped them tighter. "You see, I do know."

"He's right, Jennifer. He had your past investigated."

"Thank you, Brandon," Lucas said sarcastically. "I appreciate all you've done. But the rest of this conversation is between Jennifer and me. You may leave anytime."

"Oh, no, brother. I came in at the beginning, I'll see it through. Besides, I've just decided to resign as your personal lawyer and take on Jennifer as a client."

"Nonsense." Lucas turned back to Jennifer, a light frown creasing his forehead. "She doesn't need your services. Do you, Jenny?" He patted her clasped hands. "We can get married tomorrow. I've made a few calls and fixed everything."

"No," she whispered, the word almost strangling her.

"Then we can leave for the ranch."

"No."

"You'll love it there."

"You're bacon's burning, Lucas."

He shot Brandon a killing glance and reluctantly moved to the stove. He turned the overbrown strips and cracked two eggs into the hot skillet, sending a splattering of grease over the surface of the stove. "Honestly, Jenny. You'll love the ranch and Dad."

"No." Was the man deaf as well as blind? Couldn't he see how serious she was? Wearily Jennifer rubbed her eyes. She'd expected some resistance, but not this unwavering single-mindedness. He didn't seem to care what she wanted or thought. "No, Lucas."

"What?"

"I said no, I won't marry you."

He chuckled again and expertly flipped the two eggs, one at a time. "Of course you will."

"Lucas!" Brandon warned softly.

"Stay out of this." He slipped the eggs from the skillet and transferred them to a waiting plate, disregarding the fact that the whites looked like old lace. "After some business problems are taken care of we'll take a long honeymoon."

This wasn't happening to her. Could she have so totally misjudged Lucas? His bullying shocked her. Then she suddenly realized that it wasn't arrogance but happiness that was making him so overbearing. His eyes sparkled like a clear green pool on a bright sunny day, and his expression was that of a small boy who had just been given a puppy.

She hated herself for bursting his bubble of happiness. "Lucas, listen to me, please," she pleaded gently. "It's not you. It's just that I've never wanted to marry." The situation was awkward with Brandon avidly listening to their every word.

Lucas stopped in midstride, plate in hand and stared at her. "Of course you do. You're pregnant." He smiled proudly and went on. "You have to marry me. I'm the father."

Jennifer's heart sank. "But I'm not going to, father or no father. I thought all this out last night...." Her words trailed off as his expression changed to one of a tolerant man indulging a petulant child. "I'm serious, Lucas. There's nothing you can do."

He set the plate down before her with a loud thump. "You think not?" Damn the woman. Why couldn't she give in gracefully and let him have his fun?

Jennifer made the mistake of looking down at the breakfast he'd cooked for her. She stared into two yellow eyes and a brown strip that looked like a leering mouth mocking her. Her stomach heaved and she jumped up, pushed the chair out of the way and ran for the bathroom, with Lucas right behind her.

Several humiliating minutes later, Lucas handed her a glass of red liquid. "Here, rinse your mouth out and wash your face with cold water, and you'll feel better." His hands tightened around her waist, holding her up as her trembling knees almost gave way. Concern and pity warred in him with amusement and a slow-building anger. Damn butt-headed female! She was such a baby right now—totally defenseless.

Burying her face in the warm cotton towel, Jennifer wondered when her body had turned traitor. She hadn't been sick before, but it seemed that once her condition was confirmed, her system had decided to develop all the symptoms of pregnancy.

Before she could regain her wits and her second wind, Lucas scooped up her limp body into his arms and left the small confines of the bathroom. The motion made her lower the towel and stare pleadingly at him. His eyes were brimming with tenderness. A groan rose in her throat, only to end in a soft grunt of relief as Lucas lowered her onto the white wicker love seat. She closed her eyes and sighed as a damp, cold washcloth was laid across her throbbing forehead.

"Jennifer, you need something in your stomach," Brandon urged, and he waved a small object under her nose.

She moaned and shook her head, refusing to open her eyes.

"Come on," he coaxed. "Here," he tried again, this time emphasizing each word with a firm nudge of his hand on her shoulder.

"Don't shake me, Brandon." Her eyes opened, the lids heavy. She shifted her gaze from one man to the other as they hovered over her.

"Please try to eat, Jenny." Lucas took a cracker and handed it to her, making her accept it.

Brandon leaned over the back of the love seat and inspected her pale features. "Go on. Eat. It'll help, I promise."

She nibbled a corner, experimenting with the steadiness of her stomach. "How do you know it'll help?" she snapped. "Have you ever been pregnant?"

Both men grinned at her waspish retort. "Stop griping and eat," Lucas scolded.

Jennifer finished the cracker, surprised that her stomach didn't take immediate exception. Delicately she licked the salt from her fingers, then shifted as she heard an odd sound—half gasping, half choking. She looked up, her attention riveted at first to the peculiar expression slipping across Brandon's face. Then she looked at Lucas. The sound came again, and as she watched, Lucas's color quickly faded from a rosy flush to a pasty white, to a sickly pea green. She raised herself up, resting on her elbow as Lucas spun around and dashed back toward the bathroom.

The silence that followed Lucas's hasty retreat was broken only by Brandon's laughter. He roared, his head thrown back as he clutched the long package of crackers to his chest.

When a concerned Jennifer tried to ask to him to help his brother, a new spasm of laughter seemed to take hold of him, and he leaned weakly against the back of the love seat for support.

"Well, really, Brandon. I don't find the fact of Lucas being sick the least bit funny." She eased into a sitting position, carefully testing her stability as she moved.

Brandon wheezed for breath and waved his hand. "You'll see. Here—" he shoved another cracker at her "—eat and don't move around so much."

"Maybe you should go check on him. He's been in there a long time."

Her worried plea sent him off again and he watched her lips tighten. "I'm not the only one who's been eating since five o'clock this morning," he said. Through his watering eyes he noticed her fierce scowl and tried again to reassure her, but the sincerity of his words was ruined by his bouts of laughter. "He's a big boy, Jennifer. He'll live."

She was about to protest more vehemently, when a door opened behind her. Before she could turn around, Lucas made his way to the twin love seat opposite her own.

"Damn you, Brandon, I could hear you cackling like a madman. What the hell is so funny?" The long speech sapped what little strength Lucas had left, and he slapped the wet washcloth across his forehead, leaned back against the fluffy cushion and draped his legs over the arm of the short love seat with a sigh.

The sight of Lucas's long legs overflowing her furniture, his feet actually resting on the floor, made her bite her lip. She wanted to join in Brandon's laughter but something told her Lucas wasn't far from exploding. She swallowed a giggle. Poor man, he did look ghastly.

Eagerly Brandon pulled up a wing chair, situated it between them and handed them each a cracker.

Lucas sighed, a pitiful, childish sound for a man his size. He would have glared at both Brandon and Jennifer if it didn't take so much energy. "Okay, obviously it's going to kill you if you don't spit it out. What in hell do you find so damnably funny?"

"Haven't you figured out yet what's happened to you?" Brandon asked, his voice brimming with mischief and a certain superiority that set his brother's teeth on edge.

Lucas groaned. "For heaven's sake. No games...not now. Of course I know what happened," he snapped.

"I don't think so," teased Brandon, struggling hard to keep a straight face.

Lucas, resigned to his brother's quirky behavior, gave in. "What, then?"

"Morning sickness!" he announced succinctly, and handed his two patients another cracker.

Jennifer nibbled automatically, her gaze shifting from one man to the other with growing interest.

Lucas glared at his brother as if he'd just lost what little sense he had left. "Sometimes, Brandon, your jokes go too far."

"I'm serious, and I'm willing to back my statement with five thousand dollars. Are you willing to try to disprove it? I'll even throw in a side bet that if history repeats itself you won't get over your morning sickness till Jennifer does. Is it a bet?"

A deep frown lined Lucas's brow. There was something familiar about what Brandon was telling him. "No."

"Smart man!" Brandon doled out more crackers to Jennifer and Lucas and helped himself to one. "Don't you remember Mom laughing and telling us that Dad suffered the same malady with all three of us? She used to tease him about it." He looked over at Jennifer and smiled. "It's really sort of a family joke, or maybe a curse. Dad would laugh about it, but it seemed he went through hell. After each of us was born he said he'd swear to Mom that there would be no more. And Mom would only smile secretly."

Jennifer couldn't believe what she was hearing. They were both stark raving mad. She leaned on one elbow and looked from Lucas to Brandon. "Do you mean to tell me that you're telling the truth?"

The idea of Lucas suffering along with her was not unappealing. In fact, the more she thought about the prospect of him having to share her agony, the more it pleased her. She began to chuckle, flopped back on the cushions and asked, "Did your father have labor pains, too?" The thought set both her and Brandon laughing again.

"It didn't extend that far. Pity, too—would have been interesting."

Lucas gave them both a sour look. "I'm glad you two find this all so amusing. I damn well don't." He expelled his breath disgustedly, sat up too quickly for his queasy stomach, then froze. A cold sweat dotted his forehead, and he eased back down shakily, accepting a cracker from his brother. "If what you say is true, then at least I can be one hundred percent sure that the child is mine...my flesh and blood." He closed his eyes, unaware of the bomb his thoughtless words had set off.

Brandon groaned and buried his face in his hands at his brother's insensitive gaffe.

"Bastard," Jennifer hissed, her eyes spitting fire. "This is not your child."

"Of course it is," he replied, so smugly that when Brandon groaned again, he opened his eyes and faced two very angry determined expressions. "What's wrong?" Then he realized what he'd said so unthinkingly and tried to retract his words. "I'm sorry." He rubbed his face vigorously, then stared at Jennifer. "You're not the only one who's finding things happening too fast. It's got me crazy and saying everything all wrong. But don't you dare lie there and try to tell me this child is not mine and I can't take care of both of you."

"You can't. You forfeited all rights," she reminded him, and wondered why her triumph wasn't sweeter. She should be jumping with joy that she'd finally returned the insult he'd handed her the morning after their first meeting.

Lucas pressed his forearm against his eyes. "Brandon, what's she talking about?" His brother didn't answer, and he moved his arm only enough to open one eye. "Well?"

Brandon quickly munched another cracker, instantly losing his bravado. Who would ever have thought his little joke would have come to this?

"I'll tell you since he's suddenly decided to become mute," said Jennifer. "The paternity agreement you made me sign. Do you remember?"

Lucas nodded, then sent Brandon a searching look that ended in a baleful glare when he finally met his brother's innocent blue eyes.

Jennifer caught the exchange between the two men and wanted to smile. "You also signed another document—my agreement." Lucas said nothing, just continued to stare at his brother. "You signed away all rights and legal claims."

Sitting upright, Lucas roared, "I did not." Then he remembered the papers Brandon had had him hurriedly sign before he left for Europe weeks ago. When he'd asked for an explanation, Brandon had given him a vague mumbled response and sped him on his way with a promise to take care of everything. "My child will not be raised as illegitimate."

"My child, not yours."

He swung his legs around and placed his feet firmly on the floor. "You'll marry me tomorrow and that's that."

"Don't Lucas," Brandon pleaded, shocked at his brother's loss of control. "Stop before you say something you'll regret the rest of your life."

"You!" He pointed at Brandon with a shaky finger. "You have done quite enough, Judas."

"But Lucas—"

"Stay out of this!" Both Jennifer and Lucas snapped at him, and Brandon rapidly munched on another cracker, his eyes overbright with suppressed laughter.

Lucas leaned forward, propped his elbows on his knees and rested his chin on his clenched fist. "My child," he growled, his look daring her to contradict him again. She didn't, and he continued in a softer tone of voice, more reasonable. "How in the world do you think you can manage without my help? What about your job, money? I hate to burst your bubble, but it does take money to have a baby."

"Money, money! Always money. How I hate that word." Jennifer sat completely upright and faced him. "Everything always comes back to your damn money." She leaned forward, her expression scornful. "Unlike some people I know, I don't require a lot to live on. And if you haven't already found out in that *cheap* background report, I own this duplex. It's paid for and I collect a handsome income from renting the back apartment. If that's not enough—" Jennifer looked around her home at the priceless objects she'd always loved but could live without "—I can sell some of these antiques. As for working, let me tell you something," she snarled close to his face. "I made a living before you came along and I can make one after you're gone."

He snorted and she scowled at him, leaning even closer in her anger. "And there's always free-lance work. That means I won't have to work for you."

Her head was beginning to spin and she flopped backwards onto the soft cushions. "As for the expense of having my baby, there are always free clinics, or something." She wasn't very sure of her ground here and closed her eyes so she wouldn't have to go on.

Lucas's anger became more pronounced as he listened to her lengthy speech, knowing that all she'd said was true and that she really could manage without him. But when she started discussing having his child in such a cavalier fashion, he exploded. "Never—do you hear me—never will I have my child born on the charity of others."

"Look, you two," Brandon interrupted. "Why don't you give it a rest. You're both feeling rotten."

Lucas ignored his brother, his fixed stare studying Jennifer, a strange light in his dark green eyes. "I don't understand any of this." He looked totally baffled. "I'd be good to you. I care, and it's not as if you don't know me.

What's wrong with me that marriage is so distasteful?'' he asked softly, a sad droop to his mouth.

Jennifer stared unbelievingly at the man before her. Confused, defeated, a beaten man with slumped shoulders. Though he had her almost fooled with this image of utter dejection, she didn't miss the hard, determined glitter in his eyes. Lucas McCord had missed his calling. He should have been an actor.

The bizarreness of the entire morning struck her and she bit her lip hard to keep from laughing. Her gaze shifted to Brandon, then quickly bounced away when she saw his openmouthed admiration at his brother's performance.

"I'm sorry you can't understand any of this,'' Jennifer said. "After all, it takes a person of an exceptionally sensitive nature to know how I feel. Now Brandon understands, don't you, Brandon?''

"Enough,'' Lucas muttered when he realized his ploy hadn't worked. "Now listen—oh hell, I give up. There's no sense discussing this till you're in a better frame of mind.'' He slowly got up on his feet, tested the steadiness of his stomach, then straightened to his full height. "You will not quit working for DeSalvas. No, not one damn word. You have a contract to work out and work it out you will.''

"But Lucas, in a couple of months I'll be showing. It really would be better to go free-lance now.''

"Absolutely not. You'll work for me, and if it embarrasses you when you start to show or your friends begin to ask questions and people stare, that's your problem. It won't bother me.'' He picked up his coat and slipped it on. "Just don't make the mistake of thinking this is the end. We'll continue tomorrow and the next day and the next. I don't give up.'' His face set in a rigid expression and his lips curved in a chilly smile.

But before he left, he reached out and stroked Jennifer's hair, a sadness creeping across his face as he mourned the loss of the long silky tresses. He shot Brandon a hard look. "Put those damn crackers down and come on." Without a backward glance he marched out of her home. It was Brandon who turned and smiled, sending her a thumbs-up sign before he eased the front door shut.

Jennifer stared at the door and wondered if maybe she should leave town. Get as far away from Lucas and the DeSalvas as possible. But where would she go? Besides, she knew she could never hide from Lucas, not if he wanted to find her. She lay back and closed her eyes, wondering what it was she'd ever done to deserve such a fate. And worse still, how was she going to get through this? All her big talk had been just that—talk.

She flung her arm over her eyes to shut out the bright slats of sunlight glaring through the parted curtains. Maybe, just maybe, all she'd said wasn't talk, after all. Her eyelids began to droop, and she yawned. She'd just take a nap and think things out when she awoke.

A STRAINED SILENCE fell between the two brothers as they walked down the sidewalk to their cars. Before they parted, Brandon gripped Lucas's shoulder and turned him around to face him.

"You almost blew it in there. I've never known you to be so insensitive, arrogant and overbearing. Then, to add insult to injury, you just get up and leave. What the hell happened?"

"Love and fear," Lucas said disgustedly. "It dawned on me how vulnerable I am." He reached into his inside coat pocket, pulled out a pair of sunglasses and slipped them on. "Do you realize if someone wanted to get to me all they'd have to do is hurt Jennifer? And now with the baby..." He paused, refusing to voice his fears, afraid that once spoken they might come true. He ran a hand wearily over his stubbled chin and cheeks. "Damn, but I feel terrible."

Brandon couldn't help the chuckle that escaped. "You can't continue to bully Jennifer. Not now."

"I know," Lucas cut him off. "She's in no shape emotionally or physically to take my strong-arm tactics. She's too confused right now. Besides, I got the strangest feeling that if I continued to push she just might make a run for it and leave."

"Yeah, I got the same impression."

Lucas squinted up at the cloudless sky and frowned. "That's why I backed off and gave in." He broke off, his lips a tight line, his eyes searching the partly deserted street, looking for a car or anyone who looked as if they might be working for Kane. He muttered under his breath when nothing along the street appeared out of the ordinary.

A few empty cars parked in driveways and one in the street. An old woman in her front yard, her hair in curlers as she retrieved the morning paper. A yardman, carefully pruning the hedge across the street. A small girl pedaling her tricycle down the sidewalk as fast as her little legs would carry her while her shapely mother jogged along behind.

He caught a movement from the corner of his eye and looked back across the street as the yardman pulled his dilapidated straw hat down farther on his forehead. There was something strangely familiar about his arrogant carriage and Lucas narrowed his eyes. "Brandon..." but beside him Brandon was almost choking in amazement. "That can't be who I think it is?"

The yardman wiped his hands on his baggy khaki work pants, then tipped back his head so Lucas received the full blast from his silver eyes. "Kane?" he whispered, and almost stumbled as Brandon grabbed his arm, mumbling for him to look farther down the hedge. There, squatting near the flower bed, spade in hand, was an identically dressed smaller figure who had a definitely feminine curve to her backside. The diminutive worker pivoted, and Lucas grinned as he saw the bright flash of a smile. "What the hell are Kane and Shasta doing out here?"

Brandon let go of his brother's arm and headed for his car. "Maybe they couldn't find anyone to watch Jennifer on such short notice and decided to do it themselves. Then again, it could be Shasta's perverted sense of humor to punish Kane for not believing her about Jennifer's innocence." He laughed, slipped into his car and rolled down the window.

"Either way, you can bet she won't run out on you with those two watching. Go home, Lucas and get some rest. You look like something the cat dragged in." He gunned his car engine and grinned up at Lucas. "If I were you I'd call the doctor and see if he'd give you something for that morning sickness." He raced the powerful Corvette engine again, gave a jaunty wave and sped off.

"Damn pain in the ass!" Lucas muttered. He jabbed the key in the lock and swung open the car door. The heat inside engulfed him, almost taking his breath away. He turned on the air conditioner, laid his head on the steering wheel and waited for the cool air to take away the queasiness. He couldn't endure this every morning. Then he smiled. For his child he'd endure hell itself.

As his stomach settled down he opened his eyes and glanced over at Kane and Shasta, but he wasn't actually seeing them. Fear and anger churned inside him. His skin was clammy and the silence inside the car weighed down on him heavily. He had a feeling in his gut, a feeling of impending doom. It wasn't only the threat of thieves hanging over his head like an ax. What if he couldn't make Jennifer realize she needed him, or that she would be happy with him?

"I'm scared," he admitted, his deep voice husky with emotion. All his life he'd gotten what he wanted with little effort. But now he'd willingly give up all his past good fortune just to be sure he could have Jennifer healthy and in love with him. He swallowed. Hell, he'd bargain with the devil himself if he could guarantee nothing would happen to their child. He had to get her out of the city and on the ranch, where he could have some uninterrupted time to work things out and to keep her safe for as long as he could.

CHAPTER THIRTEEN

SUSAN MCCORD nervously paced her elegantly furnished hotel room, walking from one end to the other and back again. The only time she stopped was to light another cigarette, or when a muffled noise penetrated the well-insulated walls. Her usually immaculate appearance was marred by the fact that her silk Dior blouse had been pulled haphazardly from the waistband of her skirt. Her hair, always perfectly arranged, now drooped almost comically to one side. She was scared.

The rapid-fire knock at the door made her jump as if someone had shot a gun beside her head, but she didn't move or acknowledge the sound till the code of two long then two short knocks were completed. In contrast to her previously high energy, her steps now lagged as she walked to the door.

"Such melodrama, Susan, and so early in the day."

She stood back to allow the man to enter. As he brushed by her his arm touched hers, and she steeled herself to keep from recoiling. How she hated this man, this devil with his cunning eyes, his cruelty, his pain, his clever ruthlessness. The flash of gold in his ear had become a symbol of evil, and she'd learned to fear the man himself more than the fear of getting caught. "Well!" she demanded, and quickly closed the door.

"You're right. You're being followed."

"Oh, God." She sagged against the door and raised her hand wearily, pushing at her disorderly hair. "He knows."

"Surely you weren't naive enough to think Lucas wouldn't put a tail on you? The thing is, my sweet, he can't prove anything—not yet."

Susan inhaled and pushed away from the door. She grabbed up the half-empty pack of cigarettes and shook one out with trembling fingers. "Did anyone see you come here?" Repeatedly she flicked her lighter, and repeatedly it refused to light. In a fit of temper she snatched the cigarette out of her mouth and threw it and the lighter to the floor. She quietly contemplated her loss of control, looked up and shivered at his amused expression.

"No one followed me or saw me enter the hotel. Now where are the papers?" He made himself comfortable on the end of the king-size bed.

Susan wanted him gone, and she yanked up her leather handbag, pulled out a small folded bunch of papers and tossed them to him. "Here are the translations from the last tapes you gave me."

"Why so nervous tonight, Susan? Or is it tension? I know a sure way to fix your problems."

"Of course I'm nervous. I'm being followed and watched day and night." She glared at him and briefly fancied calling Lucas and making a deal—her freedom for this man's name. But the delicious thought died an instantaneous death as he lifted his head and stared at her. She watched his eyes narrow as if he could read her traitorous thoughts. She let her own gaze drop from his and studied the carpeted floor.

"This looks good." He glanced up from the papers. "Do you realize what DeSalvas is trying to put together?" She nodded and he mocked her intelligence with a jaunty salute. "There's no telling how much money those bastards will make on this." He slapped the papers angrily on his thigh, making Susan jerk. "Why, darling, so jumpy?" He rose and slowly walked over to her, his hand outstretched to stroke her pale cheek.

Susan spun around and reached for another cigarette, carefully avoiding his touch. She leaned down and picked up her lighter from the floor. It flamed to life on the first flick. Her back muscles stiffened at his knowing chuckle and she swung around.

"No games tonight, Susan?" he taunted, enjoying her fear.

"No." She moved her head sideways to avoid his fingers. "I'd like my money."

He reached into the inside pocket of his coat and pulled out a thick envelope, but instead of handing it over, he tapped it on his chin. "Come and get it."

Susan almost hesitated, but the thought of all that money gave her courage. She took a few steps and with lightning speed snatched the envelope from his hand. But before she could move away he had her arm in a viselike grip.

"Not so fast. Here." He handed her a familiar type-writer cartridge.

"No." She backed away as far as he would allow her to go. Her hands tightened on the envelope of money, mentally tabulating how much that would add to her Swiss bank account. "You said—" she pointed to the papers resting on the bed "—you said those would be the last. I'm leaving the country before Lucas can get any proof."

"Come on, darling. I will double the amount," he cajoled sweetly, making her shiver. "Just one more for—shall we say old lovers' sake?"

Susan shook her head and yanked her arm free of his cruel grip. She stepped back farther. "You have enough. When you sell those to your Vienna contact you'll make a fortune." She gasped as he moved with the grace and speed of a killer animal, his hands biting into her arms, causing her to close her eyes in pain.

"I don't give a damn what you think or want. But I want Lucas's defeat to be total." He laughed, a sound that brought Susan's fearful gaze to his face. "You don't know, do you? Your sweet stepsister is pregnant. Oh, yes. A neat package, don't you think? I've finally found out a way for the ultimate revenge."

It was in his eyes, the insanity that he'd previously concealed. He would take perverse pleasure in seeing Lucas ruined. Then Susan saw something else and realized the extent of his cunning. He was willing to do anything to win, anything to deliver the final crushing blow—even murder. Her legs began to tremble. "I won't be a part of any of this." She struggled to break his hold, only to have her face pulled close to his, his hot breath like an open pit to hell.

"I haven't asked you to be a partner in my coup de grace. I've found the ideal way to get Lucas. What better method than to destroy what he loves and holds dear?"

He let her go, and as Susan stumbled back she watched him pick up the cartridge from the floor and set it on the dresser. "I'll have the ribbon deciphered in two days. Then we're through. I'm leaving as soon as you pick it up."

He nodded, then turned to leave and she sagged with relief. But his next words turned her spine to ice.

"You say a word to anyone—warn Lucas—and I'll find you no matter where you try to hide. I'll find you, Susan, and you'll curse your parents for ever having conceived you. Do you understand?"

"Yes. I promise you I wouldn't think of interfering with your plans and your fun."

"Not even to save Jennifer? One supreme gesture?"

Susan shrugged, a harsh gleam in her eyes. "Never."

"Good. Two days, Susan. Then our partnership is at an end."

"Wait!" She couldn't help it. She had to ask the one question that had been plaguing her for days. "You attend all those parties, like the one the other evening. Why is it I've never seen your photograph in the papers?"

He laughed, a sound that caused her to flinch. "Why? Because I choose not to be seen, darling."

His mocking laughter only stopped as he shut the door. Susan yanked an ashtray off the coffee table and let it sail across the room. It hit the door with a satisfying thud. She picked up the envelope and began to count her money. Two days and she'd be living the life she'd always dreamed about. She'd be free, and Jennifer would be nothing more than an unpleasant memory. After all, she couldn't be responsible for a madman's act of revenge, now could she?

JENNIFER SCOWLED FIERCELY when the doorbell chimed her arms immersed to her elbows in hot sudsy dishwater. She wondered if Lucas had come back to try his luck at brow beating her without an audience? Surely not. The bell sounded again and her soft mouth pinched together in a thin line. He had his nerve coming back after he'd left her kitchen—and her emotions—a wreck. Grimly she spun around, marched to the door and yanked it open. "Cleo!" She stumbled backward in surprise at the older woman' appearance.

Cleo shifted the two brown bags in her arms, her somber expression belied by the bright twinkle of curiosity in her eyes. "These are heavy, kid. Either invite me in or I'll drop them on your doorstep."

Stupefied, Jennifer did as she was told and Cleo headed for the kitchen. "My heavens," Cleo exclaimed, "what in the world happened here?"

Jennifer followed Cleo's tall figure hestitantly, wondering what was going on. "Lucas and Brandon happened."

"Ah."

"Cleo, what are you doing—" She broke off and whirled around, her heart pounding heavily against her ribs as she heard the rumble of a male voice. Her eyes widened in amazement as Mark's broad shoulders filled her doorway.

He nodded and set his armload of brown paper grocery bags down on the floor. "I'll go fix the broken window now then be off." He kissed Cleo soundly goodbye and winked at Jennifer as he passed her on the way out her front door.

Still confused and a little stunned, Jennifer could only stand and watch Cleo begin to lift the bags onto the table and start to unpack. The sight of apples, plump green grapes and bananas shocked her out of her stupor. "Stop! What's going on and who bought all this?"

Cleo's short shining cap of black hair rose from the depths of a big bag. "Lucas bought them—and you don't look so hot. Maybe you'd better sit down for the explanation I'm going to give when you regain your equilibrium." She pointed to a nearby chair and Jennifer sat. "I'll finish cleaning up and store these away."

"You'd better tell me what's going on."

"I will, but first I'd like to thank you." At Jennifer's blank look she smiled and went on. "At JoBeth's party you politely tried to ignore the fact that Mark is considerably younger than me. I appreciate your thinking that any curiosity on your part would hurt my feelings. I could tell by your actions that the age difference didn't bother you and you like Mark." She began pulling items out of the overstuffed bags. "I don't usually explain my actions to anyone, but as a friend I'd like you to know a few things."

Jennifer nodded, genuinely touched by Cleo's openness and willingness to share part of her personal life.

Cleo caught her tender expression and returned the smile "Now I'm going to shock you. I've been married four times No gasp? Good! I'll go on. My first marriage—I was youn and he was the love of my life. Unfortunately it was not t be and Stan died. I waited a long time to remarry and al three times it was to men my own age. Boring fuddy-duddie who wanted only to be taken care of and stay home after th courtship and wedding."

Her jet-black eyes flashed with anger. "I'm in my..." Sh mumbled her age, then grinned. "Never mind how old I am But I'm not dead by a long shot. Mark is handsome and h makes me laugh. Sometimes he can be a little rough aroun the edges but—" She waved a bunch of fresh broccoli a Jennifer, then opened her arms wide in a gesture of help lessness. "And he's dynamite in bed," she whispere dramatically.

Jennifer threw back her head and laughed. "Oh, Cleo you're one of a kind."

"Of course!"

"But none of this explains what you're doing here with a this food."

"Jennifer, I don't know much about your background only what little you've told me. I want very much to be you friend." She paused, sensing Jennifer's wariness. "Yes dammit, I know you're pregnant! So what." She hurried on "Don't be so rigid in your convictions that you won't allov yourself to bend with your changing emotions. Now that' all the advice I'm going to give and if you need help of an kind, Mark and I will be deeply hurt if you don't come t us."

Reaching across the table, Jennifer squeezed Cleo's hanc "Thanks," she said hoarsely.

"Wait, you might not thank me when you hear what els I've come to tell you." She cleared her throat, suddenl feeling more like a traitor than a friend. "Tomorrow—" Cleo stopped to muster her dwindling courage. "Listen, Jennifer, I've known Lucas and his family for years, and they're wonderful people—warm, loving and always willing to lend a hand to those they care about."

"Out with it," Jennifer growled, suspicious of the pleading tone in Cleo's voice.

"Sometimes they can be a little autocratic, but they mean well."

"Cleo!"

"Lucas has instructed me to inform you that tomorrow he'll pick you up at ten o'clock and the two of you will fly to the Mariposa for the weekend."

"He'll what?"

"Pick you up and fly you to the ranch."

"I heard that. Damn, Cleo. Who does he think he is, anyway?"

"Right now, your boss," Cleo told her grimly, and the words stopped Jennifer's arguments.

"What does that have to do with going away for the weekend?" she fumed. "And why didn't he call me or wait till I came back to work tomorrow morning?"

Cleo shrugged. "All I know is there's been some trouble with security on the new project and he wants you to finish it at the ranch."

Jennifer frowned at the explanation and wondered at her doubts. The feeling persisted that she was being manipulated like a puppet and Lucas was the master puppeteer, pulling the strings, dancing her closer and closer to some goal known only to him.

JENNIFER RUBBED HER DAMP PALMS nervously back and forth over her thighs, wrinkling the already-creased white linen slacks. She kept her eyes straight ahead, refusing to take in the beauty around her, the ribbons of white fluffy clouds moving quickly by her as she skimmed across the azure Texas sky. Beside her Lucas made an abrupt turn and his hand came into her rigid line of vision. She watched, following each precise gesture as his long fingers flipped switches and adjusted a knob. Shutting her eyes tightly, she stifled a low moan.

The compact interior of the twin-engine Cessna was bone chilling. Yet a fine sheen of moisture covered her forehead and her pumpkin-and-white striped linen blouse clung to her wet back as pure fear seeped from every pore. The small aircraft hit another air pocket, sending her stomach to her toes. Her fingers squeezed the nylon harness around her and she swallowed thickly. Was Lucas deliberately trying to antagonize her? Her eyes ached from the glare of the sun and she wanted to rub the pain away, but she was afraid to remove her hold on her lifeline. Instead she gritted her teeth and forced herself to concentrate on other subjects.

She was learning things about herself every moment she was in Lucas's company. Before he'd come into her life, she'd always considered herself a calm, peaceful person. Now she found she became excited just at the prospect of tangling wits with him. So it wasn't without a reckless anticipation that she'd met him at the front door this morning, ready to continue their argument. But Lucas seemed strangely preoccupied—that, or else just stubbornly determined not to argue.

With a great effort she opened her eyes and darted a quick glance at the silent man beside her. He hadn't even mentioned her pregnancy, not even after her dawn rush to the bathroom to wrestle with her heaving stomach. She was willing to forget the subject also. Yet she was uneasy that Lucas was avoiding it. The man was maddening as hell.

Three days ago her life had been turned upside down and inside out, but she'd survived and remained in control. She gnawed her lower lip. Now she wasn't so sure of her control, not with this quiet act Lucas was giving her. The devious devil was up to something.

The plane bucked and rolled sideways. Jennifer opened her eyes and shot Lucas a killing glance. Charming. He'd been entirely too charming this morning and she was leery of his sudden benevolence. She could have sworn when Lucas and Brandon walked out of her house the other morning that she had held the upper hand in the situation. A mocking laugh broke from her, only to be cut off as the plane dipped, making her clutch her harness for dear life.

She swore vehemently under her breath, petrified to move in the narrow space, afraid she'd bump some important gadget. But oh, how she wanted to reach out and hit him. Darting another hurried glance out the window, she groaned. Surely those tiny wings were too small to carry such engines? Propellers twirled frantically, sucking the wind through their blades in a herculean effort to keep the plane airborne. Suddenly it seemed to her sensitive ears that the whole cabin squeaked and rattled as eerie, garbled voices crackled over the radio, only adding to her sense of doom. This wasn't flying—at least nothing she'd ever experienced before.

Lucas leaned sideways and touched Jennifer's arm, causing her to jump and clamp a hand on his leg. She looked at him and he smiled, pointing to the earphones and mouthpiece attached to his head. She frowned and he motioned for her to adjust her headset over her ears. Amusement crinkled the corners of his eyes as he watched her one-handed attempt to do as instructed. "Can you hear me?"

Jennifer gave a curt nod.

"Good. It's not as bad as it sounds." He caressed the oddly shaped wheel. "We've hit some air turbulence. This baby might be light and get thrown around, but she's sound." He reached down and began to pry her fingers from his kneecap. "Relax, we'll be in calm air in a minute."

She released her grip on the harness, slapped his hand away and yelled into the tiny microphone near her mouth. "Put your hands back on the wheel—now!"

He winced as her voice blared in his ear and she smiled grimly. She hated him! There were no other words to describe her feelings at this moment, and he'd pay...oh, he'd pay dearly.

Lucas looked at her as if she'd suddenly sprouted horns. He realized now that flying the small plane wasn't as good an idea as he'd thought. But he'd wanted her to get a picture of the size and beauty of his ranch from the air. He sighed. He could have driven, but he hated the thought of being confined in a car for three or more hours. "You don't like to fly?"

Despite her fears, she managed to shoot him a haughty look. "Of course I do. But I like to fly in something a little bigger—say the size of a football field. This thing feels like something the Wright brothers built."

Lucas laughed scornfully. "This is really flying, lady—by the seat of your pants."

"Just you make sure you keep those pants on. I'm too young to die."

He gave her a scorching look, then smiled as the plane settled down and stopped bucking around. "Ah, we've hit the calm air currents. I'll take you down. There's something I want to show you."

Jennifer breathed a heavy sigh of relief as her body ceased to vibrate. She made a determined effort to straighten her rumpled clothes and grumbled softly, forgetting the microphone, "Don't ever ask me to fly in this do-it-yourself kit again."

"I'm crushed. I could have brought the Lear jet but I thought you'd enjoy this."

"Hah! That, Mr. DeSalva, is the biggest lie you've ever told. You wanted to fly this crate. And that remark just goes to show how much you don't know about me."

He regarded her finicky attempts to crease her linen slacks with a twinkle in his eyes. "Look over there."

She followed the direction of his finger and her eyes widened in awe at the panorama below.

"We're almost there." He tilted the small aircraft on its side so she could get a better view. "Have you ever been in the Hill Country?" She shook her head, and he watched her shoulder-length hair swing and bounce with a moment of regret. "It's the most beautiful land in Texas—rolling hills, rivers and streams as clear and brilliant as colored glass. Look, Jenny—" He pointed in a new direction. "No, no, honey, to your right. See that river snaking its way through those trees? That's the Pedernales. Over to your left is the Blanco River. They meet and mingle and branch out all over the Hill Country. Over a hundred years ago ranchers would gather up longhorn cattle from the open range and drive them up the Chisholm Trail to market."

He leveled the plane and Jennifer let out her breath. She didn't particularly enjoy viewing the world with her body scrunched against the side of an airplane and her nose pressed flat to the window. Once more she tried to adjust her clothes but the plane dipped precariously, making her grab for her safety straps.

"There it is! Hold on tight, Jenny. I'm going to make a low pass over the house to let them know we're about to land."

Jennifer should have known what was coming by th
wolfish grin he flashed her and the obvious excitemen
shining from his eyes. But she didn't see the pleasure in th
grown man's face turn to the mischief and devilment of
young boy. Suddenly her heart was in her throat, and all sh
could make out before squeezing her eyelids tightly shu
were the fuzzy shades of various colors as the plane plunge
downward. Courageously she opened one eye a fraction o
an inch and watched in fascinated horror as a red-tiled roo
filled her view. Resigned to the inevitable, she becam
strangely calm and waited for the sound of crushing meta
and splintering glass. Instead they seemed to slow, and th
plane jerked and bumped a few times.

"You can open your eyes now. We're down." Lucas un
strapped himself, kicked the door open and jumped to th
ground.

Light-headed, Jennifer looked around. Her vision blurre
and swam, and she quickly blinked away the tears. "Get m
out of here!" she yelled through clenched teeth as she pulle
frantically at the safety harness. "Lucas, I want out—
now!" Her stomach finally settled down and she slowl
sucked in a breath of fresh air. "Of all the crazy, hare
brained things to do. Open the door this moment."

As he realized the outcome of his boyish pranks, Lucas'
grin changed to an expression of self-disgust. He yanke
open Jennifer's door, unbuckled her from the harness
helped her down and gathered her trembling body in hi
warm embrace. "I'm sorry," he mumbled contritely ove
and over again. "I don't normally do things like that. It wa
wild and foolish and just seemed to take hold of me. For
give me for being so inconsiderate." Loosening his grip o
her body, he placed his hands on her shoulders and held he
away from him. "Say something—anything. Are you okay
Is the baby all right?"

"Yes, yes and yes again. I'm fine now that my feet are firmly on the ground."

Lucas pressed his lips to her forehead, scooped Jennifer up into his arms and with long strides ate up the short distance to the station wagon parked alongside the long concrete airstrip.

"I may never speak to you again, and that's a promise you can bank on if you ever put me through anything like that again."

"Yes ma'am," he said meekly and slammed the car door.

Jennifer watched him as he walked around the back of the car and opened the driver's door, slipping in silently. "I'm fine," she sniffed, loathe to forgive him too soon. "No thanks to you."

"Good."

"What?" she demanded, indignant at his lack of sympthy. She sat up from her slouched position. He wasn't listening and hadn't really heard a word she'd said. He had folded his arms over the steering wheel and was staring off into the distance, his hungry gaze devouring the scene before him. It was an expression of a man reunited with a long-lost love, and for a brief second she felt a sharp stab of jealousy. "How could you have stayed at DeSalvas so long when you had all this?"

Lucas shrugged, then turned to look at her. "Because I never had anything to come home to. My father manages the ranch for me and does a good job."

"But…" She stopped, seeing the shutter slip over his face and his stern expression return. Had she truly detected a hint of discontent there? "Why, Lucas?" she asked, guessing at the reason behind that brief glimpse.

It was as if they shared the same thoughts. A little confused, Lucas rubbed his forehead wearily. "He quit, Jenny. After mother and Beth were killed, part of him died and he just gave up. I could never understand why. All our lives he'd drummed into us that a DeSalva never shirks his duty. Yet he did.''

"Did he, Lucas, or did he just exchange one duty for another? Maybe he needed to surround himself with memories?''

"Funny, that's what he said—about surrounding himself with them. But, dammit, Jenny. He's my father. He should have been able to overcome it. Oh, hell! What do I know? I never tried to put myself in his position." He looked at her intently. "Maybe I could now, though.''

Jennifer chose to ignore his cryptic remark and leaned back as he started the engine and pulled out onto a narrow tree-lined gravel road.

"If things had been different, would you really have stayed here and ranched?''

"Yes." Abruptly Lucas stopped the car, swung open the door and slid out, pulling Jennifer with him. Her gasp of astonishment brought a smile to his firmly held mouth. "This is paradise, Jenny, love. A place to live and love and raise children.''

CHAPTER FOURTEEN

JENNIFER STOOD MESMERIZED by the view before her. She leaned back against Lucas's body and soaked in the scene like a blind artist miraculously gifted with sight. Emerald hills rolled across the horizon, spotted with giant trees that spread their leafy shadows in a never-ending web. Sunlight danced through the thick foliage, changing colors and shapes like a ghost skipping across the land with each new gust of the soft breeze. Nature's canvas was ever changing and the only stationary jewel was a fairy-tale hacienda nestled in the center of what looked like a tropical jungle festooned with a rainbow of flowers. White stucco walls rose two stories, framed and surrounded on both levels by ornate black, wrought-iron balconies. The Spanish-tile roof soared high and peaked, the muted rose red a testament to its age.

"You can't see it from here, but the patio is from the house of one of my ancestors' ranchos in Spain. A great-grandfather shipped it over stone by stone, right down to the timbers and foundations." Before he led her back to the car, he drew her attention to a variety of out buildings and several huge barns, all with the same white stucco and red roofs.

"It's beautiful, Lucas," she whispered.

"Yes, and peaceful. Troubles seem small in comparison when you come in contact with nature." He drove down the graveled lane, then turned onto a long brick drive, coming to a halt before the entrance of the house.

Jennifer smiled, an expression of appreciation lighting her face. "Now that has to be another item that your distant grandfather brought over!" She pointed to the imposing double doors, which stood at least ten feet tall, their dark weathered oak studded and banded with massive, ancient ironwork.

"If you look close enough—" He broke off and chuckled. Jennifer was already out of the car and inspecting the doors' surface. "Can you see the indentations made by Indian arrows?" He, too, slid out of the driver's seat and pushed on a section of wood. The door swung open smoothly on well-oiled hinges.

She stepped into a long, shadowed central hall with polished Mexican-tile floors. Squat, glazed pots full of tall greenery lined the cool stone walls. At least six brass carriage lamps hung in a row on the wall, their light throwing a warm, golden glow upon the arched, vaulted brick ceiling.

"Come on, Jenny." He tugged impatiently on her arm, guiding her carefully forward. Her eyes were still glued to the unusual craftsmanship and masonry work above her head. "Jenny, it's just a house—my home, not a museum."

She pulled her arm free of his hold and nervously shook the cuffs of her blouse down. "Lucas..." She hesitated, then mentally shrugged. She had to ask sometime. "Does your father know about me...I mean the baby?"

"I don't know." He studied her anxious expression and suppressed an urge to tease. "I haven't told him, but I intend to." She nodded, and he turned and bellowed for his father.

Instead of the deep tones of a male voice there came the sound of the slap of leather on polished tiles and a melody of soft Spanish. A tiny, robust Mexican woman ran to Lucas with open arms, her black eyes filled with shimmering tears. As Jennifer watched, Lucas grabbed the woman and managed to pick her up and swing her around in his arms. Her childish giggles echoed off the stone walls, only to stop as quickly as they started when she spied Jennifer.

Spanish flowed rapidly between Lucas and the woman and though the dialect was strange to her, Jennifer caught enough to know she was being complimented on her blond hair. Self-consciously she ran her hand over her hair, and the old woman's eyes crinkled with the realization that Jennifer understood.

"Jennifer, I'd like you to meet Pilar, cook *extraordinaire*, mentor, arbitrator, stern taskmaster and wielder of a mean willow switch."

The copper-skinned woman took a swipe at Lucas with her dish towel and laughed. *"Señorita."* She acknowledged Jennifer with a regal nod of her small head, then ruined her queenly posture by giggling again.

Lucas waited patiently, then asked, "Where's Dad?"

"Oh, may the Virgin Mary forgive this old woman's silly prattle." Pilar crossed herself solemnly. "Señor Howard had a stroke and Señor Matt flew out at dawn to San Antonio, but he says he will be back tomorrow." She held the cotton cloth to her mouth, her bright eyes gleaming as she looked from Lucas to Jennifer. "He says he will meet this lady you bring home for the first time if he has to flap his arms and fly himself home." She found the idea immensely funny and began to laugh all over again, her round little body quivering with each gasp of air. With a wave of her hand she left the room as quickly as she'd entered, the leather soles on her sandals flopping rhythmically on the tiled floor.

Lucas watched affectionately as the broad backside jiggled out of sight. ''Come on and I'll show you to your room. You can freshen up and change before I take you on a fast tour of the ranch.''

LUCAS'S IDEA of a quick tour was not hers, Jennifer thought, as she sat exhausted in a tub of hot water. She wiggled her toes and sighed. With a smile she had to admit that it had been worth every little pain just to have been witness to the change in Lucas. She sank deeper into the fragrant water and leaned her head back on the tub's rim as she remembered the day's activities with pleasure.

The very air around them seemed to have worked as a cleansing balm, washing away the lines in Lucas's face. With an easy openness he had smiled and laughed and teased, making her forget her own problems for the day. Jennifer grinned and opened her eyes, only to stare dreamily off into the distance as more of the day replayed through her mind.

He'd led, pulled, tugged and cajoled, showing her around miles of outbuildings and barns. Earthy odors had assaulted her from every direction, and it was strange, but not altogether an unpleasant experience. New sights had delighted her eyes, and she remembered the warm feelings that had run through her veins as he'd proudly told her about his other life as a rancher, a man of the land.

Lucas had showed her his prize horses and waxed lyrical on their winning points and she had petted them dutifully. But she had drawn the line when his newest acquisition had lumbered over for an introduction. A monster bull, its rusty coat gleaming with hours of loving care, had swung its huge head with its sheared horns in her direction and she had backed away.

"Don't be such a baby. Come over here and pet Bluebonnet." Lucas had grinned at her reaction to the bull's name. "He's as harmless as a kitten."

"Then you tell me why he has an inch-thick ring in his nose?"

He'd tried to explain, but she'd repeatedly shaken her head and backed away. His green eyes had almost melted her heart, but when she had turned and found herself staring into round cinnamon eyes, fear raced through her veins.

Slowly she pulled her warm, relaxed body from the tepid water and began to dry off. How naive could one person be about ranch life? She laughed as a particular incident flashed into her mind. In one building she had noticed a long wall with built-in freezers and had questioned Lucas, thinking, like an idiot, that maybe they butchered their own beef. The thin, old man in charge of the maintenance had snorted, cackled and stomped off, leaving her with flaming red cheeks.

Jennifer slipped the peach satin nightgown over her head, then caught her reflection in the mirror. "Well really!" she scoffed at herself. "How was I to know there's a million-dollar business in storing and selling semen for artificial insemination and that the big refrigerated units were to keep the liquid gold frozen?" She grinned. Poor Bluebonnet. No wonder he had a ring in his nose.

She flicked off the bathroom light and quickly slid between cool sheets. Somehow she knew that by being given Beth DeSalva's room she had been accepted as family and not as a mere house guest. She snuggled down, her mind heavy with sleep. There was such a strong sense of togetherness around the ranch and it made her feel as if she were being wrapped in a protective cocoon.

Although her body was tired to the bone, her mind refused to turn off. The sheets suddenly felt too tight around her toes. She kicked and pushed till they loosened, all the while trying to stop her mind from spinning. Too many new impressions in one day. She thumped her pillow in frustration. She needed sleep, but she felt itchy, on edge. Taking several deep breaths, she forced her muscles to go limp. Then she flipped over onto her back and glanced at the bedside clock. Midnight. This was ridiculous! Throwing back the covers, she slipped out of bed, picked up her robe and shrugged into it. Soundlessly she stepped out of her room onto the balcony, smiling at the mingled fragrance of honeysuckle and gardenias. Like a beckoning finger, the clear tinkling sound of running water lured her from below, and she quickly walked across the dimly lit balcony and descended the stone steps to the circular patio. She spied a long stone bench and collapsed onto its cool surface. Maybe the dry night air would calm her jagged nerves. Exhausted she buried her face in her hands and would have cried at the injustice of the mess she found herself in, when a deep voice floated out of the darkness, making her jump.

"I couldn't sleep, either."

She could barely make out Lucas's shadow through the spray of bright emerald water from the fountain. The soft breeze flicked a strand of hair across her eyes and she pushed it back with an impatient gesture.

"Why couldn't you sleep?" When he made no move to join her, Jennifer sighed, feeling strangely relieved.

"I've been sitting here reviewing my life, trying to get my priorities straight. I guess I should have done it years ago, but I had no reason important enough to even consider it."

"Have you worked out any of your problems?" Jennifer questioned softly.

"Some. And you, Jenny? What of the problems preying so heavily on your mind tonight? Why can't you sleep?"

Jennifer gathered the lapels of her robe closer and tucked her bare feet beneath the bench. "This place...there's something special here...unexplainable. It's so peaceful and serene—maybe too serene."

"How so, Jenny?" he asked, feeling a deep excitement growing inside him. His home was founded on love and trust and a sense of family. He knew she saw it everywhere and had been touched by its presence. "Tell me, Jenny. Talk to me."

She was quiet for a long time, wondering why it was so important for her to drag up the past now. Those memories were painful. Yet there was a need to completely unburden herself for the first time. "Did the security report you have tell you about my father?"

"Yes, quite a bit."

She sighed. "I never understood him, never could get close enough even to try. He abused my mother terribly—oh, not physically. He was too career-conscious and ambitious for that. But sometimes I wonder if the physical abuse would have been much worse than the psychological torment he put my mother through. I don't think she ever stopped bleeding emotionally—not even after his death."

"And you, Jenny. Did he ever turn his abuse on you?"

She swallowed and wondered how he would take her answer, then shrugged defeatedly, a tiny movement of one shoulder. "Sometimes I prayed he would." She laughed bitterly. "Isn't that insane? But I don't think he knew I existed most of the time. He was cruel, petty and vicious, but only to my mother. And she slowly wilted under his tyranny. Haunting memories of her father's cold, controlled voice burst in her head and she flinched.

"There had to be accusations. What did he accuse your mother of, Jenny?"

Jennifer frowned. "I don't really know, or can't remember," she said slowly. "He could be so polite, so sarcastic and belittling." Her tone was more puzzled than before as she continued to question herself. "They fought, or rather he would, once they were behind closed doors. I can still hear the hated rumble of his voice." Her head came up and she tried to part the darkness between them. "What if deep down I unknowingly transferred that dislike to men in general?"

"Do you hate me, Jenny?" Lucas's question came out slowly and moved on the night air with an undercurrent of hurt.

"No!" she denied vehemently, then laughed lightly as she realized she'd fallen so easily into his trap. Her next words dropped to a whisper. Yet she knew he heard. "Of course I don't hate you." She stopped, afraid to commit herself.

"Jenny..." Lucas's low voice reached out to her, wanting only to soothe away the pain that remembering must have caused. "The report I had done was extensive. I agree your father was a cruel bastard with problems only a psychiatrist could solve, but honey..." He paused, unsure if he should continue. "Your mother had a lot to answer for, also."

"My mother! What are you talking about?" She knew her heated question lacked the fire of the wronged. Deep down she knew what he was about to say. Yet she'd always been unwilling to voice her doubts, even to herself.

"Always remember there are two sides to every problem. Your mother kept Stuart Steel perpetually in debt. Didn't you ever wonder at the cost of her wardrobe? Designer gowns were outrageously expensive even then. I believe she tried to compensate for her lack of money and circumstances by dressing in the height of fashion and surrounding herself with priceless antiques."

He raked his hand through his hair. "Didn't it ever occur to you to wonder why your family was stationed for no more than a year at each post? Debtors, Jenny. They were constantly at your dad's heels, and he tried to cover his tracks as fast as he could to keep his superiors from discovering his predicament. He was, after all, a diplomat and the businessmen were reluctant to take issue because of his political influence."

Jennifer threw back her head, stared at the bright stars that filled the sky and laughed harshly. "Are you telling me that I've misjudged him all these years?"

"Hell, no! He was a first-class bastard. But don't put your mother up on a pedestal, either. They were both human and both made horrendous mistakes. That was their life, Jenny, not yours."

The silence stretched between them, and only the water splashing against the marble rim of the fountain kept the night from closing in on her. Mutely she reflected on what he'd said, and knew in her heart he was right.

"It's time, Jenny, to put the past to rest and to think of the future."

The breeze picked up and lifted fingers of hair across her eyes. She reached up to brush them away, surprised to find her cheeks wet with tears. It was indeed time to relinquish the past. She buried her face in her hands and a hard sob shook her shoulders. She wept for the lonely, bewildered little girl who'd only wanted so desperately to win her daddy's love. She cried for all the bad dreams and childish wishes that had never come true. Her tears ran hotly down her cheeks for her mother's pain and ignorance. And finally she cried for Stuart Steel, a man, a husband and father, who was crippled by his inability to give or receive love.

Lucas's jaw clamped shut as he listened to her sobbing, knowing that as much as he wanted to comfort her, to take her in his arms and soothe away the pain, he couldn't. Whatever past demons she faced, she must face alone, once and for all. He studied his own bare feet and steeled himself against the pitiful sounds reaching out and tugging at his heart. He'd been concentrating so hard in an effort to ignore her weeping that he hadn't heard her cross over to his side, and he jumped when she touched him.

"May I sit down?" She tried to keep her eyes off his bare chest and the low-slung jeans resting on his slim hips. "What do you want from me, Lucas?"

"You."

"Why?"

"There are hundreds of reasons, but I shouldn't have to tell you, Jenny. You're going to have my child."

Her heart contracted in her chest at his words. "I see. And what if I want to hear all the reasons?"

"You have to earn the right, but one is that I love you." He waited, a strange singing in his ears.

"I'm afraid of your love, scared where it will lead."

"Tell me, Jenny." He reached out an arm to encircle her and bring her close to his side, only to let it drop behind her as he realized how stiff she was. The openness of the conversation was new to her and hard to cope with.

"I'm flawed, Lucas. I don't know if love will endure, and quite frankly the idea of marriage, though it no longer horrifies me, is still a frightening prospect." She clasped her hands together, silently waiting.

"If marriage is distasteful we won't discuss it. Love and needing are another matter. I won't push you into anything you're not ready for, but will you consider my earlier proposal of us living together? I want to be with you, Jenny, to hold you and my baby." He laid his finger across her parted lips to stifle her reply. "No, think about it carefully before you answer."

She shivered, and he wrapped his arm around her, pulling her to his side. After a moment he felt her relax and rest her head on his shoulder. "Everything will work out, Jenny, if you'll just let it happen."

She moved her cheek against the warmth of his skin and murmured, "I wish..." Her voice trailed off and she was as quiet as the night. "I wish we could start all over again, Lucas. Pretend that the first night we met never happened."

Lucas gave her a quick shake. "Don't wish that night away from me, Jenny, or ask me to forget that it ever happened." He kissed the top of her silken head tenderly. "Don't you know the memories, no matter what happens to us, will stay with me for the rest of my life? I'll grant you the way it happened was as unconventional as hell and threw everything out of kilter, but things will work out."

Where was the logical-minded realist she'd known? Here was a man with dreams. She sighed and closed her eyes. Maybe it wasn't such a bad idea, after all. She'd had her own fantasies lately. The breeze picked up, blowing an early-morning dampness across her skin, and she felt the chill.

"You're cold." Lucas climbed to his feet, drawing her up with him. "Come on. I'll walk you back to your room."

They made their way up the stone stairs and round the balcony, each lost in thoughts. As they came to a stop outside Jennifer's open door, she reached up and stroked the side of his face.

"It's taken me a long time to admit what a wonderful man you are." He turned his head and kissed the palm of her hand. She smiled sadly. "All my life I promised myself I'd never make the mistakes my mother did. I'm sorry, Lucas. I've made a mess not only of my life, but yours, as well." She dropped her hand and stepped back through the doorway.

"Jenny, let's straighten this out once and for all so in the future there will never be any misunderstandings between us." He followed her into her room and softly closed the double doors. "There's not a person alive who could make me do something I didn't want to do. You think you seduced me that first night?" He stroked her hair and moved closer. "If I hadn't wanted you, do you actually think I would have gone along with your little game? As for messing up my life—how could you possibly do that when you're the one person I've ever truly wanted?" He smiled at her, his teeth a white flash in the moonlit room. "And how can you say our child is a mistake?"

Jennifer grinned at his teasing tone, watching as he turned around and walked toward the door. He made her feel so good about herself, and she needed him. Her mouth opened, but nothing came out. After years of repressing her feelings, she found it almost painful to reveal herself. "Lucas," she called quickly, and waited till he faced her. "Don't go."

"Why, Jenny?" He remained across the room, his green eyes shining like emeralds in the light from the partly opened door.

Jennifer swallowed thickly, her heart knocking like a heavy fist against her chest. Doubts assailed her and she hesitated, staring at him with pleading eyes. "I want you."

Lucas gave her a wry grin. "You can do better than that, Jenny, love."

She inhaled and squeezed her eyelids closed. "I love you." The words were only halfway out of her mouth before she found herself wrapped in a strong embrace.

He buried his face in her hair and moaned, the sound of a man who has just been handed the world. "Oh, Jenny, be very sure."

"I am Lucas, and I won't lie to you. I'm scared, too. But you're right. I have to give up the past and face the future." She ran her palms up and over the warm golden flesh of his chest, then dropped her arms, quickly untied her robe and let it fall away. Shrugging off the straps of her nightgown, she stepped out of the pool of satin. "I've missed you, Lucas." Her voice dipped low and seductive, bringing his gaze up to meet the hunger in her eyes. "Take me to bed. Make love to me. It's been too long."

His hands trembled with want and love as he reached out and ran his fingers lightly along her breasts to her waist. Tightening his grip, he guided Jennifer backward a couple of steps till they reached the edge of the bed. His mouth covered hers and his arms wound around her as he eased her onto the wide expanse of the bed.

Her fingers buried themselves into his thick hair, urging his mouth closer and his tongue deeper. She moaned at the feel of his hands on her, touching, seeking. Then she broke away. "I...I..."

He kissed her quick and hard as he hovered above her. "It's difficult to say sometimes, but it will get easier."

"I do love you."

"See."

He smiled, a tender smile that made her catch her breath. What had she done to deserve so much? There was a sudden stinging behind her eyelids and she squeezed them shut, savoring the feel of his hands on her body.

They needed no preliminaries. She opened herself to him, sighing as he entered her. She arched beneath him, welcoming him deeper as her legs wrapped around his hips, her arms clinging to his broad back. She loved him, and the fact that he returned the feeling held its own special contentment.

Please, she prayed, *don't let this be a dream. Don't let him ever change or leave me.* Before he could set the pace of their lovemaking, she felt a lifetime of hurts wash away. She wept, her tears sliding wet and hot down her flushed cheeks.

"Jenny! Sweet Jenny. There's nothing to cry about." Lucas brushed the damp tentacles of hair from her face.

Jennifer swallowed, trying to put into words what was happening to her, but when nothing came from her parched throat she could only smile in wonder. The smooth muscles under her fingers bunched, and she let her hands slip down his back, loving the hard curves of his buttocks. She gazed into his glittering eyes and pulled him deeper inside her. "You make me feel so alive. I think I'm scared that it won't last."

Lucas groaned as she moved, her words barely registering in his dazed mind. He shook his head sharply. "Oh, it will last. I promise." His voice was a ragged whisper as he rocked against her, his hands gripping her hips, holding her tightly to him.

The trembling began again, but this time it was different, a greater force building, arching for release. Her eyelids fluttered shut, and in her mind she could hear a million wings of eagles soaring for the sun.

Hours later, bright slats of sunlight knifed across her closed eyes with a persistent intrusion that made her groan. Turning over, she also fought to ignore the grumbling of her stomach. A smile curved the corners of her mouth at the slight tenderness between her thighs. They had made love till the first signs of dawn streaked the morning sky from black to purple. Her stomach made an all-too-familiar flip-flop, and she tried to will the sickness away. She opened her eyes to get her bearings in case she had to make a dash for the bathroom. Then she noticed a small saucer on which were stacked a dozen soda crackers. She snatched a couple and began to munch away, eyeing the glass filled with chipped ice and a dark brown liquid that was also on the bedside table. But it was the folded sheet of paper she reached for, and she smiled with pleasure as she read:

Good morning, Jenny. The day calls, so hurry up and pull yourself together. We're going on a picnic. Thought the cold Coke would help. It seems to work for me.

Love, Lucas

Jennifer picked up the glass and sipped slowly, then more rapidly as the nausea subsided. Picnic, indeed! She wondered when he planned to finish the project. It was time she had a long conversation with one Lucas M. DeSalva about coercion and lies. A little voice told her she was being manipulated by an expert. Falling in love and admitting it was one thing, but she'd be damned if she was going to start obeying his every command.

"ARE YOU GOING TO bait that hook or sit looking at it all afternoon?

Jennifer felt Lucas's amused gaze on her every move.

"Fish don't crawl up on the bank to take a bite of that worm, you know."

"I know that!" she grumbled, then bit her lip as she looked down at the fat worm squirming on the lid of an old coffee can. She didn't like the idea of threading the poor creature on the sharp hook, but she wasn't going to be cowardly, either.

"Why not admit you can't do it?"

The laughter in his voice made her swing her head around and shoot him a dirty look. "Can, too." She gritted her teeth as she fastened the worm on the hook. "See." She swung the line out, and it almost touched Lucas's nose.

He chuckled and grabbed the rod from her hands. "You're dangerous, lady. I think I'll cast for you." With an expert flick of his wrist he sent the hook flying to the center of the river.

Carefully Jennifer cleaned her hands on a damp towel. She watched his movement, enjoying the easy flow of muscles under the white cotton Western shirt and the skintight jeans he wore. "When are we going to start working on the papers you brought?"

"What papers?" he asked absently, caught his mistake and laughed. "Think you're pretty smart, don't you? Okay, I lied. Forgive me?" He turned his head, his eyes shining with pleasure.

"Absolutely not. Lucas, you can't run my life like this."

"Whoa there. I wasn't interfering, just trying to tilt the odds in my favor a little. You can't condemn a man for that?" He put the rods on the grassy slope and walked back. Hunkering down in front of her, he took her hands in his. "Don't pout. It isn't like you. I did it for both of us. If I hadn't, there's no telling how long your stubbornness would have dragged on.

Jennifer pulled her hands free, flopped back on the blanket and gazed up through the overhanging branches of the tree they had chosen to picnic beneath. She snatched up a half-eaten chicken leg and began to munch. "I guess I'll forgive you...this time."

"Magnanimous of you," he said sleepily.

She held the bone away for inspection and frowned. "Do you know that's the fifth piece of chicken I've eaten?" She rolled over onto her side to face Lucas. "If I had to eat Pilar's cooking all the time I'd get fat."

"You'll get that way in a few months, anyway, so a few extra pieces of chicken won't hurt." He reached over and patted her stomach, then felt her go stiff at his words. "I know I promised not to pressure you into a decision, Jenny, but that doesn't mean I can't talk about the baby. I won't tip-toe around the subject just because you're still unsure. By the way, have you reached a decision yet?"

Jennifer laughed and sat up. She pulled her legs to her chest and rested her chin on her knees. Her gaze followed the gentle grassy slope down to the clear stream, which made its way lazily over rocks and huge protruding roots of an ancient cypress tree. The land was so beautiful it actually hurt her eyes to look around. A bee buzzed past her face on its way to a field of colorful wildflowers across the water. She batted at the light brush of wings against her cheek and turned back to Lucas. A warm smile touched her lips as she noticed his closed eyes and the shallow, even rise and fall of his chest. She gave him a hard poke in the side to test the depth of his slumber.

Lucas groaned in protest and flicked her hand away. "I believe you're a sadist. You wore me out last night, and now that I want to take a nap you decide to talk."

She ran her fingers over his ribs and grinned at the deep rumble of laughter.

Lucas grabbed her arms and pulled her over onto his chest. Without a pause, he flipped her over and rested his body along hers to hold her secure. "Temptress. You're very brave this afternoon. Take a deep breath, Jenny, and tell me what comes to mind." He grinned at her puzzled expression and urged, "Go on. Close your eyes and sniff."

"Christmas," she said. "Cedar and pine...and stories by a big roaring fire."

"It's that way all year round. Can you deny our child the right to develop and grow in an atmosphere such as this?"

"Lucas."

His thumbs made small circles on her neck. "Okay, okay. I'll stop the hard sell—for now." He breathed warmly in her ear and she shivered. "Think about it, though." The tip of his tongue trailed a path from her neck to the swell of her breast, his breath teasing her nipple erect through her blouse, and she moaned deep in her throat.

Strong hands caressed her rounded derriere, pulling her closer to the hard ridge of his arousal. Every inch of her flesh felt alive. His hand slipped between her thighs and she gasped. It seemed brazenly wanton to make love in the daylight, but she would deny Lucas nothing. "Lucas, no one will see us, will they?"

"This is my private retreat and everyone on the ranch knows better than to come here unless it's a dire emergency. Now what do you find so amusing?" he whispered close to her ear. Suddenly his entire body stiffened, and he

cursed as the pounding on the ground matched the thudding of his heart. "Hell and damnation!" He quickly
moved away from Jennifer's side. "Button your blouse.
Someone's coming."

"Hello, you two!" Brandon yelled as the big chestnut
horse he was riding broke from a stand of tall pecan trees
and slowed to a prancing walk. A wicked smile touched his
generous mouth as he took in the scene before him. "Did
I interrupt something?"

"You better have a damn good excuse," Lucas snarled.

"I need to talk to you for a second, Lucas. Alone. Hi
Jennifer, you're looking wonderful. The Hill Country air
must agree with you."

Jennifer sat with her knees pulled to her chest, her violet eyes mere slits. Refusing to answer, she tried to calm
her shaking insides, but she felt cheated and glared at the
culprit she held responsible.

Lucas shifted his weight, his leg propped high to hide his
aroused state. "Couldn't you have waited till we returned
home?"

"No, it's important, or I wouldn't have ridden all this
way."

Lucas sighed, slowly stood and ambled over to the side
of the horse. He took hold of the leather bridle and listened as Brandon began to whisper. "What!"

Jennifer jumped at Lucas's roar. His face as dark as a
cloud, he stomped back to her, yanked up the picnic bas-
ket and threw it into the back of the Jeep. "Come on,
Jenny. We have to get back."

"What's happened?"

"Just get the blanket and get in—please."

She settled herself in the bucket seat, flinching at the
grinding gears and clutching the dashboard as the Jeep

shot forward. "Lucas, what's wrong? Has something happened to your father?"

"No." He slowed down, then pulled to a stop beneath the hanging limbs of a weeping willow. "Jennifer, not only has Brandon decided to visit the ranch, he tells me that JoBeth isn't far behind him. I'm sorry. I wanted this time for ourselves. Now it's ruined."

"It's all right, Lucas," she lied. But it wasn't, and her voice must have revealed her feelings, because Lucas banged an angry fist on the steering wheel. Jennifer was still unsure of the depth of Lucas's involvement with JoBeth. Staring off into the wild tangle of vegetation, she remained quiet as Lucas drove back onto the dirt road. There was a large lump in her throat from jealousy and fear. JoBeth Huntley was a force to be reckoned with. She had everything, and Jennifer was scared of the hold she might have on Lucas, no matter how he denied it.

"Lucas?" But she never finished her question as the Jeep ground to a gravel-spraying stop at the back of the hacienda. JoBeth Huntley walked toward them on the arm of a tall, dignified gentleman who was a much older version of Lucas. Matthew DeSalva leaned heavily on his cane. His green eyes, identical to Lucas's, stared at Jennifer with a bright twinkle that brought a wide answering grin to her lips. Lucas's father knew everything, and judging by his open smile, he heartily approved.

Jennifer only had time enough to stab Brandon with a dagger glance before her attention turned to JoBeth. Her jaw clenched and she managed to keep a smile plastered on her face as JoBeth greeted Lucas like a long-lost lover. And maybe he was, she thought.

Lucas pried himself from JoBeth's clinging embrace, shot Brandon a bewildered glance that said, "What's gotten into her?" He caught Jennifer's blank expression and gently pushed JoBeth aside, wanting only to explain and wipe away the hurt he saw in her eyes. But his chances were foiled as his father, judging the situation correctly, hurriedly introduced himself and led Jennifer away with a promise to show her the loft.

Lucas watched them disappear, then stared at JoBeth with hard angry eyes. Once again he was denied the chance to vent his ire as JoBeth, realizing the depth of his anger, spun around and sprinted after his father. "Don't make a move, Brandon," Lucas warned. "You'd damn well better explain what the hell is going on."

Brandon shrugged and handed the horse reins to the waiting Mexican boy. "I couldn't help her following me, Lucas, not once she found out where you were." He ran a hand impatiently through his hair. "But I'll tell you this. Something's wrong with that woman. She's been acting strange for the past two days—bitchy—edgy." He laughed, a sound that contained little humor. "I think she's crazy, more so than before." He walked over to Lucas and threw his arm around his shoulder. "Come on. I need a good stiff drink."

They entered the library through the open patio door. Lucas waited till Brandon had fixed them each a drink and returned to sit across from him.

"How's the campaign to win the fair lady going?"

"None of your damn business," Lucas answered gruffly, but he couldn't restrain the smile that twitched his lips. "I guess by that overjoyed look on your face that you spilled the beans and Dad knows it all?"

Brandon raised his glass and toasted his own genius. "He knows only the important parts, though."

"You've got a damn big mouth, brother."

"All the better to serve you with, *brother*."

Lucas sipped his drink, eyeing Brandon warily over the rim. "Okay, out with it. What did you mean riding up and dropping the bomb that Susan's gone. Gone where?"

"That's just it. We don't know. Kane called to tell us she slipped his tail and disappeared. He picked up her trail later on an airline heading for London. That was twenty-four hours ago and as far as he's been able to track her. After that, nothing." Brandon grimaced as Lucas threw his drink out the patio doors. "Temper, temper."

"Where the hell is she?"

"That's the odd part. Susan McCord just suddenly vanished. She never checked into a hotel, never made a reservation on another airline. It's as if she'd dropped off the edge of the world."

"Bull!" Lucas retorted.

"Kane said the same. He also said for someone to disappear so totally without leaving a paper trail of checks and credit cards is a professional setup. In other words, Susan or her contact acquired a false passport. Kane was willing to bet one of his Samantha Grey paintings that she's taken on a new identity."

Lucas cursed long and low. "Yes, and by God there's no telling how much of my money she's got socked away in a Swiss bank account."

"Our money," Brandon reminded him. "Anyway, we're out of the woods now. I told Kane not to proceed with setting up the surveillance equipment in Jennifer's office. He argued that he didn't think our troubles were over yet." Brandon set down his glass, stood up and stretched like a pleased tomcat. "He's wrong, though, isn't he?"

"No." An icy hand clutched Lucas's insides, and he gulped down his drink. "I think we're in something far worse than the stealing that's been going on. Whoever is behind this is ready to initiate the final move. I feel it here.'' He tapped his heart.

''Surely you don't think Jennifer is still in any danger, do you?''

''Yes, but not here at the ranch. Our lunatic's plans are centered in Houston. How am I going to keep Jenny here till we find who's trying to destroy us? I've said all along that whoever was after us wanted more than to steal our secrets. He wants to take what I hold most dear, and I'll be damned if he's going to hurt Jennifer.''

''Don't you think it's time to tell her what's been going on?''

''Hell, no! How am I going to convince her that everyone wasn't conspiring against her? No, no. After we catch this madman, then maybe I'll tell her.''

''And what if she finds out?''

''She won't.'' He prayed silently that he could keep it from her until he had time to complete the story and make sure she would understand that he had never suspected her.

CHAPTER FIFTEEN

IT TOOK JENNIFER only five steps away from Lucas to know for certain she'd reached a decision. With the first step she saw again the look in his eyes when she'd finally confessed that she loved him. The second step brought a barrage of memories of how tender and understanding he'd always been. On the third step she thought of his smile when it was boyish and loving, and she knew she'd never want to do anything to change it. The fourth step filled her with a strange power, knowing that JoBeth might have everything but she wasn't going to have Lucas. With the fifth and final step, jealousy bit deeply, and she realized that her love for Lucas was all that really mattered to her. Now all she had to do was tell him.

"Come along, Jennifer. I know my son has neglected to show you my special room." Matthew tightened his grip on her arm and led her through the center of the house to the living room. "We can talk better in here." He stopped and glanced over his shoulder as JoBeth followed closely. "This is old hat to you, honey. Why don't you go say hello to Pilar before she has her feelings hurt and gets her nose bent out of shape at the insult?"

Jennifer watched mutely as JoBeth's eyes moved from her to Matthew then back again. It couldn't have been more obvious that the DeSalvas's longtime friend resented Matthew's obvious acceptance of Jennifer.

"I don't think she likes the idea of sharing Lucas's attention or, for that matter, anyone else's in this family. So go easy on her for a while. JoBeth's a sweet girl and worth having as a friend." Matthew watched the retreating woman with understanding in his eyes, noting the straight angry back and the lack of swing in her walk. "Though I bet she'd make a formidable enemy. But enough of this."

He turned slowly around and with the repetitive three-legged tap of man and cane he crossed the tile hall, only to stop when he came to the entrance of the living room. "Brandon told me you were going to do your dissertation on the Spanish crown's influence on modern-day Texas land titles. I think I have something here that will interest you."

The first thing Jennifer noticed was the spaciousness of the room and how oddly it was divided. In one half was beautiful parquet floor, decorated with couches and over-stuffed chairs in soft, serene shades of peach and buff, artfully arranged around an intricately carved stone fireplace.

Massive oak beams crisscrossed the ceiling, and above the mantle hung tin and wood *retablos*. It didn't surprise her when Matthew said the altar pieces dated as far back as the seventeenth century. But it was the other half of the room that drew her attention, with the soft butter-colored stone floor and walls and the high reading loft with shelves of books bound in rich leathers.

"The back portion of this room, the stone walls, floor and loft, are the original part of the house built a year to the day the Alamo fell to Santa Anna's army. There's a cornerstone with the initials of the *maestro albañil* and the date carved in it." He guided Jennifer up the worn stone steps and hurried over to an old armoire. "Sit down while I find what I'm looking for."

Jennifer sank into the deep folds of a much-used leather chair and waited impatiently as Matthew continued his search.

"Ah. I think these will interest you and may be helpful in your research on the remaining original Spanish land-owners in Texas." Eagerly he handed her sheets of documents encased in plastic. "After I had these carbon dated and authenticated I had them sealed to protect them from further deterioration."

Picking up one of the stiff sheets, Jennifer almost gasped aloud as her eyes scanned the bottom of the page and noted with awe the wax seal and official ribbons.

"Yes, the 1744 Spanish crown's land grant to the De-Salvas." Matthew smiled warmly. "The original grant deeded us this land, showing boundaries that ran all the way to the Gulf of Mexico. Larger, I might add, than the King Ranch. But because of our nationality we weren't able to hold on to the biggest portions. My ancestors believed that next to family, only the land was worth dying for. They were wise enough to change alliances with the ever-changing owners of Texas. And though forced to relinquish some of their land to appease the current government in power, they gave up only what they considered less profitable land and held on to the choicest acreage." The laughter lines in his face deepened as he recalled the cunningness of his family.

Jennifer laid the document reverently on the round oak table and watched him laugh. It was as if she were being given a glimpse of Lucas thirty years down the road, and what she saw warmed her heart.

Matthew reached over and patted her hand. "There are hundreds of documents, letters from family and friends living at court. Even a set of diaries by some great, great spinster aunt who escaped the tyranny of a Spanish queen.

We've never had them translated because of the difficulty with proper Castilian court Spanish and also because my wife was reluctant for them to leave our possession. But you now—that's different. Brandon tells me you're very talented in this field. Maybe after you and Lucas decide what you're going to do you'll think about it as a job."

"Mr. DeSalva—"

"Matt, please, Jennifer. Don't worry." He rose slowly to his feet with the aid of the thick cane. "I won't ask you questions, but I want you to know that it's been a long time—too long, actually—since I've seen my son so relaxed and happy. We DeSalvas love passionately, Jennifer and only once." He smiled sadly, a dullness dimming the bright green of his eyes, and pointed to the armoire. "That's a fact of history you'll quickly come across when you see the family tree."

The pain left his face and his eyes twinkled.

"It's fortunate we've all produced large families. Now I'm going to leave you to pore over these to your heart's content. No, don't get up. These old bones need some rest." Carefully he maneuvered himself down the narrow worn steps. At the bottom landing he stopped and looked up. "I'll see you in the library for an aperitif before dinner. Be early, and maybe we'll have time to talk before my son claims you."

We DeSalvas love passionately and only once. Jennifer felt sad that he'd never found another to share his life. Yet there was excitement in the beat of her own heart at the idea of being loved with such passion. Was it possible for a woman who never really knew what love was to be lucky enough to find it? She prayed silently that her hopes weren't pipe dreams.

The afternoon sun beat hotly through the loft's round window, warming her thoughts. She yawned, thinking that maybe Matthew had the right idea. A nap was an inviting proposition. She replaced the documents, promising herself she'd return before dinner and have another look.

The big bed and the coolness of her room were an irresistible invitation. She quickly bathed, slipped on her robe and was about to crawl between the beckoning sheets, when the bedroom door opened and JoBeth walked in.

"Resting this time of day? Doesn't ranch life agree with you? Or are you sick?"

"Just tired." She watched as JoBeth prowled the four corners of the room, as if she were checking to see if Jennifer had moved anything.

"This is usually my room when I'm here."

A small frown creased Jennifer's brow. "I'm sure Lucas would have given me another had he known you would be here." She was puzzled by the challenge in JoBeth's voice. Then she remembered how close JoBeth was to the DeSalvas and conceded that she must be feeling usurped. But there was something else in her manner that gave Jennifer pause for thought.

"I see you've decided which man you're going to trap. Was the choice difficult? I mean, Jean-Paul and Brandon are equally as appealing as Lucas. Of course, Lucas—"

"JoBeth!"

"—Lucas has more money."

Jennifer sat down heavily on the side of the bed and stared silently at the woman across from her for a long second. "I know how you feel about Lucas."

"Do you?" JoBeth retorted dangerously, her eyes snapping with fire.

"I'd hoped we were going to try to be, if not friends, at least civil to each other for Lucas's and Brandon's sake."

"Boy! You've got some nerve." JoBeth's voice was like a low growl. "After what you've done! Let me tell you something." She twisted around and stared into the vanity mirror, smoothing her hair, yet keeping her gaze steadily on Jennifer. "Lucas is mine. He belonged to me before you came along and he'll—"

"Don't say it, JoBeth!" Jennifer surged to her feet. She didn't know if she was stopping a pack of lies. All she knew was that she didn't want to listen.

"Don't say what?"

Both women jumped and spun around to face Brandon, both as tightly strung as a pair of she-cats ready to fight.

"Don't say what, Jo?" he demanded harshly. "What was she about to tell you, Jennifer?"

But before Jennifer could open her mouth, JoBeth butted in. "I was about to tell her about Lucas and me."

"Well, that's okay, isn't it? Because there's nothing to tell." His eyes narrowed on JoBeth's stubborn, angry face.

"Do you know what she's done?"

"Shut up, JoBeth. As usual, you don't know what you're talking about. So just shut your malicious little mouth."

Jennifer looked back and forth between the two of them as they stood facing each other. She knew now why JoBeth was so upset. She'd found out about her pregnancy and thought Lucas was being trapped. "JoBeth, listen to me," she pleaded gently, knowing the pain the woman must be going through.

"No, Jennifer." Brandon sliced the air with an angry gesture of his hand. "She's wrong and you don't owe her an explanation. Simply put, it's none of her damn business. Come on, Bets, lets leave Jennifer so she can rest." He glared at JoBeth daring her to defy him. "Now, *Bets*," he commanded, and the hated nickname worked like magic, sending JoBeth through the doorway and stomping down the hall. "Don't worry, Jennifer, I'll take care of this." He started to close the door, then paused. "Whatever she said before I interrupted—well, just disregard it."

Flopping backward, Jennifer stared up at the ceiling. She tried to put herself in JoBeth's place and knew she would probably have acted the same way. Yet surely if JoBeth knew of Jennifer's pregnancy, she also knew that, baby or not, she didn't have the power to force Lucas into anything. One thing Jennifer was sure of, she was going to settle this misunderstanding as soon as possible. Her relationship with Susan still haunted her, and though JoBeth wasn't actually family, the woman loved the DeSalvas and was close to all of them. Jennifer didn't want the responsibility of having caused a rift in their relationship.

Her eyelids grew heavy and she rolled over, pulling the covers with her as she snuggled down. A smile of mischief curled her lips, and her last thought before she drifted off to sleep was that she was going to have to tell Lucas of her decision and put him out of his misery.

HER DREAMY PROMISE was easier said than done, Jennifer thought, as she frowned irritably across the living room at the subject of her thoughts. Lucas stood by the fireplace dressed casually in chocolate-colored slacks and open-collared, beige-and-brown, pin-striped silk shirt. It wasn't his clothes that drew her attention, but the fact that an overdressed JoBeth hung, glittering in a sequined gown, on his arm. Jennifer looked down at her own dress with regret. The cornflower-blue silk with tiny white dots, blouson top, dolman sleeves and dropped shirred waist couldn't begin to compete with JoBeth's dress and she was loath to get anywhere near the woman.

"Don't frown, and don't drink your wine so fast," Brandon admonished. "Lucas said that was all you get tonight. Come on, smile. Forget JoBeth and whatever game she's playing tonight.'' Brandon grinned, his eyes bright with humor.

"I take it from her accusations that she knows about the baby?''

Brandon mulled over her question for a second. "She must, but not from me! I swear, Jennifer. I have a big mouth only when I think it will help. I've never discussed you and Lucas with her, and I know Cleo wouldn't either. Funny, though, I wonder just who did tell her?''

JoBeth's continual interference every time Jennifer tried to get close to Lucas took its toll. She tilted her wineglass, found it empty and grimaced. Her eyes narrowed on Lucas and he looked up, meeting her heated gaze. He immediately slipped from JoBeth's grasp and rudely walked away. Jennifer watched him approach her with that peculiar catlike walk of his, and her breath quickened.

"From that look I'd say JoBeth had better back off.'' He smiled, thoroughly enjoying her open show of jealousy.

"You could say that. I suddenly find I can be as possessive as you.''

"Good.'' Lucas plucked the empty glass from her hand before the lovely old crystal went sailing across the room toward JoBeth's head. "I worry about her, though, Jenny. There's something wrong, but I can't get her to tell me. All she'll say is that she's willing to help me anyway she can. Damned if I know what she's talking about. Maybe Dad can get it out of her. One thing—she wanted to know entirely too much about us.''

"What did you tell her?''

"The truth. That I'm in love. Have you decided?''

She smiled. "I—'' She didn't finish, but snapped her mouth shut as JoBeth slipped between them.

"Has Lucas showed you the portrait of his mother and sister, Jennifer? No? Then maybe Brandon will be a good sport and show you now."

"I've never been 'good' in my life, *old sport*," Brandon remarked as he and Matthew joined them.

JoBeth immediately bristled with hostility. "True, but at least you admit your faults, and a liar you're not. There seems to be an overabundance of them lately. Cheats, thieves, liars—people who would stoop to anything to achieve their purpose."

"Why, thank you, Bets, somewhere in that jumble of words I think I detect a compliment."

"Don't hold your breath—and stop calling me 'Bets.'" She glared at Brandon. "Why haven't you given Jennifer one of your famous nicknames? I bet I could come up with a stack of names that would fit to a tee." An awkward silence fell and before she could say anything more, Matthew took hold of her arm and led her away.

"You see?" Brandon looked accusingly at Lucas. "I've never known her to be so cunningly spiteful. She doesn't accuse anyone openly, but the implications are there all the same." He took a hearty gulp of his drink. "I'd like to turn her over my knee. Damn spoiled brat."

Lucas chuckled and Jennifer was forced to smile. "You try it, brother, and she'll probably scratch your eyes out. One of these days you're going to really see JoBeth as she is."

"I know what she is."

"Do you? Come on, Jenny. Let my thickheaded brother brood over his blindness for a while." He touched her arm lightly and steered her out onto the patio.

The scent of jasmine and roses filled the night air, and Jennifer inhaled deeply, the enticing fragrance calming her nerves.

"Okay, lady, ever since you walked into the living room you've had a smug look on your face. What are you up to?" He slipped his arm around her waist and held her close as he led her to a nearby stone bench.

The warmth of his body was as comforting as the night, and she leaned into his embrace. "I did a lot of thinking this afternoon."

"There you two are. Pilar said dinner is about ready." JoBeth joined them, sitting down beside Lucas as easily as if she'd been invited.

Enough was enough, Jennifer thought. "JoBeth I don't know who's put your tail in a vise, but I would prefer to be friends." She eased out of Lucas's hold and stood.

JoBeth rose, too, facing her.

"However, if you don't leave us alone, I'm going to throw you in that damn fountain, headfirst." She took a threatening step forward.

"You wouldn't dare! Lucas wouldn't let you!"

"Yes, I would."

Jennifer took another step closer and JoBeth backed away, then spun around and marched through the patio doorway.

"I'd have given a million dollars to have had a camera." Lucas buried his face in his hands and his shoulders shook with laughter. When he was finally able to raise his eyes they glittered with love. "You've changed just in the hours we've been here. Brandon was right. Ranch life and Hill Country are good for you."

"I have changed, haven't I?" she said, a little surprised and thrilled that the changes had come so naturally.

Lucas reached out and grabbed hold of her wrist, pulling her down into his lap. "Now out with it. You've teased me enough. You've decided to live with me, haven't you?"

She leaned back in his arms and laughed up at the stars. "Yes, I—" She got no further. Lucas's warm mouth covered hers in a long deep kiss that said all that was necessary. At the sound of bells ringing, Jennifer began to giggle. "I'm hearing bells. I don't believe it."

"Damn right, but it's the dinner bell." He hugged her tightly as if suddenly afraid to let her go. "This is a hell of a time to tell me. If we don't go in they'll come out here to see what's wrong. Listen, Jenny, I don't want to tell Dad tonight, not with JoBeth making a pest of herself. And there are some things I need to clear up with Brandon after dinner. So later, when everyone's gone to bed, I'll come to your room and we'll talk it all out."

He scooped Jennifer into his arms and stood, carrying her till she laughingly demanded to be put down. Slowly he let her body slide down his, making her feel the heat of his desire. "Hell of a way to go to dinner," he grumbled, and hugged her close once more. "You'll never regret this decision, Jenny. Now you can start thinking about marriage, because that's what I want more than ever. No." He covered her mouth with his hand. "Don't answer yet. Just promise me you'll think about it?"

She nodded.

"You'll wait for me?" She moved her head again, smiling this time and he replaced his fingers with his mouth.

FOR THE THIRD TIME THAT DAY, Jennifer found herself back in the big canopy bed. Yet this time she was not the least bit tired, as she impatiently waited for Lucas.

The bedside clock read eleven and she sighed, picked up the book from her lap and began to stare at the printed pages once more. A noise from Lucas's room brought her head up. She held her breath and listened, straining to hear any little sound that would alert her that he was on his way, but nothing else happened and she looked at the book again.

Earlier she'd accused Lucas of being a devious devil. Now she was more certain of it. He'd known all along he was going to try to coerce her into marriage. She grinned slightly, a little surprised that the idea wasn't totally repugnant to her. She had changed!

The muffled crash of something hitting a hardwood floor broke the silence, and Jennifer glanced over at the wall that divided her room from Lucas's. Suddenly she couldn't remember if she was supposed to wait for him here or in his room. Either way she intended to see Lucas this night. Throwing the covers back, she slid out of the bed, retrieved her robe and headed for the door.

Once in the darkened hall, she stopped and looked both ways, feeling like a thief tiptoeing through the house. What if Matthew happened to come from his room and came upon her nightly stroll? The thought made her clamp her hand over her mouth to keep from giggling out loud. He'd more than likely laugh at her embarrassment rather than ask questions.

She hesitated outside Lucas's door, her hand clutching the cold brass doorknob, her heart pounding in her ears as an odd premonition seemed to stop her from entering. It was only a second before she pinpointed her reluctance. An airy thread of a familiar fragrance seeped through the half-opened doorway, making her stomach muscles tighten. She felt as if the scent were suddenly choking the very breath from her body and blurring her vision.

Surely her distorted sight was deceiving her and she wasn't seeing Lucas's clothes strewn on the floor with various articles of female clothing. She looked from one item to the next. A pair of panty hose snuggled up to Lucas's socks. A floor-length, half slip rested beside a striped silk shirt. A pair of bikini panties nestled next to a pair of jockey shorts. Her gaze trailed after the line of discarded clothing. With each item her head pounded harder, till the pain behind her eyes became unbearable. She swallowed and kept her eyes glued to the foot of the wide poster bed, knowing that she didn't want to see what lay beyond.

A swath of moonlight spilled into the room, highlighting everything with an unnatural brightness. Her vision swam with tears. She blinked them away and slowly raised her eyes till they rested on the mounds of covered flesh. The scene struck her with a force that almost doubled her over, and she grabbed the dresser edge for support.

Lucas and JoBeth lay curved together under the thin sheet as naturally as if they had been made for each other. The pounding in her temples sounded like a huge brass drum and the high-pitched scream that never left her mouth vibrated around in her head, making her vision whirl in crazy colors. Her stomach gave a sickening lurch and she blinked hard to clear her mind. Was she having a dream? But when Lucas moved his arm, pulling JoBeth further into the curve of his body, she knew it was a living nightmare and she was standing in the middle of it, wanting to die from the pain.

A silent sob escaped her lips, and anger began to claw at her. How dare he! How could he? After all his sweet words and promises. Why? The plea went unanswered. Dazed and sick at heart, she backed out of the doorway, pulling it quietly shut behind her. She pressed her hot forehead to the cold wood. Swaying on her feet, she stepped away from the door, hands on the wall for support. But her knees wobbled dangerously and she leaned her shoulder against the wall for balance. Why? Why had she been lied to and manipulated, charmed and seduced into believing he loved her? Nothing made sense, except that she could never, would never, be able to face Lucas again.

Jennifer wrapped her arms around herself and stood in the drafty hallway, rocking back and forth, racked by questions she had no answers for. Yet out of the chaos one thought became clear. She had a baby to protect. A child who would never know its father. She would make sure of that, even if she had to leave Houston and start over again. No one would ever get close enough to hurt her again. Anger eased the pain, and Jennifer realized she had to get away.

She forced herself to stand up straight and inhaled deeply. Determination stiffened her backbone, and memories of the past hardened her heart. She'd been hurt before, but this was the last. Never again would she allow herself the luxury of caring for a man so much. She took in another deep breath and let it out with a shaky sigh. With steady steps she headed down the hall past her room to another door. She pushed it open and hit the light switch. Bright light blazed in the room, bringing the man in the bed to an upright position.

"What the bloody hell is going on?" Sleepy blue eyes opened wide as Brandon focused his gaze on Jennifer's white face. He pulled the covers to his chin. "Dammit woman, don't you know not to come barging into a man's bedroom?"

Her lips tightened. "Oh, yes. I just learned that particular lesson the hard way. Take me home, Brandon. Take me back to Houston. Now!"

"Are you crazy? It's—it's almost midnight. Besides..."

Jennifer laughed, a sound that sent a chill crawling up Brandon's back.

"Is midnight still the bewitching hour," she asked, "or is it the *witching* hour?"

"What happened? What has my brother done?"

In a calm voice devoid of all emotion, she told him. At his look of disbelief, she tightened her clenched fists together till the knuckles became transparent. "Then go look for yourself."

"I will. Throw me my jeans and turn around."

Vaguely she heard his movements as she stared off into space. Even when he had left the room she didn't bother to move, but stood stiffly, her body as numb and cold as her emotions.

A grim-faced and angry Brandon returned a few minutes later. He tried to hold her and comfort her, but she cringed and stepped away from his touch. He studied her blank expression, her eyes dark as the night, filled with confusion and disgust. "Go pack your things. We'll leave as soon as you're ready."

The night made a mockery of her feelings as the two of them drove down the darkened road. The stars were bright, the moon full and the night creatures were singing in joyful song. Moonlight madness, she thought, then remembered her own foolishness the first night she had met Lucas. Her moment of madness.

"Jennifer, I think we should go back," Brandon said, once they had reached the main highway. "Running away is crazy. Lucas should have a chance to explain. Listen, we celebrated tonight and toasted a few to our future. Maybe he drank more than I thought."

She winced, knowing the reason for his celebrating—his victory. He had gotten what he wanted. "I won't go back, and if you try to make me, I'll get out of this car and walk home."

"Jennifer."

"No! Just drive and don't talk to me about Lucas, JoBeth or anything." Her voice trembled and she swallowed the sob that threatened to crack her control.

The remainder of the drive to Houston was completed in the silence she asked for, and just as the sun began to push the night away, Brandon turned into her driveway. He unloaded her luggage and checked her home to make sure all was safe.

"Promise me you'll get some rest, Jennifer? All this tension can't be healthy for you."

"I will," she said dully.

"All the way here I've been thinking something's wrong with this. I'm going back to the ranch and strangle Jo-Beth—after I get the truth from her."

"Fine."

He took a step toward her, saw another shudder rack her body and stopped. "I'll call you. Now please get some rest."

She walked him to the door and smiled pleasantly. "Thank you for driving me home, Brandon."

When the door closed, she looked around her home with new eyes. Her mother's treasures were pathetic reminders of a life her own was paralleling too closely. "Rest," Brandon had said, but she knew she'd never want to close her eyes again as long as she lived. If she did, she would see Lucas and JoBeth together. The sickening scene would replay itself with never-ending pain for the remainder of her days.

Trying to keep her mind a blank, Jennifer repeatedly told herself that she'd been happy before she met Lucas and she could be happy without him. She wandered aimlessly around, touching familiar objects, forcing her thoughts on the past in an effort to blank out the present.

But her past seemed a hazy blur now, a life that belonged to someone else.

An hour later she shook herself out of the daze she'd been in. She remembered the stack of material waiting for her at the office on Monday and almost laughed out loud. She had no intention of returning to DeSalvas, but she would go in today and finish what she'd started. Then she would feel free to walk away, knowing she hadn't shirked her duty, no matter what the circumstances.

JENNIFER PULLED INTO DESALVAS parking lot, turned off the car engine and rested her damp forehead on the steering wheel. She rubbed her sticky palms on her jeans and sighed resignedly. She didn't think she could still be shocked. Not after what Lucas had done to her. Yet here she sat in the cool, air-conditioned confines of her car, an emotional wreck.

She leaned back into the seat and stared with blind eyes at the tall building, turning a golden bronze in the hot morning sun. As she rubbed hard at the ridges the steering wheel had made on her hands, she thought in disgust of her dawn trek across town.

Like some demented soul with a death wish, she'd driven to Susan's house earlier, only to find it deserted and completely emptied of all furnishings. She had made her way from window to window, gazing in at bare walls and floors. It had taken the next-door neighbor to finally convince her that Susan had sold the place and moved out.

With some perverse sense of self-destruction she had wanted to tell Susan she had been right about Lucas, so she drove to the only other place Susan might be—McCord's Translations. She still had a key, so she let herself in, knowing by the echoing of her footsteps that the same emptiness would greet her. Where had Susan gone?

Jennifer opened her car door and swung her legs out. For a moment she remained seated, staring up at the DeSalvas' building. She'd been happy there, made good friends and had learned to drop the shield she'd built around herself. She shrugged. It was all behind her now. With forced movements, she strode up the wide curved steps, past the security guard's vacant desk and into the waiting elevator.

In a few minutes she was walking the long, lonely hall toward her office, head bent, eyes on her feet. A chill rose up her backbone as she realized how spooky an abandoned building could be, and she briefly wondered where the guard had been. As she drew close to her goal a low murmuring of voices sent her heart racing and she slowed her steps. The voices were real, and she let out her breath softly as she recognized them to be Kane's and Shasta's. She took one more step, then stopped as what they were saying and doing penetrated her thoughts.

Shasta handed her husband the grill for the air-conditioning vent and Jennifer followed their every movement, noting the camera lens tucked neatly in the open duct. Her mouth opened wide in horror as she realized what her friend was doing to her office.

"I still don't think we'll catch the thief this way." Shasta handed her husband a screwdriver and smiled at his grunt of disapproval. "Jennifer never would—"

"Hand me that other size screw," Kane interrupted. "Do you have any idea the amount of money DeSalvas lost because of that bitch's thieving? Millions! Lucas hired us…"

"Millions?" Jennifer whispered. "Thieves?" The words rang like a huge bell in her head. "Lucas"? They thought she was stealing from Lucas! Lucas thought she was a thief! Jennifer groaned and Kane and Shasta spun around.

"Oh, God, no, Jennifer," Shasta began. "It's not what it looks like."

Jennifer felt as if she were going to be sick, and she backed up as Shasta stepped toward her.

"Please, for heaven's sake, listen to me. Lucas *never* thought you were involved other than someone using you as a cover. Please listen to me, dammit. You have to understand—"

Jennifer took another step backward, then stopped, her bright eyes looking from Kane's blank expression to Shasta's white face then back again to Kane. "You followed me—the first day I met Lucas. Somehow you knew I would be meeting him, and you trailed me from the moment I left my house."

"Yes."

"But Lucas never thought you had anything to do with stealing and selling his secret project. Tell her Kane."

"Secrets? The new project." Jennifer was stunned by the revelations. They thought she had stolen parts of his plans for his new project.

"Jennifer, Lucas loves you. Please, if you believe in anything, believe that. Tell her, Kane!" Shasta spun around, and out of sheer frustration at her husband's silence, she kicked him in the shin. "Say something, dammit."

"He can't, can he, because he thinks I'm guilty?"

"No!" Shasta shouted. "He did once, but not anymore. Please..." She held out her hands, but Jennifer backed closer to the open door.

"And you, Shasta—my good and honest friend. All the time we had lunch and talked you were just trying to find out if I was your thief, weren't you?"

"I won't deny I did at first, but as soon as I got to know you I knew you weren't capable of any of this. I was your friend then. I still am."

"Oh, no." Jennifer took another step and this time crossed the threshold. "What about Brandon and Cleo?"

"Cleo never knew. I only used her to help find out about the clothes you have. Like us, Brandon saw early on that you couldn't be involved."

"And Lucas. My God, Lucas!" Jennifer closed her eyes at the injustice of it all. For the first time in her life she'd gambled on love and her return had been a slap in the face. Never, never again, she vowed in anguish.

Jennifer's eyes filled with fat tears of pain, and she spun around and ran. Ran from Shasta and her false friendship, from Kane and his accusing eyes. She ran from the devils of the past and the misery of the future. When she finally stopped, she found herself on a different floor, in a tiled rest room, crouched like an animal in a corner, listening to the distant footfalls of her trackers.

Once the quiet surrounded her, Jennifer's restraints broke and she buried her face in her hands and cried at Lucas's brutal betrayal. He'd lied and cheated and all for what? Money! Money and secrets! She raised her head and wiped her cheeks with the back of her hand. She *hated* them all. She'd never stolen a thing in her life. *But someone had, and had tried to make it look as if she were responsible*. Who? The first name to pop into her head was *Susan*. Like an avalanche memories began to return—bits and pieces of conversation. She shook her head at the farfetched fantasies. Obviously the thefts were still going on though Jennifer had left McCord's months ago.

She stood up slowly, wincing at her cramped muscles. Someone was taking information from her office, she concluded. It was the only way to make her appear guilty.

Who would deliberately do such a thing? Better still, she thought, who would hate her so much that they wanted to frame her? She quickly washed her face and stared into the mirror. She was going to find out who and how and why if it killed her. But to do that she needed to search her office. Maybe she could find some clue that Kane and Shasta had overlooked. Her lips tightened to a straight white line as she stepped out of the eleventh-floor men's rest room. She tried the elevators, and when the buttons didn't light up or show any signs of movement, she headed for the stairway and the floor above her.

The hallway was deserted as Jennifer quietly moved toward her office. She stopped and frowned at the door—it was partially closed. With a trembling hand she gently pushed it open. Inch by inch it moved, till suddenly the knob was yanked from her grasp. Something hard and warm clamped around her wrist and she was jerked forward, almost losing her balance and falling to her knees till the hand pulled her back to her feet.

"What are *you* doing here?" she asked, and tried to pull free. When the grip on her hand tightened she looked up and froze. She was staring down the small round barrel of a handgun. Her mouth went dry with the worst fear she had ever faced in her life. "Not you! *Please* not you."

CHAPTER SIXTEEN

THE SATURDAY-MORNING TRAFFIC, though sparse around the Galleria at such an early hour, was already moving sluggishly in the humid heat. Lucas could see the waves of the sun's rays radiate off the hood of Brandon's Corvette. He gave a savage yank to the steering wheel and scowled murderously at the beautiful redhead in the car beside his, who was trying to flirt with him. Shifting gears, he gunned the powerful engine and shot forward, his bloodshot eyes staring straight ahead. Finally, his goal in sight, he slowed and wheeled the car into the DeSalvas parking lot. In the next second he spotted Jennifer's Mustang and slammed on the brakes, leaving two wide black stripes on the pavement as he screeched to a halt behind her car.

Lucas closed his eyes tightly, thanking some invisible hand of fate for allowing him to find her on his second stop. Throwing open the door, he struggled to release his long body from the cramped confines of his brother's car.

He sprinted across the parking lot, a wolfish grin transforming the stern, tight line of his mouth. Brandon would be wild with fury when he found his car gone. Served him right, he thought, angrily rubbing the sore spot on his jaw. He'd had to get to Houston fast and the airplane would have taken too much time with the refueling, filing a flight plan, landing at Houston's airport and fighting the freeway across town. He'd actually made better time in the

Corvette, especially since he'd broken practically every speed limit there was.

The tall glass entranceway yawned wide and familiar. Lucas quickly yanked opened the heavy doors and loped across the marble floor. His steps echoed hollowly and he called out for the security guard as he ran. When only the continued sound of his footfalls met his summons he bellowed, "Frank." Never missing a step, he cursed under his breath at the silence and headed for the elevators.

"Lucas!" Kane yelled from the open doorway of Masters Security.

Lucas veered and changed direction. "Where's Frank? He's not supposed to leave his post unless he's relieved." A frown deepened across his brow, and his tired, heavy-lidded eyes glittered with suppressed anger.

"One of Masters' bodyguards is searching for Frank." Kane motioned for him to come into the office, but Lucas shook his head and started to turn around.

"I don't have time to stop, Kane. Jennifer's here and I have to find her."

"You'd better take the time to listen to Kane, Lucas," Shasta stepped from behind her husband's tall frame. "We've got big problems." She grabbed his hand and urged him in. "Come on."

Lucas hesitated and Shasta began to tell him what had happened earlier with Jennifer. He listened, but his attention was caught by Kane, who was fiddling with the knobs of a television monitor.

"Did you hear what I said, Lucas?"

"Yes, go on."

"That's all, except she knows only enough to be damning—to you."

Staring down at his feet, Lucas slowly shook his head and sat down in the straight-backed chair. "I guess she had to find out sometime, but dammit, not like this. She must feel as if she's been used and betrayed.'' He raked his fingers through his hair, his mouth a grim white slash as he thought of what she must be going through—the hurt and doubts. She'd learned to trust her own instincts, and now this newly acquired confidence would be destroyed. ''There's no telling what damage this has caused,'' he mumbled softly, but both Kane and Shasta heard the stress in the deep voice. Lucas raised his head, the pain evident in his dark green eyes. ''Where is she?''

Shasta swallowed, feeling his misery and shame at her own duplicity. ''She's still in the building,'' she said helplessly. ''It's just a matter of finding her. Maybe when she's had some time to reconsider—'' She broke off as a commotion at the doorway drew their attention.

Bob Waters, one of Masters' trained bodyguards, struggled in under the almost dead weight of the injured security guard. ''I found him tied up in the utility closet with a large lump on his head.''

''Jenny!'' Lucas whispered, panic in each syllable. He surged to his feet, then immediately froze, along with everyone else in the room. The monitoring unit Kane had been working suddenly burst into life.

''What are you doing here?'' the disembodied voice called out over the office speakers, and Lucas flinched, thinking that for the first time in his life he was going to pass out. But he forced his eyes on the screen, watching the confusion in Jennifer's expression give way to the realization that the man standing with his back to the camera had a gun pointed directly at her heart. When he heard her anguished pleas, ''Not you—please, not you'' he sprang into action, bellowing and shouting orders.

Shoving Kane out of the way, he charged for the elevator, punching buttons like a madman, cursing each second's delay. But nothing happened, and when he felt Kane's hand on his shoulder he knew without being told that the man with the gun had disabled the elevators. He looked around wildly, patted his pockets and began running toward the private elevator. Jamming his hands in his jeans, he searched frantically for his key, disregarding the coins and folded bills that trailed in his wake.

He rounded the corner and stopped, his mouth dry as a desert, his heart thumping like a jackhammer against his ribs. Shasta was on her knees, a small set of burglary tools laid out before her as she worked feverishly on the tangle of colored wires that had been ripped from the open steel panel.

Kane grabbed Lucas's arm and pulled him away. "The stairs," he shouted, and as he passed Bob Waters he snatched up the walkie-talkie held out to him. "Call the police. Come on, Lucas. I hope you're in shape, man, because we've got twelve floors to cover in a hurry."

Lucas inhaled deeply to clear his mind, telling himself to take one landing at a time. He set his foot on the first step, prepared to take off, when Jennifer's voice reverberated off the stone walls.

"Why?" she asked in a stricken voice.

A chuckle resounded throughout the stairwell, a sound so filled with viciousness that Lucas bounded up the stairs at a speed that soon had Kane panting.

JENNIFER'S EYES moved from the weapon pointing at her to the face above. An earring, a small circlet of gold, winked at her almost playfully as it caught the light. The picture before her was a grotesque contradiction: a handsome, elegantly dressed man holding an ugly gun. But it was the jet eyes that held her attention and filled her with terror. She'd always considered herself a fairly brave per-

son. In the middle of the night when a strange noise jarred
her out of a sound sleep, didn't she immediately jump up
to check under the beds, behind the half-closed closet door
or behind the shower curtain? Now, though, she stood
rooted to the spot, paralyzed with fear as she realized that
death didn't necessarily come on fleet silent feet. She stood
frozen in fear, unable to move.

"This really is a bloody confusing mess for you, isn't it,
Jennifer, darling? Everyone running around trying to get
evidence against you and Susan, never once suspecting me.
The perfect crime, wouldn't you say, love? Susan does the
stealing, we line our pockets and I finally get to crush Lucas in the process."

He chuckled deeply and her throat ached from the hard
lump of panic. She swallowed thickly. "Why, Jean-Paul?
For the money?" She reached out for the desk to steady
her shaking legs.

"Mais non! Please, *ma chérie,* do not make a move. I'd
hate to put a bullet through your little heart before I'm
ready."

Jennifer sucked in a deep breath of air, thinking frantically that this was all a mad joke and any minute he would
begin to laugh. But she knew she was wrong. It was no
crazy joke, and the only thing mad was the look in Jean-
Paul's dark eyes. She shifted her gaze carefully and stared
at her typewriter, noting the open cover and the missing
ribbon cartridge. "You have what you've come for. Please
leave."

"Like hell. You are a bloody fool, darling." He smiled
teasingly and shook his head.

The gun waved back and forth carelessly, and she held
her breath, her eyes watering a little as she listened to the
sing-song voice switching from the heavy clipped British

accent to the soft tones of the French then back again. Had he totally lost contact with reality?

"I'm sorry, Jennifer. You are caught in the middle. Your stepsister and I have enjoyed the fruits of our partnership and she has taken her share and flown away. But me now, I have to stay to settle the old score, you understand?"

"No, I don't. Susan had everything."

"But the greedy bitch wanted more. You were only a means to an end—to accomplish her goals. Don't waste your last thoughts on her. She knew my plan and couldn't have cared less what happened to you."

"Why you, Jean-Paul? Lucas considers you his friend." She choked on her words, remembering the way Lucas liked to reminisce about past exploits the two men had shared. A tremble began to move up her legs as she saw the malicious pleasure her fear brought him. His face was right out of an El Greco, and was hideous in its relish of victory. "What do you want from me, Jean-Paul? Do you want me to beg for my life and the life of my child? I will."

"Non," he said sadly, "it will do no good. Lucas has to be taught a lesson."

"Why? Please, please answer me that."

He shrugged elegantly, his voice a sweet purr that sent a chill up her back. "He has taken everything from me—my land, my self-respect, my heritage. Now I take what he holds most dear."

"But Jean-Paul, Lucas saved your vineyards. He bought them and gave you an interest."

"Shut up," he screamed. "Do not tell me this. It was because of him that I speculated with my inheritance in the first place." He fell silent, drifting off into his own private hell. Then he jerked back to the present, his expression a twisted mask of bitterness. "I found the letter in his briefcase...a letter on a new venture. His notes asked

Brandon to check further, that it looked promising." Jean-Paul broke off, his eyes wide, the pupils dilated with mal-evolence. "Be very careful and do not make a move if you wish…" He trailed off, then chuckled and waved the gun at her like a chastising finger. "You play with me like on television. You think if you keep me talking long enough help will come." He leaned forward and whispered con-spiratorially. "No one will rescue you, my darling. I have taken precautions."

Jennifer flinched as alcoholic fumes fanned her face. She'd hoped he would only use her as a hostage or a shield to make good his escape. But now, looking into the depths of his madness, she knew she'd never leave the office alive. He was going to kill her, had planned it for a long time and had no remorse whatever. She thought her knees would buckle and closed her eyes in sheer terror. "What have I ever done to you, Jean-Paul, that makes you want to hurt me?"

"Nothing. I adore you and so does Lucas. That, *chérie*, is the key. Lucas loves you and the child you carry. He will be the one to suffer, not you."

"Oh, God." She squeezed her eyelids tighter, waiting, wondering if there would be any pain when the shot fi-nally came. There was a roaring in her ears, and some-where between the pounding of her heart and her shallow breathing she imagined she could hear Lucas's voice. She said his name with a whimper and swayed on her feet.

LUCAS AND KANE hit the twelfth-floor landing at the same time, both gasping loudly as their lungs fought for oxy-gen. Lucas struggled with the door, his hands shaking vi-olently with exhaustion. He knew, as did Kane, that they couldn't stop to work out a plan. He'd heard everything being said in Jennifer's office and knew they had no time.

The door opened and he lunged out into the hallway, Kane right behind him. Shasta emerged from the elevator at the same time and ran after them. He felt as if he were moving through a sea of molasses, each step painfully slow. His chest burned with each breath, and his parched throat ached, but still he pushed himself harder to speed up his steps.

Jennifer's office seemed a million miles away, and as he rounded the corner he prayed that the sound of his pounding footsteps and the deafening rasping of his breathing would only startle Jean-Paul into turning around, not firing the gun immediately. As if of the same thought, he and Kane flew through the open doorway, their feet leaving the ground simultaneously as they sailed across the room, taking a startled Jean-Paul off guard and tackling him to the floor.

Lucas lay across the struggling, cursing Frenchman's shoulders, his hand clamped around Jean-Paul's wrist as he tried to shake the gun from his grasp. He wheezed and grunted in his effort to keep the madly bucking man down, knowing that even with Kane's help they were both too weak to restrain him for long. His body and mind were too drained to think clearly, and all he could do was hope their combined weight would hold him till help arrived. He opened his eyes and dizzily watched a pair of worn, dirty sneakers come into his line of vision. Helplessly he looked up and watched as Shasta, assessing the situation, snatched the gun away. With a quick, efficient movement she spun it around, grasped it by the barrel and applied a hard tap to the side of Jean-Paul's head.

The spate of filthy cursing stopped and the body beneath Lucas went limp. Lucas turned his head slowly, met Kane's disgusted expression and they both began to laugh. A wild, crazy sound of relief filled the room.

Jennifer watched the scene play out before her in slow motion. But when Lucas and Kane began to laugh, it was as if something snapped inside her. She buried her face in her hands and began to cry. They were laughing, and she'd been seconds away from death. Nothing made sense anymore. She swayed on her feet, then felt the steadying strength of Lucas's arms wrap around her.

Her hands dropped away from her face and she glared down at the dark head resting against her stomach, his breath a hot whisper through her silk blouse. Her fingers curled into her palms and she began to beat her fist on his shoulders. "I hate you. I hate you."

"Sh, honey. Jenny, stop."

"No. I hate you."

He grabbed her hands and rose slowly to his feet. "You don't hate me. You're just scared and mad."

"Why, why didn't you tell me what was happening? If you'd loved me you would have told me what you suspected Susan of doing. She was my stepsister," she said irrationally. A deep sob escaped her lips, and she pressed her fingers against her mouth, trying to hold back her emotions. Struggling to regain control, she dropped her hand and stared at Lucas without expression.

"Oh, no, you don't. You're not going to erect that damn wall between us again." In one quick movement that surprised even himself, he grabbed Jennifer, pitched her over his shoulder and strode out of the office. "Kane, take care of the police when they get here. I've a few things to settle with Jenny. Then they can get her statement."

"Put me down, Lucas DeSalva. You put me down this minute!" She pounded his back, wiggling and squirming in an effort to escape, only managing to bump her head as they entered the one working elevator.

She'd seen him in many moods, but this one was new to her. There was a purpose to his step, a relentless glint in his eye and an obstinate thrust to his chin.

He jammed the key into the lock and kicked open the door to his suite, marched in and dropped her like a sack of potatoes on the leather couch. "You move and I swear you'll regret it till your dying day."

"Your threats are meaningless, when I've just looked death in the face," Jennifer shot back dramatically, earning herself another bark of laughter. She watched nervously as he stripped off his sweat-soaked shirt, balled it up and threw it on the floor as though throwing down a gauntlet. He gave her another challenging look and headed for his bedroom. Before she could gather her wits and make her exit, he was back, a towel wrapped around his neck, his chest bare and dry. She edged down the couch, closer to the door, when his steady stare stopped her.

"Go on, make a run. You've been running away from things all your life. This wouldn't be something new. Except I'm going to stop you." He smiled, a twist of his lips that dared her once more to defy him. "I might be dead on my feet, but I can still handle you. We're going to straighten this mess out once and for all. Then we'll go on with our lives—together."

"Never," she snapped.

"Oh, yes, lady." He walked to the bar, filled a glass with water and gulped it down.

She would have loved to quench her thirst but stubbornly refused to ask for a drink.

Lucas's hard green gaze ran over her, taking in every detail, checking that Jean-Paul hadn't done her any physical harm. He raised his eyes to hers, and they stared at each other for a long while before he looked down to refill his glass. Casually he downed the drink, then slowly strolled toward her and sat down. Jennifer inched farther away, but his hand snaked out, grabbing her wrist and hauling her onto his lap. "Jenny, ordinarily I'm not a patient man, but knowing your problems and background, I've been patient and understanding. But a man can take just so much. I love you. Anything I've done was to protect you from further harm."

"Ha! You call shacking up with JoBeth right under my nose for my own good?"

"Okay. We'll start with that explanation."

"No!"

"Fine. Where, then?" She fell mutinously silent, and he sighed, his arm tightening around her stiff body.

"Jean-Paul," she finally said, wanting to put off his lies about his affair with JoBeth as long as possible.

Lucas closed his eyes with the pain of remembering what his friend had tried to do to him. "I heard everything he said to you while Kane and I were doing our marathon run up twelve flights of stairs. We never suspected he was involved. Oh, we knew Susan has an accomplice, but—"

At the mention of her stepsister's name Jennifer's head dipped. "She knew he was going to kill me," she whispered. "She hated me so much she didn't care."

"Susan was as crazy in her own way as Jean-Paul. And that's the only reason I can give you for what he's done. Somewhere, somehow he stepped over the fine edge of sanity. I don't know why, and after what he tried to do to you I don't give a damn what happens to him. But he'll have plenty of time in jail to think about it. Texas is tough on attempted murderers, extortionists and industrial spies and thieves."

He touched her chin and turned her face to his so he could watch her expressive eyes. "Jenny, I never, ever thought you were involved in stealing from DeSalvas. How could I? I loved you and knew you would never do something so totally against your nature." He told her everything from the beginning, sparing nothing and no one in his explanation. "I know your feelings are hurt about Brandon, Shasta and Kane doubting your innocence, but I think you'll agree the circumstances were solidly stacked against you. So before you condemn them, think of the way they must have felt. They liked you, even though they thought you guilty, but it still didn't change the way they cared for you."

Jennifer nodded at his explanation, but it would take time to straighten out all her feelings and to understand just what had happened. "Where's Susan?"

"Gone, skipped the country. But not for long," he whispered savagely. "I'll find her and she'll pay for what she's done to you."

Jennifer shivered and turned her head away, only to have her chin clasped between strong fingers and pulled back to face him. She gazed into his eyes, wanting desperately to believe him, yet still doubting. After all, there was still JoBeth to answer for. She freed her face from his grasp and tried to move out of his arms.

"Don't look at me with that blank expression, goddammit. I know what you're doing and it won't work. You can't hide from me anymore, Jenny. You have to face facts."

He was right. She was faced with both sides of the coin of love and hate. Hate for Lucas and what he'd kept from her—how he'd manipulated her life. He'd saved her, but he'd also been the major cause of her troubles. Yet there was the other side: the love she felt for him. "Damn you, Lucas!" she snarled at his surprised, smiling face. "How could you sleep with her? And after all the things we talked about?"

"That's it, honey. Spit it out. Get mad! Hit me, but dammit, get it all out in the open. Tell me you feel something—anything."

"I do feel—and it hurts like hell." It was true. The pain of his perfidy was worse than anything she'd ever experienced. She lunged forward, breaking his hold on her with the unexpected action. Surging to her feet, she stepped out of his reach and spun around. "How do you think I felt? Not three hours after you told me you love me, I find JoBeth in your bed, naked."

"She wasn't naked! She just made it appear that way."

Jennifer frowned fiercely at the tiny twitch of his lips and started to raise her arm. But Lucas was already on his feet, catching her by the wrist and hauling her up against his chest. His eyes glinted and the grin that had previously lightened his features froze in place.

"Why was JoBeth in your bed and just how long have you been having an affair with her?" Jennifer demanded.

"I ought to take a leaf from Brandon's book and turn you over my knee for that remark."

"Well, what did you expect?" she asked in a sarcastic tone that brought his eyebrows together. "Did you really think because of my past that I'd remain passive and overlook the incident? Maybe at one time in my life I would have, but not now. You made me love you! You accomplished what you set out to do. Now you're answerable to me for your actions where my feelings are concerned." She glared at him, then let out a yelp as Lucas yanked her closer. His hand clasped the back of her head and his mouth met hers.

The kiss demanded a response she was determined to withhold. She brought up her balled fists, placed them on his chest and pushed as hard as she could. She gave an angry moan and increased the pressure, but her efforts only added fuel to his wild passion. His tongue dove deeper into the moist cavern of her mouth, tasting, savoring, and she felt her body turn traitor and begin to respond. Her fingers unfurled and began to stroke the warm flesh of his shoulders.

How she loved the velvety feel of his skin and the contrast made by the rough texture of the dark triangle of hair on his chest. When his arms loosened their grip and his lips slid down the line of her jaw, she drew back.

"That only proves that my body seems to have a mind all it's own. It's this—" she tapped her temple "—that you have to concern yourself about. I want some straight answers. Now!"

"Yes, ma'am." Lucas reached out and lovingly caressed her cheek with the back of his hand. "Let's sit down, before I fall down." He settled her once more on his lap, and when she started to protest he gave her a sharp shake. "Jenny, JoBeth is like a sister to me. I've never had an affair with her, nor have I wanted to. Don't you know she's in love with Brandon? Has been since she was about nine years old. She uses me because she knows it drives Brandon crazy trying to figure out our relationship."

"Then why was she in your bed—it didn't look very sisterly from where I stood!"

Lucas grinned and rubbed his face tiredly. "What a farce that was. If you had stayed you would have died laughing."

She shot him a hurt, skeptical glare and he smiled back warmly. "I doubt it, Lucas. You might begin by telling me why you never came to my room the way you promised."

He pulled her into a more comfortable position, nestling her against his body, wanting only to hold her close and safe in his arms. "I...damn! This is hard to admit, but the truth of the matter is I had too much to drink. I was so relieved and happy that I told Brandon about your decision to live with me. He toasted me a few, and of course I couldn't refuse. Honestly, Jenny, I was only going to lie down for an hour to get my head together. But I guess we tipped a few too many.''

A silence fell between them and Jennifer shifted and snuggled farther into his embrace. ''So, you went to sleep and awakened to find JoBeth?''

''Not quite. Can you imagine what it's like for a man my age to be rudely awakened by his father whacking him across the backside with his cane? I think I immediately reverted to my childhood, because for a brief moment all I could think of was that Brandon had managed to get me in trouble once again. In the next second I opened my eyes and low and behold, there's JoBeth curled up on the other side of the bed, sniffling and crying hysterically. He rubbed his face again, trying to suppress a smile.

''It was absolute chaos for the next two hours. You were gone, Dad had a note from Brandon explaining what he'd found earlier and JoBeth was still crying bucketsful. I was hungover and damned confused. But after a whole pot of Pilar's coffee everything began to straighten out. It took another hour to get JoBeth calmed down enough to get a couple of coherent sentences out of her. Then, of course, Brandon comes busting in, clips me a good one on the jaw and rounds on poor JoBeth.'' He shook his head and chuckled in amazement that he'd been able to shout everyone down long enough to completely understand what had happened. ''A three-ring circus would have been tempting at that point.''

Jennifer couldn't grasp the humor in the situation and continued to stare at him with a neutral, polite expression. Yet inside she was burning with anger. All she could see was JoBeth curled in Lucas's arms, and the memory brought a fire to her violet eyes that Lucas didn't miss.

"Jenny, Jean-Paul told JoBeth you're pregnant. He convinced her that any one of us—me, Brandon or him—could be the father. He also told her you had selected me to trap because I was the richest. I know it's a weak story, with all sorts of holes in it, but you have to remember her attachment to our family. All she could think to do was try to come between you and me. She said she knew it wouldn't do any good to talk to us or offer you money. Jean-Paul had spread his sickness too cleverly. She was sorry, Jenny, sorrier than you'll ever know, once she realized just how much I love you. I don't believe I've ever seen her so confused and ashamed."

Jennifer relaxed against his chest and closed her eyes. They'd all been taken in and had suffered because of Jean-Paul. She didn't have the heart to condemn JoBeth. The man was demented, so filled with hate he had used anyone he could to serve his purpose. "Where's JoBeth now?" She had some vague notion of trying to see her to let her know she understood.

Lucas eased Jennifer backward and moved to lie down beside her. The activities of the past twenty-four hours were beginning to take their toll and he had to shake his head to keep awake. He reached out and touched her shining hair, running his fingers through the silky mass. "The last I saw she'd locked herself in the bathroom and refused to see or talk to Brandon. Now enough of them. Am I forgiven?"

"I guess." She looked down, watching as he began to unbutton her blouse. When his lips caressed the valley between her breasts she touched his hair, lightly at first. Then her fingers tangled in the thick black softness. "I love you," she whispered.

"I know." Lucas grinned and nuzzled the top of one white breast, then laid his head down with a tired sigh. "While I was running up those twelve flights of stairs, not knowing what Jean-Paul was going to do and scared to death something might happen to you, I realized one important fact. Our agreement isn't what I want at all."

Jennifer squeezed her eyes shut, feeling the world spin crazily beneath her. With his next words the earth righted itself, and she smiled radiantly.

"I want us to get married!"

He refused to raise his head and remained perfectly still except for the finger that absently circled the globe of her breast. "I've talked it over with Brandon and he agrees with my plans. We can move to the ranch and he'll take his place as president of DeSalvas. Oh, I'll remain chairman of the board for a while, then gradually resign that post to him, also. I know I agreed just to live together, Jenny, but it won't work. We both need the strong, secure foundation—"

"Yes," she whispered, stroking the side of his face.

"—That marriage can give. We live—" His head snapped up. "What did you say?"

"I said yes!" She looked solemnly into his amazed face, trying to hide her happiness.

"Just like that? No arguments, no dithering, no tears and protestations of being hemmed in?"

"No." A tender smile touched her lips. "I won't lie and tell you I'm not scared, but the alternatives are unbearable. What happened today made me realize that life is made to live to the fullest. Good, bad or indifferent, life's too short not to take a chance on love."

Lucas kissed her, holding her close, feeling the steady beating of her heart beside him. "I'll make a promise to you, Jenny. If at any time in our marriage you feel trapped and unhappy, I'll let you go." He touched his fingers to her lips. "No, I mean it, so don't say anything you might regret later." He tucked her head into the curve of his shoulder and raised his gaze to the wide expanse of windows and the clear azure sky beyond. He'd be forgiven this one last little lie, he knew. But Jenny needed an escape hatch, a hold on her freedom. Lucas smiled, his eyes glimmering like a clear river stream. He would never let her go, not till they put him six feet under the earth.

Jennifer chuckled, suddenly feeling ridiculously young and happy. "Don't you think we should celebrate this occasion?" She hugged him fiercely, her bones melting with the heat of his closeness. "Maybe a prenuptial honeymoon. Or should we call your father first? Brandon will tease us and somehow convince himself it was all his doing." A soft rumbling answered her, and she saw that Lucas had fallen asleep. She kissed the top of his head tenderly and smiled. He'd saved her life, in more ways than one. With his constant love and understanding he'd shown her what it was to be truly free. For that she'd love him all the rest of her days.

EPILOGUE

"WHAT THE HELL DO YOU MEAN you can't get a Life Flight helicopter out here? Of course it's a life-and-death situation!" Lucas bellowed into the telephone as he walked to the limit of its long cord then back again. "Listen carefully, lady, my wife is in labor—she's going to deliver twins at any time. We have to get her out of here!" He listened intently, barely breathing as he pressed the receiver to his ear. "Yes...yes," he growled impatiently, struggling hard to control his temper once again. "I'm well aware there are high winds and ice warnings out. I've been trying to get my own plane up for the past three hours. But a helicopter just might make it."

Lucas fell silent, his jaw knotting at what he was hearing. Did the woman think he was some country bumpkin? Of course he knew what was happening with the weather. Like everyone in the Hill Country he'd had the television and radio on to listen to reports on the worst winter storm in a century to blanket Texas. Hail, sleet and mounds of snow swept through the usually warm climate, stunning everyone with their unexpectedness and intensity. There were power failures all over the state, transportation was reduced to a standstill as the roads iced over, airports were closed—and aircraft grounded.

Matthew DeSalva stood at the patio window, a silent sentinel, watching hail the size of golf balls bounce and shatter on the frozen ground. His shoulders slumped as he heard the sheer panic in his son's voice.

"I'm perfectly calm!" Lucas yelled, then snapped his mouth shut. "What do you mean you'll talk me through the delivery when the time comes?" He slammed the phone down and began pacing the length of the Persian rug once more.

"Son, you've got to pull yourself together. It's not going to do Jennifer any good to see you falling apart."

"I know, Dad." Lucas raked his hand through his hair and around the back of his neck and continued to pace back and forth. What was he going to do? He stopped and stared off into the distance, remembering how happy Jenny had been when she'd finally talked him into having their child by natural childbirth. They'd spent hours curled up in their big bed going over the lessons. He'd decided it would be an unforgettable experience to watch his first-born come into the world. But their plans had been abruptly called off when the doctor told them Jenny was going to have twins.

After two days of shock, he'd called his friend Boston Grey for some reassurance and support. After all, Boston had survived the birth of quadruplets. The news of twins had thrown everybody at the ranch into a festive celebration—everyone but Lucas. He was suddenly scared, knowing their chances for trouble were doubled now. Though Jennifer took the news in stride, he'd begun to dog her every step like a lunatic.

Lucas bumped into his father, who was pacing from the opposite end of the room. They did a little dance, bobbing from side to side, then parted. When he turned and collided with Matthew for the third time, they went through their strange footwork again. "For heaven's sake, Dad, go walk the floor somewhere else."

"Sorry," came a mumbled reply.

"What's taking so long getting her ready?"

Matthew shrugged, knowing no answer would appease Lucas, and he sighed with relief as he spotted Pilar standing in the doorway.

"You best go up, Señor Lucas." She twisted the ever-present dish towel, her usually immaculate hairdo slipping from its tight knot atop her head.

Lucas's face paled. "How is it, Pilar, that a woman knows nothing about childbirth?" he asked in an accusing tone.

Plump, rounded shoulders hunched upward. "I take care of the little ones, never the mothers. Besides, I have a weak stomach." She quickly spun and waddled out of the room, panic-stricken at the thought of being asked again to help.

"Dad?" Lucas turned beseeching eyes on Matthew and received a firm headshake to his unspoken question. He turned around and headed for the stairs, thinking of Jennifer alone in the big bed waiting for him. Once outside the door he stopped long enough to force his expression into one of calm confidence.

Jennifer watched Lucas enter with a smile, a soft loving curve to her lips that sent his heart thumping harder. He was scared, she thought, and her smile widened. "Did you get the hospital? Are they sending a helicopter?" She'd known the answer long before he'd insisted on putting the call through, but she hadn't argued, hoping the job would keep him busy and his mind off the coming event. She'd been just as scared as he, but somehow his vulnerability had turned her apprehension to a strength she hadn't known she possessed.

"We're on our own, Jenny." He sat gingerly on the side of the bed, picked up her hand and kissed her palm.

She felt the tremors in his clasp and wrapped her fingers around his. "It's all right. We'll do it ourselves."

"Honey—" His voice cracked and he cleared his throat.

She touched his lips with her fingers. "You've delivered foals before." She stopped as her breath was cut short by pain. "There can't be all that much difference."

Lucas groaned, wrapped his arms around her and buried his face in the swell of her breast. "You're not one of my damn horses. I don't think I can do this, Jenny."

Jennifer tilted her head to one side so she could see the panic in his eyes. "Afraid—you, Lucas?"

"Damn right!" His head jerked up as another contraction swept through her, and his eyes pleaded with hers. He thought he'd go mad at the trust he saw there.

Jennifer's breathless laugh echoed in the quiet room. "I'm afraid you don't really have a choice, darling." She arched and began panting once more. "You know what to do. We studied all the books."

"That was for delivery in a hospital with the doctors in attendance. I learned only the—ah, hell—" he broke off in anguish as another pain sent her grasping the edge of the bed. "Right!" He stood, rolled up his sleeves and began shouting orders. The room felt overly hot and was suddenly filled with people as Matthew and Pilar appeared at his side, willing to give a hand if they could.

It was a long night, and even though the contractions came fairly close together it was an even longer labor than they'd anticipated. At times Lucas was convinced Jenny was going to die. There were endless hours of breathing and panting with Matthew gently wiping away the perspiration from Jennifer's pale face with cool cloths.

Lucas cajoled, begged and cursed the fates that had given him everything and now seemed tempted to take it all away. But Jennifer wouldn't let him break. When a pain was too strong and she couldn't stop the scream and he wanted to die, she'd open those violet eyes and smile at him with so much love and trust that it humbled him and kept him from breaking down completely.

After what seemed a lifetime, Lucas finally held up a squirming body, listening with wonder to the loud, angry cry. He vaguely heard Pilar babbling as he handed his son over to be cleaned up. "What's she saying, Dad?" But Matthew could only stare at the squawling bundle as Pilar held the child for Jennifer to see.

Matthew gave a nervous, choked laugh and wiped Jennifer's forehead. "A boy, and by the looks I'd say about six pounds," he said.

Jennifer smiled tiredly. "Our little Matthew," she murmured. "Lucas," she called softly through clenched teeth, "are you ready to do it again?" A grin forced its way across her pained expression as she watched Lucas's eyes widen. They were both aware that if there was going to be trouble it would be now.

Minutes later, Lucas held his tiny daughter in his hands, gazing at her red face, which was puckered indignantly at her treatment. As he placed her carefully in the second makeshift incubator, his eyes went from one healthy child to the other. His daughter quieted under Pilar's ministrations, and the room fell silent. Lucas laid a heavy hand on his father's shoulder. Matthew was sitting between his grandchildren, keeping a vigilant eye on both.

Lucas returned to Jennifer's side and pulled a chair up to the edge of the bed. He picked up her hand and kissed it, silently thanking her for his children. A loud sigh of exhaustion escaped his lips and he rubbed his stubble-covered jaw. If anyone had told him nine months ago what he would have to do, he would have laughed and called them insane. Jennifer always said he had changed her life, but his was the one that had changed. Dreams were meant to come true, after all. He had the woman he loved; he was back at the ranch leading the life he'd longed for, and now he had his children. He leaned forward and laid his head next to Jennifer's.

Jennifer opened her heavy-lidded eyes, turned her head and gazed at Lucas, bent over awkwardly, his head cradled on his folded arms, sound asleep. She gently ran her hand over his hair, trying to return it to some semblance of order and he lifted his head.

Pale and haggard, with lines etched deeply at his mouth and between his eyes, he smiled. "We did it," he whispered in awe.

She touched his face, letting her fingers trace the signs of strain and worry. Out of the corner of her eye she saw Matthew and Pilar tiptoe out of the room. "I'm very proud of you, Lucas. Are they all right? All their fingers and toes?"

"Healthy as horses," he chuckled, and kissed her cheek. "You know, we never did decide on a girl's name."

"I have." There was a long thoughtful pause before she went on, a little unsure of his reaction. "Catherine Elizabeth." She hoped it would please him to name their daughter after his mother and sister. Lucas lowered his head and as she watched him his shoulders began to shake. "Lucas?" she whispered, and he lifted his head, his eyes brimming with bright tears that flowed unchecked down his cheeks.

Jennifer gathered him in her arms, realizing this was probably the first time he'd ever cried openly for the loss of his sister and mother. She hugged him closer to her and blinked away her own tears.

The door swung open suddenly and they both looked up as Brandon rushed into the room, his coat and boots caked with snow and ice.

He jerked to a stop and grinned sheepishly at interrupting their private moment, but curiosity won out, and he craned his neck, trying to get a look at the new additions to the family.

"Don't you know how to knock?" Lucas asked him testily, but his eyes were bright, clear and laughing. "And how did you get here? When I talked to you early yesterday in Houston there was no way you could get through."

Brandon pulled off his gloves and shot them a wicked grin. "Never tell the new president of DeSalvas he can't do something. I made it to San Antonio, bought a new Jeep, then left it at the entrance to the ranch. I've tracked through two miles of snow to see my niece and nephew." He bounded over to the incubators and gazed down. "Well, now, what do you know—Uncle Brandon." He rolled the title around on his tongue and took another look, beaming as if he had something to do with their birth. His bright gaze shifted to the two grown people, and he began to chuckle. "Looks to me as if Jennifer has decided to stay awhile, after all."

Jennifer squeezed Lucas's hand and they stared lovingly at each other. "Just for a lifetime."

H·A·R·L·E·Q·U·I·N

FIRST·CLASS
Sweepstakes

OFFICIAL RULES

1. NO PURCHASE NECESSARY. To enter, complete the official entry/order form. Be sure to indicate whether or not you wish to take advantage of our subscription offer.

2. Entry blanks have been preselected for the prizes offered. Your response will be checked to see if you are a winner. In the event that these preselected responses are not claimed, a random drawing will be held from all entries received to award not less than $150,000 in prizes. This is in addition to any free, surprise or mystery gifts which might be offered. Versions of this sweepstakes with different prizes will appear in Preview Service Mailings by Harlequin Books and their affiliates. Winners selected will receive the prize offered in their sweepstakes brochure.

3. This promotion is being conducted under the supervision of Marden-Kane, an independent judging organization. By entering the sweepstakes, each entrant accepts and agrees to be bound by these rules and the decisions of the judges, which shall be final and binding. Odds of winning in the random drawing are dependent upon the total number of entries received. Taxes, if any, are the sole responsibility of the prize winners. Prizes are nontransferable. All entries must be received by August 31, 1986.

4. The following prizes will be awarded:

   (1) Grand Prize: Rolls-Royce™ *or* $100,000 Cash!
   (Rolls-Royce being offered by permission of
   Rolls-Royce Motors Inc.)

   (1) Second Prize: A trip for two to Paris for 7 days/6 nights. Trip includes air transportation on the Concorde, hotel accommodations...PLUS...$5,000 spending money!

   (1) Third Prize: A luxurious Mink Coat!

5. This offer is open to residents of the U.S. and Canada, 18 years or older, except employees of Harlequin Books, its affiliates, subsidiaries, Marden-Kane and all other agencies and persons connected with conducting this sweepstakes. All Federal, State and local laws apply. Void in the province of Quebec and wherever prohibited or restricted by law. Winners will be notified by mail and may be required to execute an affidavit of eligibility and release, which must be returned within 14 days after notification. Canadian winners will be required to answer a skill-testing question. Winners consent to the use of their name, photograph and/or likeness for advertising and publicity purposes in conjunction with this and similar promotions without additional compensation. One prize per family or household.

6. For a list of our most current prize winners, send a stamped, self-addressed envelope to: WINNERS LIST, c/o Marden-Kane, P.O. Box 10404, Long Island City, New York 11101

Harlequin Intrigue

Because romance can be quite an adventure

WORLDWIDE LIBRARY IS YOUR TICKET TO ROMANCE, ADVENTURE AND EXCITEMENT

Experience it all in these big, bold Bestsellers— Yours exclusively from WORLDWIDE LIBRARY WHILE QUANTITIES LAST

To receive these Bestsellers, complete the order form, detach and send together with your check or money order (include 75¢ postage and handling), payable to WORLDWIDE LIBRARY, to:

In the U.S.
WORLDWIDE LIBRARY
Box 52040
Phoenix, AZ
85072-2040

In Canada
WORLDWIDE LIBRARY
P.O. Box 2800, 5170 Yonge Street
Postal Station A, Willowdale, Ontario
M2N 6J3

Quant.	Title	Price
_____	WILD CONCERTO, Anne Mather	$2.95
_____	A VIOLATION, Charlotte Lamb	$3.50
_____	SECRETS, Sheila Holland	$3.50
_____	SWEET MEMORIES, LaVyrle Spencer	$3.50
_____	FLORA, Anne Weale	$3.50
_____	SUMMER'S AWAKENING, Anne Weale	$3.50
_____	FINGER PRINTS, Barbara Delinsky	$3.50
_____	DREAMWEAVER, Felicia Gallant/Rebecca Flanders	$3.50
_____	EYE OF THE STORM, Maura Seger	$3.50
_____	HIDDEN IN THE FLAME, Anne Mather	$3.50
_____	ECHO OF THUNDER, Maura Seger	$3.95
_____	DREAM OF DARKNESS, Jocelyn Haley	$3.95

YOUR ORDER TOTAL	$_____	
New York and Arizona residents add appropriate sales tax	$_____	
Postage and Handling	$___.75	
I enclose	$_____	

NAME _____

ADDRESS _____ APT.# _____

CITY _____

STATE/PROV. _____ ZIP/POSTAL CODE _____

WW3

She fought for a bold future
until she could no longer
ignore the...

ECHO OF THUNDER

MAURA SEGER

Author of **Eye of the Storm**

ECHO OF THUNDER is the love story of James
Callahan and Alexis Brockton, who forge a union that
must withstand the pressures of their own desires and the
challenge of building a new television empire.

Author Maura Seger's writing has been described by
Romantic Times as having a "superb blend of historical
perspective, exciting romance and a deep and abiding
passion for the human soul."

Take 4 books
& a surprise gift
FREE

SPECIAL LIMITED-TIME OFFER

Mail to **Harlequin Reader Service**®

In the U.S.
2504 West Southern Ave.
Tempe, AZ 85282

In Canada
P.O. Box 2800, Station "A"
5170 Yonge Street
Willowdale, Ontario M2N 6J3

YES! Please send me 4 free Harlequin Superromance® novels and my free surprise gift. Then send me 4 brand-new novels every month as they come off the presses. Bill me at the low price of $2.50 each—a 10% saving off the retail price. There are no shipping, handling or other hidden costs. There is no minimum number of books I must purchase. I can always return a shipment and cancel at any time. Even if I never buy another book from Harlequin, the 4 free novels and the surprise gift are mine to keep forever.

Name   (PLEASE PRINT)

Address   Apt. No.

City   State/Prov.   Zip/Postal Code

This offer is limited to one order per household and not valid to present subscribers. Price is subject to change.   DOSR–SUB–1

What readers say about
HARLEQUIN SUPERROMANCE™

"Bravo! Your SUPERROMANCE [is]... super!"
R.V.,* Montgomery, Illinois

"I am impatiently awaiting
the next SUPERROMANCE."
J.D., Sandusky, Ohio

"Delightful...great."
C.B., Fort Wayne, Indiana

"Terrific love stories. Just
keep them coming!"
M.G., Toronto, Ontario

1. How do you rate _____
   (Please print book TITLE)

   1.6 ☐ excellent   .4 ☐ good   .2 ☐ not so good
   .5 ☐ very good   .3 ☐ fair   .1 ☐ poor

   J123456789

2. How likely are you to purchase another book:
   in this *series* ?   by this *author* ?
   2.1 ☐ definitely would purchase   3.1 ☐ definitely would purchase
   .2 ☐ probably would puchase   .2 ☐ probably would puchase
   .3 ☐ probably would not purchase   .3 ☐ probably would not purchase
   .4 ☐ definitely would not purchase   .4 ☐ definitely would not purchase

3. How does this book compare with similar books you usually read?
   4.1 ☐ far better than others   .2 ☐ better than others   .3 ☐ about the
   .4 ☐ not as good   .5 ☐ definitely not as good   same

4. Please check the statements you feel best describe this book.
   5. ☐ Easy to read   6. ☐ Too much violence/anger
   7. ☐ Realistic conflict   8. ☐ Wholesome/not too sexy
   9. ☐ Too sexy   10. ☐ Interesting characters
   11. ☐ Original plot   12. ☐ Especially romantic
   13. ☐ Not enough humor   14. ☐ Difficult to read
   15. ☐ Didn't like the subject   16. ☐ Good humor in story
   17. ☐ Too predictable   18. ☐ Not enough description of setting
   19. ☐ Believable characters   20. ☐ Fast paced
   21. ☐ Couldn't put the book down 22. ☐ Heroine too juvenile/weak/silly
   23. ☐ Made me feel good   24. ☐ Too many foreign/unfamiliar words
   25. ☐ Hero too dominating   26. ☐ Too wholesome/not sexy enough
   27. ☐ Not enough romance   28. ☐ Liked the setting
   29. ☐ Ideal hero   30. ☐ Heroine too independent
   31. ☐ Slow moving   32. ☐ Unrealistic conflict
   33. ☐ Not enough suspense   34. ☐ Sensuous/not too sexy
   35. ☐ Liked the subject   36. ☐ Too much description of setting

5. What *most* prompted you to buy this book?
   37. ☐ Read others in series   38. ☐ Title   39. ☐ Cover art
   40. ☐ Friend's recommendation 41. ☐ Author   42. ☐ In-store display
   43. ☐ TV, radio or magazine ad 44. ☐ Price   45. ☐ Story outline
   46. ☐ Ad inside other books   47. ☐ Other _____ (please specify)

6. Please indicate how many romance paperbacks you read in a month .
   48.1 ☐ 1 to 4   .2 ☐ 5 to 10   .3 ☐ 11 to 15   .4 ☐ more than 15

7. Please indicate your sex and age group.
   49.1 ☐ Male   50.1 ☐ under 15   .3 ☐ 25-34   .5 ☐ 50-64
   .2 ☐ Female   .2 ☐ 15-24   .4 ☐ 35-49   .6 ☐ 65 or older

8. Have you any additional comments about this book?
   _____ (51)
   _____ (53)

Thank you for completing and returning this questionnaire.
Printed in USA

NAME _____
(Please Print)

ADDRESS _____

CITY _____

ZIP CODE _____

BUSINESS REPLY MAIL

FIRST CLASS   PERMIT NO. 70   TEMPE, AZ.

POSTAGE WILL BE PAID BY ADDRESSEE

NATIONAL READER SURVEYS

2504 West Southern Avenue
Tempe, AZ   85282